MR. BOSTON

Official Bartender's Guide

Pocket Edition

Edited by
Jonathan Pogash
with
Rick Rodgers

Photography by Ben Fink

D0898927

Copyright © 2012 by Sazerac North America, Inc. All rights reserved.
Photography © 2012 by Ben Fink

MR. BOSTON, and the Mr. Boston Character Logo, are trademarks of Sazerac North America, Inc. SAZERAC is a trademark of Sazerac Company, Inc.

Published by John Wiley & Sons, Inc., Hoboken, New Jersey

Published simultaneously in Canada

For general information about our other products and services, please contact our Customer Care Department within the United States at (800) 762-2974, outside the United States at (317) 572-3993 or fax (317) 572-4002.

Wiley publishes in a variety of print and electronic formats and by print-on-demand. Some material included with standard print versions of this book may not be included in e-books or in print-on-demand. If this book refers to media such as a CD or DVD that is not included in the version you purchased, you may download this material at http://booksupport.wiley.com. For more information about Wiley products, visit www.wiley.com

Design by Memo Productions, NY

Library of Congress Cataloging-in-Publication Data

Mr. Boston pocket edition / edited by Jonathan Pogash with Rick Rodgers.

    p.   cm.

    Includes bibliographical references and index.

    ISBN 978-0-470-88233-7 (cloth), 978-1-118-29811-4 (ebk.)

    1. Bartending. 2. Cocktails. I. Pogash, Jeffrey M. II. Rodgers, Rick, 1953-

    TX951.M73 2011

    641.8'74—dc23

                       2011021014

Printed in United States of America

10 9 8 7 6 5 4 3 2 1

Anyone who is pregnant or in a vulnerable health group should avoid recipes that use raw egg whites or lightly cooked eggs.

CONTENTS

INTRODUCTION

Welcome!

We are pleased as punch to present the 68th edition of the *Mr. Boston Official Bartender's Guide*. For over three-quarters of a century, the "little red book" has been the go-to manual for making perfect drinks. It has been endorsed, consulted, and considered a basic tool by both professional and avocational bartenders. In fact, over 11 million copies have been printed since the very first printing of what was then called the *Old Mr. Boston Deluxe Official Bartender's Guide*. That rare, hard-to-find first edition, which debuted soon after the repeal of Prohibition, was compiled and edited by Leo Cotton, a purchasing agent for the Mr. Boston® liquor brand. Mr. Cotton was as meticulous about his work as he was passionate about cocktails. His foreword in the original book remains timeless:

> With repeal came the inevitable avalanche of cocktail books, most of them published without regard to accuracy or completeness. A survey proved the need for a cocktail book that would be authentic and accurate. The task of compiling this *Official Bartenders Guide* was thereupon undertaken and now after almost one

year of tedious work it is presented to the thousands of bartenders throughout the country and to that portion of the American public who desire a truly official source of information for home mixing.

The *Official Bartenders Guide* was compiled and edited in collaboration with four old-time Boston Bartenders whose background and experience make them authorities on the correct ingredients to be used and the proper manner of serving cocktails. This experience plus the fact that every cocktail has been actually tested makes this truly an *Official Bartenders Guide*.

Leo Cotton's enthusiasm was such that his editing side job became a near-full-time vocation; he updated the *Official Bartenders Guide* through its 49th edition until he retired in 1970.

Though Leo Cotton died in 1990, his spirit lives on in this latest edition. The current cocktail renaissance, which began in the early 1990s, has brought with it a return to classicism in the art of cocktail making. The popularity of cocktails has increased dramatically over the last decade. What began as the "cocktail revolution" is now a whole new "cocktail culture." Every major city has cocktail lounges where the drinks are crafted with care from the very best ingredients. Newspapers such as the *New York Times* and the *Washington Post* have regular and well-read columns on the appreciation of fine spirits. Websites on every aspect of imbibing abound.

All of which amounts to the enjoyment of a heck of a lot of spirits. According to the Distilled Spirits Council of the

United States, distilled spirits grew in 2010 after a slight slump the year before, with sales up 2 percent to $19.1 billion and volume also rising 2 percent to 190.7 million cases. The council also reported that despite a weakening economy, growth is expected to continue this year as consumers migrate away from beer to cocktails.

What on earth is in all those cocktails that we are drinking? Just about everything. Spirits distributors have responded to our enthusiasm with flavors old and new, bringing out explosively exciting products like elderflower liqueur and organic spirits and, at the same time, bolstering lost categories like rye, pisco, cachaça, crème de violette, and Old Tom gin.

Categorically, vodka is still the most popular spirit for the masses, representing about 31 percent of the market, but other spirits like rum and whiskies have increased their sales. Rum, too, has taken off in a new direction that's positively old in origin—thanks to a renaissance in using sugarcane instead of molasses. If you see the words "rhum agricole" on a bottle or menu, it refers to how pure-cane rum is known on the French island of Martinique, while Brazilians call their pure-cane spirit "cachaça." Batavia arrack, a Javanese ancestor of rum, made from sugarcane and fermented red rice, is showing up on more bar menus, especially when the establishment's accent is on Asian cooking. In fact, it was named one of the "New Staples" by the *New York Times*.

On the whiskey front, rye has returned from its post-Prohibition banishment with such a vengeance that producers can't make enough of it. And new small-batch whiskies seem to debut every year now, with distilleries offering an array of boutique finishes. Single-malt Scotch and bourbon are still going strong.

How we're mixing these spirits into cocktails today is also remarkable. Mixology has returned to its culinary roots, embracing the zeitgeist and techniques of today's chefs, including taking farm to glass—as opposed to table. Once bartenders start working with someone who understands flavor combinations, like a chef, the drinks become more flavor-driven than spirit-driven. And that means mixers are more important than ever. With the introduction of high-quality, all-natural tonics and artisan sparkling juices, many bartenders have abandoned their soda guns—and all of the high-fructose corn syrup concoctions they spout—for "cleaner" mixers sweetened with cane sugar or agave nectar. This can change how drinks are made *and* how they taste.

All of which means that in this edition you won't find prefabricated mixers that didn't exist when this book was first published. In other words, you won't find references to "sour mix," "daiquiri mix," or "Collins mix." The use of superfine sugar has been almost entirely eliminated in favor of simple syrup (an easy-to-make combination of sugar and water), as the latter is more thoroughly mixed into a cocktail with less effort. When used with fresh citrus juices, it will make a highly superior substitute to the quick-fix mixes that invaded this book through its many incarnations. And, in acknowledgment of the attention to detail that many bartenders practice behind the bar, we've included from-scratch versions of many delicious flavored syrups, from lemongrass syrup to homemade grenadine, the better to bring your bartending skills up a notch. We've also been sure to include drinks in the current edition featuring spirits infused with tea, vanilla, and other flavors.

What you will find in this 68th edition are nearly 150 completely new recipes reflecting the most popular spirits, liqueurs, and juices of the moment. Scores of the best bartenders, bar chefs, and mixologists from around the world contributed recipes, tips, and advice for nothing more than thanks in print. We'd like to think their contributions were an homage to the book that first inspired many of them to start mixing drinks at the beginning of their careers.

In addition to the new recipes, the myriad details of the overall subtle changes that went into rebuilding this book might be lost on the novice or first-time reader of this guide. But our hope is that professional or veteran *Mr. Boston* readers will be pleasantly surprised by this latest incarnation. We'd like to think that Leo Cotton would be pleased to see how much of this book reflects the spirit of his original edition (which, by the way, didn't contain a single vodka cocktail).

By the time Cotton wrote the first edition of this book, the great-granddaddy of American cocktails, "Professor" Jerry Thomas, was long gone—and with him many of the techniques that set his service apart from lesser-mortal barmen back in the late nineteenth century. Indeed, ask any serious bartender or mixologist today who inspires their showmanship and creativity, and the answer will probably be "Jerry Thomas." Or perhaps it will be Thomas's twentieth-century incarnation, Dale DeGroff, who may not have single-handedly revived the cocktail classicism movement of the 1990s but certainly was and continues to be one of the most passionate, dynamic bartenders alive today.

Before you continue reading, please take a moment to think about both the responsible use and serving of alcoholic drinks. The consumption of alcohol dates back many centuries and in many cultures throughout the world is part of social rituals associated with significant occasions and celebrations. The majority of adults who choose to drink do not abuse alcohol and are aware that responsible drinking is key to their own enjoyment, health, and safety, as well as that of others, particularly when driving. Be a responsible drinker, and if you're under the legal drinking age, our non-alcoholic drinks chapter is the only one for you.

So, congratulations! You're well on your way to enhancing your expertise as a professional bartender or a properly prepared host.

Cheers!

JONATHAN POGASH

RICK RODGERS

May 2011

ACKNOWLEDGMENTS

The editors would like to thank the following superstars who joined forces to produce the seventy-fifth anniversary edition of the *Mr. Boston Official Bartender's Guide*:

There are so many people at John Wiley & Sons to thank: First and foremost, our editor, Pamela Chirls, for her motivation, wisdom, and enthusiasm. Jillian Gaffney, for keeping the pieces of the puzzle that is a manuscript under control. And to Memo Productions for their elegant design that tips a glass to the past.

Photographer Ben Fink and food stylist Jamie Kimm brought the cocktails to life in the thirst-inducing photos with talent and flair.

Peter Collins and our friends at *The Sazerac Company*, for keeping the traditions of the Mr. Boston Official Bartender's Guild alive and very much in the modern age.

Hal Wolin, bartender and member of *The Cocktail Guru* team, for assisting with testing and evaluating recipes.

Anthony Giglio and Jim Meehan, for their past editing of this book and their tips on this current edition.

The United States Bartenders Guild (USBG), for creating a community of like-minded professional bartenders. And to the many USBG members (whose names are given with their drinks) who generously contributed cocktail recipes to this book.

Jonathan would like to thank:

My mentor, gaz regan, for teaching me about classic cocktails and proper bar technique . . . and for ensuring I always buy him a drink whenever I see him.

My father, Jeff Pogash, not only a mentor, but an inspiration, for nudging me into the wild and wacky liquor business without even batting an eyelash . . . and for placing a drop of Champagne on my lips when I was born. Foreshadowing? I think so.

Rick Rodgers, my conspirator on this edition, for keeping me on track and for allowing my words to dazzle on the page . . . and for his endless humor whilst under an innumerable amount of deadlines.

And to my beautiful wife, Megan FitzGerald (and our soon-to-be bundle of joy), for her love, dedication, and endless support throughout. I love you!

Rick would like to thank:

Pamela Chirls (again) for the invitation to work with her on the book that brought me full-circle to my former career as a food service professional/bartender. Jillian Gaffney (again), for taking the time to show me new tricks with my Mac. And Suzanne Fass, copyeditor *deluxe*.

My partner, Patrick Fisher, who mixed many a Rob Roy on the rocks with orange bitters for me during the writing of this book. Come to think of it, he's mixed me a few before and after, too.

My late father, Dick Rodgers, whose spirit guided me to find his 1963 edition of Mr. Boston hidden away in his bar. The memories of our cocktail-time chats always bring a smile.

To my dear friend Carl Raymond, for pointing me to Astor Center in New York City and their excellent mixology program, and where I discovered the talented Jonathan Pogash.

Thanks, Jonathan, for proving to me that it is never too late to relearn long-forgotten skills, and for making me the best bartender in Maplewood, New Jersey. I am far from the only guy in town with crème de violette and pimento liqueur—which says volumes about the state of mixology today.

BAR BASICS

EQUIPMENT

The right tools make mixing drinks easier, but some tasks simply can't be done without the right gizmo.

Boston Shaker Two-piece set comprised of a 16-ounce mixing glass and a slightly larger metal container that acts as a cover for the mixing glass when shaking cocktails. The mixing glass can be used alone for stirring drinks that aren't shaken. This is the shaker of choice for professional bartenders.

Barspoon Long-handled shallow spoon with a twisted handle, used for a number of bartending techniques beyond stirring. The handle's curves help rotate the spoon during mixing, and the spoon bowl guides poured liqueurs into position for layered drinks.

Hawthorne Strainer Perforated metal strainer for the metal half of a Boston shaker, held in place by a wire coil.

Julep Strainer Perforated spoon-shaped strainer used in conjunction with a mixing glass.

Cocktail Shaker Two-part container with a tight-fitting lid. While styles vary widely, the most common shaker (also called a cobbler) has a top with a built-in lidded spout that serves as a strainer. The metal *Parisian-style shaker*, preferred by many home bartenders, has a sleek Art Deco look, lacks the top spout, and must be used in conjunction with a Hawthorne strainer.

Electric Blender Absolutely necessary to make frozen drinks, puree fruit, and even crush ice for certain recipes. Choose a top-quality blender with a heavy base, as lightweight blenders tend to "walk" when blending thick mixtures.

Cutting Board Either wood or plastic, it is used to cut fruit upon for garnishes.

Paring Knife Small, sharp knife to prepare fruit for garnishes.

Channel Tool Use this gadget to create relatively thin ribbons of citrus zest for twists.

Muddler Looks like a pestle, the flat end of which is used to crush and combine ingredients in a serving glass or mixing glass. Can be made of wood, metal, or even hard rubber.

Microplane Grater Useful for zesting fruit or grating nutmeg.

Bottle Opener Essential for opening bottles that aren't twist-off.

"Church Key" This metal tool is pointed at one end to punch holes in the tops of cans (these days most likely to be fruit juices), while the blunt end is used to open bottles.

Corkscrew There are a myriad of styles from which to choose. Professionals use the "waiter's corkscrew," which looks like a penknife, the "Screwpull," or the "rabbit corkscrew." The "winged corkscrew," found in most homes, is considered easiest to use but often destroys the cork.

Citrus Reamer This tool for juicing fruit comes in two styles. The strainer bowl style has the pointed cone on top, or there is the wooden handle style with the cone attached, which must be used with a wire strainer to remove the seeds. However, if you plan to use a lot of fresh fruit juice (and nothing is better for your drinks than freshly squeezed lemons or limes), get an inexpensive electric juicer or a metal standing lever-type juicer to whip through mountains of citrus.

Jigger Essential for precise measuring, it typically has two cone-shaped metal cups conjoined at the narrow ends. The best ones are marked to represent a quantity of fluid ounces (quarter, half, whole, etc.), fractionalized by lines etched in the metal. While jiggers come in a variety of sizes, the most useful jigger has 1½ ounces (1 jigger) and 1 ounce (1 pony). For smaller measurements in an unmarked jigger, just half-fill the larger cup for ¾ ounce, and the smaller cup in the same way for ½ ounce. Glass jiggers, which usually hold 2 ounces, are clearly marked, but could break in a busy professional bar. For consistency's sake, get out of the habit (if you have it) of free-pouring drinks, and take out the jigger every time you make a cocktail.

Measuring Spoons and Cups A set of measuring spoons (in 1 tablespoon, 1 teaspoon, ½ teaspoon, and ¼ teaspoon sizes) will be needed for smaller amounts of ingredients that are not measured by the fluid ounce. When measuring large amounts of liquids for punches or hot drinks, transparent liquid measuring cups in 1-cup and 2-cup capacities will come in handy.

Ice Bucket with Scoop and Tongs A bar without ice is like a car without gas. Use the scoop—never the glass—to gather ice in a mixing glass or shaker and tongs to add single cubes to a prepared drink.

Lewis Bag A heavy canvas bag with a mallet used to crush ice. Put ice cubes in the bag, close it, and pound away. It is low-tech, but it works.

Wire Sieve Used in conjunction with a Hawthorne strainer to ensure that the solids are removed from shaken cocktails. The strainer should be fit over the glass without an immoderate amount of overhang.

Miscellaneous Accoutrements Sipsticks or stirrers, straws, cocktail napkins, coasters, and cocktail picks.

GLASSWARE

Clean, polished glasses show off good drinks to great advantage. The best glasses should be thin-lipped, transparent, and sound off in high registers when "pinged." In practice, these five glasses could be used to make most of the mixed drinks and cocktails found in this book:

Y *Cocktail Glass* Also known as a martini glass, this glass used to hold 3 to about 4 ounces, but now it holds at least 6 ounces and often much more. The drinks in this book are formulated for the classic-sized cocktail glasses, which are worth the effort to find, as chilled drinks won't warm up as quickly as when they are served in the bigger glasses.

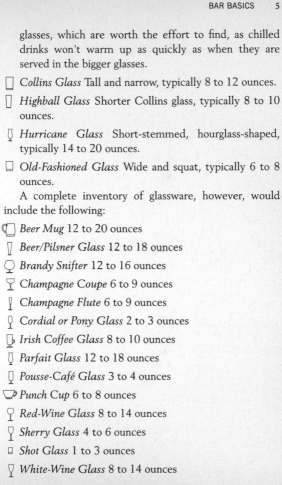

Collins Glass Tall and narrow, typically 8 to 12 ounces.

Highball Glass Shorter Collins glass, typically 8 to 10 ounces.

Hurricane Glass Short-stemmed, hourglass-shaped, typically 14 to 20 ounces.

Old-Fashioned Glass Wide and squat, typically 6 to 8 ounces.

A complete inventory of glassware, however, would include the following:

Beer Mug 12 to 20 ounces

Beer/Pilsner Glass 12 to 18 ounces

Brandy Snifter 12 to 16 ounces

Champagne Coupe 6 to 9 ounces

Champagne Flute 6 to 9 ounces

Cordial or Pony Glass 2 to 3 ounces

Irish Coffee Glass 8 to 10 ounces

Parfait Glass 12 to 18 ounces

Pousse-Café Glass 3 to 4 ounces

Punch Cup 6 to 8 ounces

Red-Wine Glass 8 to 14 ounces

Sherry Glass 4 to 6 ounces

Shot Glass 1 to 3 ounces

White-Wine Glass 8 to 14 ounces

TAKING STOCK

Here's what you'll need for a well-stocked bar.

Bitters

Angostura bitters
Peychaud's bitters
Orange bitters

Fruit Juices

Limes and lemons for freshly squeezed juices
Orange and grapefruit juices (refrigerated or fresh)
Cranberry and pineapple juices (packaged)

Savory Ingredients

Tomato juice and/or tomato-vegetable juice (canned)
Prepared horseradish
Hot red pepper sauces
Worcestershire sauce

Sweetening Ingredients

Simple syrup (page 20, or use store-bought)
Superfine (bartenders') sugar
Granulated sugar
Sugar cubes
Maple syrup, preferably Grade B, and agave nectar
Cream of coconut (Coco Lopez)

Various flavored syrups, especially orgeat or almond
Grenadine (page 22, or use store-bought)

Dairy/Egg Ingredients

Half-and-half
Heavy cream
Milk
Butter
Large Grade A eggs

Sodas (preferably in individual-serving bottles)

Soda water
Tonic (quinine) water
Various sodas, such as cola and lemon-lime

Garnishes

Lemon wedges
Lime wedges
Assorted citrus wheels
Orange and lemon twists
Pineapple wedges and/or chunks
Maraschino cherries, preferably Italian preserved
    Marasca cherries
Pitted green olives
Celery sticks
Cocktail onions
Fresh herbs, such as mint, basil, and rosemary

TECHNIQUES

Chilling Glassware

Always chill before you fill—even your cocktail shaker—and mix the drink. Use either of these methods.

1. Put the glasses in the refrigerator or freezer a couple of hours before using them.
2. Fill the glasses with ice and water and stir. Let stand while making the drink, then discard the ice water before filling the glasses.

Mixing Drinks

Shaking is appropriate for many, but not all, drinks. Forget the old warning about "bruising the liquor," for spirits cannot be affected by shaking. However, shaking will effervesce the cocktail ingredients, and there are many times when you want the drink to remain clear. Mixing drinks can also be accomplished by stirring, as well as by two less common techniques, swizzling and rolling.

No matter which mixing procedure you use, remember that the ice does more than chill the drink. As the ice melts, it slightly dilutes and mellows the alcohol to actually make the drink more palatable. This is easy to test with deeply chilled vodka from the freezer—a habit that many people have affected to make a well-chilled martini. Pour one martini directly from the chilled bottle, and stir up another with ice in a mixing glass and strain it into a second glass. Taste them side by side. Thanks to the milder flavor, most people will prefer the ice-stirred drink. Even drinks that are served on the rocks are often shaken first and then strained into a glass over fresh ice to control the amount of melting (as the fresh ice won't melt as quickly as the shaken ice).

Shaking Drinks As a rule of thumb, shake any drink made with juices, syrup or sugar, egg, or cream to be sure that the ingredients are thoroughly combined. Pour the ingredients into the glass mixing part of the Boston shaker, with spirits first, then juices, and then the sweeteners and other flavorings, such as bitters. If you are trying to learn a drink recipe by heart, you can alter the sequence to go from largest amount of ingredients to the smallest, as that seems a reasonable and reliable way to remember a long list. Pouring the ingredients into the mixer glass before adding the ice premixes them before the more thorough shaking.

Now add ice to the mixer to fill it about two-thirds full, as you want to leave room for the ingredients to be able to move freely during shaking. Egg-based drinks, such as Flips, are an important exception. In their case, the ingredients are first combined and shaken without ice to make an emulsion and then the ice is added for a second shaking to chill the drink. And never shake a drink with soda, as the action will burst the bubbles, but add the soda to top off the drink after it is poured.

Place the metal half of the Boston shaker over the glass while it's sitting on the bar. Holding the glass firmly, clap the upturned end of the metal half twice with the heel of your free hand to form a seal. (To test the seal, lift the shaker by the metal top slightly off the bar to see if it holds; if not, repeat the procedure and try lifting again.)

Turn the conjoined shakers over so that the glass is on top and the metal half rests on the bar. Grasp the shakers with the metal half sitting securely in the palm of one hand and the other hand wrapped securely over the top of the glass half, then shake hard with the glass half of the set on top. (In case the seal breaks, the liquid stays in the bigger metal half.) Shake vigorously, for a count of eight, rendering the drink effervescent and with just the right amount of melting. With egg-based drinks, you may need to shake for about a minute, until you can see that the ingredients are mixed well and evenly colored.

After shaking, clasp one hand around the equator of the conjoined shakers and then, using the heel of your other hand, hit the metal shaker bluntly at the point where it meets the mixing glass to break the seal. If it doesn't work the first time, try again at another spot.

You can use a cobbler or Parisian shaker to shake drinks, but most professionals prefer the Boston shaker because it is sturdy, easy to clean, and the glass reveals how the drink is mixed at a glance.

Stirring Drinks When the drink is comprised of spirits alone, stir the ingredients so they remain clear and unclouded by shaking. After you've assembled your liquids and ice in the mixer glass, insert the barspoon, letting the handle of the spoon rest on the edge of the glass. Move the spoon around the edge of the glass in a circle for at least thirty seconds to completely chill the cocktail, while also allowing sufficient time for a small amount of the ice to melt.

Swizzling Any drinker knows the swizzle stick—the long decorative plastic rod jutting out of a tall (also called long) cocktail that serves as a stirrer. A proper swizzle stick is actually made from wood, getting its name from the long, straight branches of the Caribbean swizzlestick tree, or allspice bush. The swizzle stick lends its name to an entire category of iced thirst-quenchers that are stirred in a special way to frost the outside of the serving glass.

A barspoon, which is long enough to reach the bottom of the deepest glass, can be used as a swizzle stick. Pour the ingredients into the serving glass (usually a Collins or hurricane glass) and add the ice. Insert the barspoon. Place both palms around the twisted part of the handle. Move your hands back and forth and up and down to quickly rotate and lift the spoon until the glass is nicely frosted. When serving the drink, hold it by its rim with a cocktail napkin, so as not to mar the frosting.

Rolling Drinks This technique prevents drinks that call for thick juices or fruit purees from foaming. (It is also somewhat of a timesaver and gives the bartender an occasional break from shaking.) Pour the ingredients over ice in the mixing glass of a Boston shaker. Pour the drink back and forth between the glass and metal shaker half two or three times until combined. Strain the drink into the prepared serving glass.

Other Techniques

Coating a Glass Cocktails are created from a well-considered mix of ingredients, and sometimes a whisper of a particular spirit is all that is required. Coating the glass with a small amount of liquor accomplishes this step. Pour just a splash of the liquor into the serving glass, swirl to coat the inside, and pour out the excess liquor. Don't worry if it doesn't coat every inch of the glass interior. The idea is to provide background flavor in each sip.

Flaming Liquors The secret of setting brandy (or other high-alcohol spirits) aflame is first to warm it and its glass. Fill the glass with very hot tap (preferably boiling) water and let stand while heating the liquor. Next, heat the required spirits in a small saucepan over low heat. When the liquor is very warm, remove the saucepan from the heat. Discard the hot water from the glass. Pour the liquor into the warmed glass. Ignite the liquor with a match (preferably a long match) using extra care, as the invisible fumes above the liquor may ignite before the liquid itself. Let the flame burn out on its own, but don't let the flame burn too long or it will affect the flavor of the liquor. If it burns longer than 45 seconds or so, place a heatproof saucer over the top of the glass to cut off the oxygen and smother the flame.

Take precautions when flaming drinks. The flames shoot high suddenly. Look up and be sure there's nothing "en route" that can ignite. That includes your hair and sleeves. Have an open box of baking soda handy to pour over flames in case of accidents. Use pot holders to protect your hands from the hot glass and saucepan.

Floating Liqueurs Creating a rainbow effect in a glass with different colored cordials requires a special, but easy to master, pouring technique. Place a long barspoon, with rounded side of the spoon bowl facing up, in the glass at the level where you want the first liqueur. Let the tip of the spoon bowl touch the side of the glass. This breaks the velocity of liqueur as it pours and helps it spread evenly. Slowly pour the liqueur over the spoon bowl into the glass.

For the next layer, place the tip of the spoon just at the surface of the poured liqueur and pour in the next cordial so it layers on top of the first. Repeat until all of the layers have been poured. You can also use this technique to float lightly whipped cream on top of a drink.

Muddling Fruits and Herbs Crushing releases more flavorful oils into the drink than shaking. Plastic or wooden muddlers are easily found at kitchenware shops. Use the wider, flat end of the muddler to do the mashing in the mixing glass. Muddled drinks are often strained before serving, but in the case of the Caipirinha, the muddled ingredients sometimes remain in the serving glass.

Rimming a Glass Creating an edible crust around the edge of the serving glass is called rimming and is a direct connection to the antique Crusta cocktail, which used sugar for the encrusting. The technique was revived, with coarse salt instead of sugar, for the Margarita. In fact, until recently, the Margarita was the only cocktail that was regularly served in a rimmed glass, and even then as an option. Bartenders now regularly use rimming to add another layer of flavor to their specialty cocktails. The sugar or salt can be mixed with other ingredients, such as spices or herbs, for even more sensory pleasure.

Rimming separates the pros from the amateurs. The crust must only cling to the outside of the glass. If it is inside the glass, the inner crust will fall into the drink and overseason it. Use coarse (kosher, never iodized or fine) salt and superfine (granulated is fine) sugar for average use. Some drinks may have special requirements for particular ingredients, like sanding (coarse-crystal) sugar. Pour the salt or sugar into a small saucer to a depth of at least ⅛ inch.

Using a wedge of fresh citrus (chosen to complement the flavor of the drink) or a small amount of the required liquor on a paper towel, carefully moisten only the outside rim of the serving glass. Then, holding the glass sideways, dab the rim into the salt or sugar while turning the glass until the entire rim is covered. Finally, hold the glass over a sink and tap the glass gently against your free hand to knock off any excess rimming ingredients. The result is a delicately encrusted rim that looks almost frosted.

SERVING DRINKS

If you're the least bit theatrical, this is the time for it. Just remember: Always use the Hawthorne strainer (spring-form) with the metal part of the set for shaken drinks, and the julep strainer (holes) with the glass half for stirred cocktails.

Straining from the Metal Shaker Place the Hawthorne strainer in the mixer, acting as a cover. Then put your forefinger and middle finger over the strainer while grabbing the shaker with your thumb, ring, and pinky fingers. Hold the shaker tightly and strain slowly at first to avoid splashing out of the glass. When straining into a cocktail glass, pour the liquid in a circular motion around the inside of the glass to help avoid spillage. As the pour slows toward the last ounce, draw your hand up high over the middle of the cocktail glass, emptying the last of the liquid with a snap of the shaker.

Straining from the Glass Shaker Place the julep strainer over the top of the glass with the concave side facing up. Grab the glass toward the top with your thumb and last three fingers, and then curl your forefinger over the handle of the strainer, holding it firmly in place. Strain following the directions above.

Double-Straining Muddled or shaken cocktails sometimes contain tiny flecks of solid ingredients that must be removed before serving. Double-straining through a sieve does a better job than a single metal cocktail strainer. Hold a wire sieve over the prepared glass. With your other hand, pour the drink from the strainer-covered shaker through the sieve into the glass.

Opening Champagne or Sparkling Wine

When the bottle is well chilled, wrap it in a clean towel and undo the wire around the cork, holding the cork down with one hand while loosening the wire with the other—never letting go of the cork. Pointing the bottle away from people and priceless objects, grasp the bottle by the indentation on the bottom. Leveraging the pressure between both hands, slowly turn the bottle until the cork comes free with a gentle pop. The idea is to release as little carbon dioxide from the bottle as possible, as the more pop, the more gas is released into the air, reducing the amount of bubbles. Pour slowly into the center of the glass.

Opening Wine

Cut the seal neatly around the neck with a sharp knife just below the top. Peel off, exposing the cork. Wipe off the cork and bottle lip. Insert the corkscrew and turn until the corkscrew is completely inside the cork. With a steady pull, remove the cork. If the cork crumbles or breaks, pour the wine through a tea strainer into another container for serving. The host or hostess should taste the wine to check its quality before offering it to guests.

How Many Drinks to Plan

Whether you're hosting an intimate dinner party or throwing a bash for a crowd, the buying guide charts in this section can make it easy for you to determine how much liquor and wine you'll need. A rule of thumb is one drink per hour per person, with a little extra added as insurance. Remember, liquor has a long shelf life, even opened, so it is better to buy more and store leftovers than to run out. With wine, open the bottles as needed, as unopened bottles can also be stored for another use, but opened bottles must be consumed in the next few days after the party. Always encourage the practice of designated driving at your festivites.

	For Four People	For Eight People	For Twelve People
LUNCH	4 cocktails/ wine before lunch	8 cocktails/ wine before lunch	12 cocktails/ wine before lunch
	4 glasses of wine with lunch	8 glasses of wine with lunch	12 glasses of wine with lunch
	4 liqueurs after lunch (optional)	8 liqueurs after lunch (optional)	8 liqueurs after lunch (optional)

COCKTAILS	6 cocktails/ wine per hour	12 cocktails/ wine per hour	18 cocktails/ wine per hour
DINNER	6 cocktails/ wine before dinner	12 cocktails/ wine before dinner	18 cocktails/ wine before dinner
	8 glasses of wine with dinner	16 glasses of wine with dinner	24 glasses of wine with dinner
	4 cocktails/ liqueurs after dessert	8 cocktails/ liqueurs after dessert	12 cocktails/ liqueurs after dessert
EVENING	6 cocktails/ wine per hour	12 cocktails/ wine per hour	18 cocktails/ wine per hour

How Many Bottles of Wine for Dinner

Table Wines, Champagnes, Sparkling Wines average 2 servings, 5 ounces each, per person

People	4	6	8	10	12	20
750 ml	2	2+	3+	4	5	8
1.5 liters	1	1+	2	2	2+	4

Generally, bottle quantities recommended provide some small overages of wine from 10-ounces-per-guest formula; "+" indicates somewhat less than the formula and you may desire to have an additional bottle on hand.

How Many Drinks Per Bottle

Cocktails, Mixed Drinks 1.5-ounce liquor servings

Bottles	1	2	4	6	8	10	12
750 ml	16	33	67	101	135	169	203
Liter	22	45	90	135	180	225	270
1.5 liters	39	78	157	236	315	394	473

Table Wines, Champagnes, Sparkling Wines 5-ounce wine servings

Bottles	1	2	4	6	8	10	12
750 ml	5	10	20	30	40	50	60
Liter	6	13	27	40	54	67	81
1.5 liters	10	20	40	60	81	101	121
3 liters	20	40	80	121	161	202	242
4 liters	27	54	108	162	216	270	324

MEASURES

Standard Bar Measurements (U.S. fluid ounces)

1 pony	= 1 ounce
1 ounce	= 3 centiliters
1 jigger shot	= 1½ ounces
1 mixing glass	= 16 ounces
1 splash	= ½ teaspoon

Other Measures

1 dash	= 6 drops
12 dashes	= ½ teaspoon
1 teaspoon	= ⅙ ounce
2 teaspoons	= ⅓ ounce
1 tablespoon	= ½ ounce
2 tablespoons	= 1 ounce
¼ cup	= 2 ounces
½ cup	= 4 ounces
1 cup or ½ pint	= 8 ounces
2 cups or 1 pint	= 16 ounces
4 cups, 2 pints, or 1 quart	= 32 ounces

Bottle Size Measures

Split	= 187 ml	= 6.4 ounces
Half-bottle	= 375 ml	= 12.7 ounces
Fifth	= 750 ml	= 25.4 ounces
Liter	= 1000 ml	= 33.8 ounces
Magnum	= 1.5 liters	= 2 wine bottles
Jeroboam	= 3 liters	= 4 wine bottles
Rehoboam	= 6 wine bottles	
Methuselah	= 8 wine bottles	
Salmanazar	= 12 wine bottles	
Balthazar	= 16 wine bottles	
Nebuchadnezzar	= 20 wine bottles	
Sovereign	= 34 wine bottles	

BASIC RECIPES

SIMPLE SYRUP

Makes about 1 c.

The bartender's sweetest ally. You can add other ingredients to the basic recipe to create an almost endless list of flavored syrups. (For an amazingly quick version that doesn't require cooking, use the Quick Simple Syrup variation.) Large bars can multiply this recipe to make as much as needs dictate, but don't make any less, as it keeps for weeks. While we encourage you to make simple syrup, superfine sugar will work at the proportion of 1½ tsp. sugar to ½ oz. of syrup.

1 c. granulated sugar

Bring sugar and 1 c. water to a boil in small saucepan over high heat, stirring to dissolve sugar. Boil without stirring for 1 minute. Let cool. Pour into a very clean covered container and store in refrigerator for up to 2 months.

Chile Syrup: *Add 1 tbsp. crushed hot red pepper flakes to the hot syrup in the saucepan and let cool. Strain and store in refrigerator for up to 3 weeks.*

Cinnamon Syrup: *Substitute Demerara sugar for the granulated sugar. As soon as the syrup comes to a boil, add 4 (3-inch long) cinnamon sticks. Reduce heat to very low and simmer for 5 minutes. Let cool. Strain and store in refrigerator for up to 3 weeks.*

Demerara Syrup: *This syrup gives a richer, molasses-like sweetness and an earthy color to cocktails. Substitute 1 c. Demerara sugar for the granulated sugar. Store in refrigerator for up to 2 months.*

Ginger Syrup: *A deliciously spicy syrup that works in many cocktails beyond the predictable tiki drinks. Add ¼ c. peeled, coarsely chopped fresh ginger to the saucepan with the sugar and water and bring to a boil. Let cool. Strain, pressing hard on the solids. Store in refrigerator for up to 3 weeks.*

Honey Syrup: *For a more subtle sweetness, use this syrup. Don't use a strong honey, such as chestnut, or its flavor may overpower the cocktail. Simply shake ⅔ c. mild honey and ⅓ c. water together in a covered jar until the honey dissolves. Store in refrigerator for up to 2 months.*

Lavender Syrup: *Be sure to use edible culinary lavender, now available in the spice section of many supermarkets, and not lavender intended for potpourri. Add 3 tbsp. edible dried lavender to the saucepan with the sugar and water and bring to a boil. Let cool. Strain and store in refrigerator for up to 3 weeks.*

Lemongrass Syrup: *Cut off the woody tops from 5 lemongrass stalks and peel off and discard the outer layers. Coarsely chop the tender bulbous bottoms. Add to the hot syrup in the saucepan and let cool. Strain, pressing hard on solids. Store in refrigerator for up to 3 weeks.*

Rhubarb Syrup: *Add ½ c. thinly sliced rhubarb to the saucepan with the sugar and water and bring to a boil. Let cool. Strain and store in refrigerator for up to 3 weeks. Makes about 1¼ c.*

Vanilla Syrup: Add 3 vanilla beans, split lengthwise, to the hot syrup and let cool. Using the tip of a small knife, scrape the seeds from each vanilla bean half into the syrup. Discard the beans. Store in refrigerator for up to 3 weeks.

Quick Simple Syrup: The only difference between this and the cooked syrup is that the cooked version is best for infusing with flavorings. Be sure to use superfine (also called bartenders' or bakers') sugar, available at supermarkets in the baking aisle. Combine 1 c. superfine sugar and 1 c. water in a covered jar. Shake well until the sugar dissolves. Store in refrigerator for up to 2 months.

☐ HOMEMADE GRENADINE

Makes about ¾ c.

Sure, you can buy the commercial stuff. But with pomegranate juice on every supermarket shelf (look for bargain-priced juice at grocers with Middle Eastern products), why not make your own? The flavor is superior.

½ c. pomegranate juice
½ c. superfine sugar
A few drops orange blossom water (optional)

Combine pomegranate juice, sugar, and orange blossom water, if using, in a covered jar and shake well to dissolve sugar. Store in refrigerator for up to 2 months.

COCKTAIL CLASSICS

BEING A BARTENDER requires far more than memorizing a few recipes and learning to use some basic tools. Sure, you might be able to mix a drink, but that is no guarantee you will consistently produce truly great drinks.

A bartender is in many ways like a chef—taking individual ingredients and mixing them together to create an artful blending of flavors. The best cocktails are a form of cuisine in their own right.

Just as a great chef must have a command of the foundations of cooking, like a mastery of classic French sauces, the bartender must understand the basic techniques, processes, methods, and products involved in the craft. And this includes an understanding and appreciation of the classic cocktails. These recipes are the foundation for nearly every existing drink and provide the basis for creating new and distinctive drinks.

The following eight cocktails form the basis for most modern cocktails. Understand their histories, variations, and processes, and you'll be well on your way to a better appreciation of your craft as well as being able to create original cocktails that may someday take their place among the greats.

THE OLD-FASHIONED WHISKEY COCKTAIL

Unlike other cuisines of the world, the cocktail is only a few hundred years old. While we don't know precisely when or where the cocktail made its official first appearance, we can trace it back as far as 1806. There, in a popular New York publication called *The Balance, and Columbian Repository*, we find the cocktail defined.

In the May 13 edition, an editor responded to a letter from a devoted reader about the term "cock-tail" as it appeared in the previous week's edition, saying:

> As I make it a point, never to publish anything (under my editorial head) but which I can explain, I shall not hesitate to gratify the curiosity of my inquisitive correspondent: Cock tail, then is a stimulating liquor, composed of spirits of any kind, sugar, water and bitters—it is vulgarly called a bittered sling.

At the core of this, you see the definition of the cocktail: "spirits of any kind, sugar, water and bitters." While the term "cocktail" has since been broadened to include far more drinks, and with a far less distinct definition, this original definition is one of which all bartenders should be aware. As the cocktail evolved, this earliest of cocktails became known simply as the Old-Fashioned.

There are many who claim the Old-Fashioned was invented at the Pendennis Club in Louisville, Kentucky. One of the oldest records of a recipe going by the name of Old-Fashioned is from *Modern American Drinks* by George J. Kappeler, published in 1895:

☐ THE OLD-FASHIONED WHISKEY COCKTAIL

Dissolve a small lump of sugar with a little water in a whiskey-glass; add two dashes Angostura bitters, a small piece ice, a piece lemon-peel, one jigger whiskey. Mix with small bar-spoon and serve, leaving spoon in glass.

Remembering the earlier stated definition of a cocktail, what is an Old-Fashioned but "spirits of any kind [whiskey], sugar, water and bitters"? To draw an even closer connection, many recipes of that time would also indicate that other spirits could be used in an Old-Fashioned in order to make an Old-Fashioned Brandy Cocktail, or an Old-Fashioned Rum Cocktail.

In the first known bartender's guide, *How to Mix Drinks* (Dick & Fitzgerald, 1862), Jerry Thomas writes:

♀ WHISKEY COCKTAIL

Use a small bar glass.
3 or 4 dashes of gum syrup
2 do. Bitters (Bogart's)
1 wine-glass of whiskey, and a piece of lemon peel.

Fill one-third full of fine ice; shake and strain in a fancy red-wine glass.

To translate some unfamiliar terminology, gum syrup (sometimes called gomme syrup), is a sugar syrup thickened with gum arabic. The abbreviation "do." stands for "ditto" and refers to the word "dashes" in the line above. Bogart's is a type of bitters that is no longer produced commercially. A wine-glass held 2 ounces.

This is the same cocktail as the Old-Fashioned and leads to the conclusion that the Pendennis Club didn't actually invent the Old-Fashioned, but simply provided their customers with a whiskey cocktail made the old-fashioned way. Drinking and storytelling go hand in hand, so treat any tale of cocktail invention with a bit of skepticism.

Here's a contemporary version of the Old-Fashioned.

☐ OLD-FASHIONED WHISKEY COCKTAIL

2 oz. rye or bourbon whiskey
¼ oz. simple syrup
2 dashes Angostura bitters
Garnish: Lemon twist

Pour rye or bourbon, syrup, and bitters into a cracked-ice-filled old-fashioned glass and stir. Add lemon twist.

This Old-Fashioned reflects the way this cocktail should taste. Simple syrup is used because it's easier than muddling the sugar in the glass and also provides a more consistent sweetening. Unlike many modern renditions, there is no cherry or orange muddled in with the bitters and sweetener at the beginning and there is no soda or water at the end. The water melting from the ice is just the right amount to even out the rough edges of the whiskey.

The beauty of this recipe lies in its simplicity and authenticity. Hundreds of years ago, spirits were so rough that sweeteners were needed to mask their flavors. Today, spirits are of much higher quality and don't need to be masked; instead the sweetener is being used to counterbalance the alcoholic bite, as well as fill out the flavor profile in areas where the spirit doesn't touch.

Bitters, as we have seen, are at the very heart of the definition of a cocktail. Prior to around 1900 it was almost unthinkable to have a cocktail that didn't include bitters in some form. Bitters, when added in small amounts, offer complexity to the overall flavor of the drink.

Finally, the water that is added to the Old-Fashioned and other cocktails through the ice serves to tone down and mellow the overall flavors as well as soften the bite typical of a straight spirit. Topping the drink off with additional water, as is often done, only results in a very diluted drink. The ice alone is sufficient.

But what about that cherry and orange? They were not part of the original drink. You'll find an orange slice being used instead of a lemon twist in the 1930 printing of *The Savoy Cocktail Book* by Harry Craddock. (Craddock was an American bartender who migrated to the bar at the Savoy Hotel in London during Prohibition. We all can be thankful that he chronicled most of his recipes in his book.) For the next several decades you'll see lemon, pineapple, orange, and cherry all make an appearance, either separately or in various combinations, but always as a garnish. Exactly when the practice of muddling the fruit came into fashion is hard to determine, but it doesn't appear to be referenced in print much before the 1990s.

The modern maraschino cherry didn't come onto the scene until the early 1900s, just before Prohibition. It was intended as a "temperance" replacement for the brandy-soaked marasca cherries, which previously had been in common use. Prohibition made the original version impossible to obtain in the United States, and so maraschino cherries quickly replaced them in baking and garnishing. Muddling them into the drink does little to improve the flavor or the aesthetics of this drink, even if you use imported Marasca (true maraschino) cherries.

The orange is a slightly different story. If you glance over many of the historical recipes, you will occasionally see a dash of orange curaçao added. Muddling a slice of orange into the Old-Fashioned extracts similar essential oils to those found in orange liqueurs. Or, add a twist of orange peel to the drink. Garnish the drink with a half orange-wheel and cherry, permitting the fresh fruits to play the ornamental role for which they were intended.

THE MANHATTAN COCKTAIL

The Manhattan appears to have come onto the scene about 1882, at which time it was mentioned that a cocktail made from just whiskey, sweet vermouth, and bitters was coming into vogue. It went by not only "Manhattan," but also "Turf Club Cocktail" and "Jockey Club Cocktail." The "Manhattan" moniker almost certainly comes from the Manhattan Club of New York, with the other clubs eager to have their names attached to the drink as well.

Like the Old-Fashioned, the recipe for the Manhattan is deceptively simple—just whiskey, sweet vermouth, and bitters. And likewise, the art of making a great one is in the details.

Here's how to make a Manhattan for today's palates:

♈ MANHATTAN

    2 oz. rye whiskey
    ½ oz. sweet vermouth
    1 dash Angostura bitters
    Garnish: Maraschino cherry, preferably Italian

Stir with ice and strain into chilled cocktail glass. Garnish with cherry.

You'll note two peculiarities in this recipe. The first is the use of rye whiskey; the second is that it is stirred.

As indicated earlier, this drink originated in New York, and in those days the rye whiskey distillers were located in the East, making rye whiskey the spirit of choice. Bourbon, from Kentucky and the surrounding area, was far less common in New York. Today, bourbon may be the default spirit of the Manhattan, but rye has been making a comeback and is worth seeking out. Many people substitute Canadian whisky for rye, but the two are actually quite a bit different. For one thing, rye whiskey must be made from at least 51 percent rye, while Canadian whisky contains far less. This doesn't mean that you can't make a Manhattan with Canadian whisky, or bourbon for that matter, but they will yield vastly different results.

Stirring versus shaking is an age-old debate, and it plays a big role in getting the proper results in many cocktails, specifically a Manhattan. Both shaking and stirring are intended to chill the drink and melted ice improves the overall flavor. But because this drink should be clear, and not foamy, stirring is preferred.

Just as the Old-Fashioned could be made with different spirits to create slightly different variations on a theme, there are also variations of the Manhattan. Initially, the Manhattan was designed to use sweet vermouth. But if customers wanted it made with dry vermouth instead, they would ask for a "dry" Manhattan. And asking for a "perfect" Manhattan indicates a 50/50 mixture of sweet and dry vermouth.

Like its progenitor the Old-Fashioned, this Manhattan contains bitters. And while the vogue for the past decade was to provide bitters on a "by request" basis, this vital ingredient should be provided as a standard ingredient.

THE MARTINI COCKTAIL

Making its appearance only a few years after the Manhattan, the Martini is a cocktail that has come to be the icon of this genre, so much so that almost any drink in a stemmed cocktail glass is now dubbed a Martini by the drinking public.

There are many stories surrounding the origins of the Martini, but its true origins appear to lie with its forgotten sibling, the Martinez. In *The Bar-Tender's Guide* (1887), "Professor" Jerry Thomas writes:

℣ MARTINEZ COCKTAIL

TAKE:
1 dash of Boker's bitters
2 dashes of Maraschino
1 pony of Old Tom gin
1 wine-glass of vermouth
2 small lumps of ice

Shake up thoroughly, and strain into a large cocktail glass. Put a quarter of a slice of lemon in the glass and serve. If the guest prefers it very sweet, add two dashes of gum syrup.

Again, a bit of translation is required to understand this drink in today's context. Boker's bitters, an aromatic bitters, and Old Tom gin, a sweetened gin popular in the late 1800s, haven't been made for the past few decades, but are now newly available. A wine-glass usually referred to a 2-ounce pour. The vermouth, while not specified, was probably Italian, what today's drinkers would call sweet or red vermouth. This Martinez was hardly "dry."

By the 1890s recipes for a drink now known as the Martini were appearing. In *Modern American Drinks: How to Mix and Serve All Kinds of Cups and Drinks* (1895), George J. Kappeler writes:

🍸 MARTINI COCKTAIL

Half a mixing-glass full of fine ice, three dashes orange bitters, one-half jigger Tom gin, one-half jigger Italian vermouth, a piece lemon peel. Mix, strain into cocktail-glass. Add a maraschino cherry, if desired by customer.

From this we can see that the Martini, containing just gin, sweet vermouth, and bitters, was really a gin version of the Manhattan. And like the Manhattan, when ordered normally it would be made with sweet vermouth, and when ordered "dry" with dry (French) vermouth.

While the Manhattan has pretty much survived to the modern day with its recipe intact, the Martini has not fared so well. It was following Prohibition, when untrained amateurs took to the bar, that the concept of "dry" when applied to the Martini came to mean using less dry vermouth. Today some bartenders use none at all. Orange bitters, once a required component of the Martini, were forgotten, to the point of extinction. They have only resurfaced in the last few years.

One could hardly consider a glass of plain cold gin a cocktail deserving of the name Martini. To rediscover the sophisticated balance and complexity that is possible with the Martini, it is necessary to return to its roots.

ℶ TRADITIONAL MARTINI (SWEET)

1 oz. gin
1 oz. sweet vermouth
1 dash orange bitters
Garnish: Lemon twist

Stir with ice and strain into chilled cocktail glass. Add lemon twist.

ℶ TRADITIONAL MARTINI (DRY)

1 oz. gin
1 oz. dry vermouth
1 dash orange bitters
Garnish: Lemon twist

Stir with ice and strain into chilled cocktail glass. Add lemon twist.

Try each of the above exactly as indicated. As with any culinary product, the quality of the ingredients that go into it will greatly affect the outcome, so be sure to use a good gin and good vermouth.

There are several aspects of these recipes that you will notice as being significantly different from what you might be used to. For one thing, there are only 2 ounces total of liquid being used here; this obviously will result in a drink that will look rather lost in today's 5- to 8-ounce cocktail glasses. In the days before Prohibition, the typical cocktail glass was about 4 ounces in size, so the recipes above, with the addition of water from mixing, resulted in a perfectly sized drink.

Another difference you'll see is what appears to be a massive amount of vermouth being used. The result is a drink that bears little resemblance to today's Martini. Push your prejudices aside and instead focus simply on the overall taste of the drink itself, and you'll find the vermouth is not only enjoyable but in perfect balance with the gin.

As noted, the Martini should be stirred, like the Manhattan, to retain its clarity.

And while the olive is the more popular modern garnish, the olive brine affects the delicate balance of the drink. We prefer, at least initially, to get to know this drink with this more understated lemon twist.

Perhaps more than with any other cocktail, the ratios of the ingredients in a Martini require precise balance. No one ingredient should outshine the other, and all ingredients should be playing together in the final product.

The Martini recipes listed here would be inappropriate to serve to a random customer who simply asked for a "Martini." But through the careful understanding of not only the history of this drink but its blending of complex flavors, you'll gain new insights into the mystique of this cocktail. You will find Martini recipes that will be at home in a modern bar in the gin and vodka chapters.

It is also important to recognize how a cocktail recipe can change over time. A few words need to be said about cocktail histories. Like any recipe, it can be difficult or impossible to establish the details of a cocktail's invention. There are often a few claims on a single drink. Knowing a fact or two about a drink may help a bartender keep the huge catalog straight.

Some cocktail titles are actually numbered to differentiate between the various versions. For example, the Alexander No. 1 identifies the original formula for the creamy drink with crème de cacao, which was made with gin. Alexander No. 2 is actually a Brandy Alexander.

The Corpse Reviver is another drink that has had a number of incarnations. In this book, we have included our favorite versions of a cocktail, but haven't listed an entire sequence if one of them isn't up to our standards.

Regardless of the well-established history of morphing cocktails, some artisan bartenders, whose goal is to create perfectly crafted, tasty drinks, take the attitude that the Vodka Martini simply does not exist. The reasoning is that if a Vodka Martini is made in the manner that most people order it (very dry), the drink is essentially flavorless. When a bartender is doing his or her job right, the goal should also be to give the customers what they want, regardless of personal likes and dislikes. Even the Very Dry Vodka Martini, the drink that craft bartenders love to hate, can be improved upon by using a small-batch vermouth or a "blond" aperitivo (such as Cocchi Americano). Make the Martini lover a Vesper (page 105) according to James Bond's original recipe, and get ready for some interesting conversation on how to really make a Martini.

MARGARITA, DAIQUIRI, AND SIDECAR

As we've seen through the Old-Fashioned, Manhattan, and even Martini, drinks in the mixed drink category known as "cocktail" always included bitters as one of their ingredients. In those days, there were many different categories of mixed drinks, with the category itself defining much of the recipe. Forgotten monikers like Daisy, Fizz, Cobbler, Crusta, and the still-surviving Sour were each categories of their own. And many of them are coming back as bartenders stretch their talents (see page 40).

Mixed drinks reached both their apogee and their nadir during Prohibition. To disguise the flavor of so-called bathtub gin and other ill-prepared spirits, more and more ingredients were added to drinks. The term "cocktail" grew to such popularity that it eventually came to encompass many of the drinks that were previously from other categories. The "Sour" is one such category, and it even has vestiges in many modern cocktail names, like the Whiskey Sour.

The traditional sour was made using a spirit of any kind, a sweetening ingredient, and a souring ingredient. The sweetener could be as simple as just sugar or syrup, or it could be a sweet liqueur or cordial. The souring ingredient was normally lemon juice, but it could also be lime juice or grapefruit juice, or some combination of these.

Today, the Margarita is the reigning sour. Like most cocktails, the history of the Margarita is often debated and never resolved. A commonly repeated story has it being invented in 1948 by Margarita Sames for a large party she was holding in Acapulco, Mexico. There is a competing story that claims it was created in 1942 by Francisco Morales, who called this drink a "Daisy," which in Spanish is "Margarita." These and many other conflicting stories all claim to recount the origins of the most popular tequila-based cocktail. But they all agree that the original recipe consists of tequila, Cointreau, and lime juice, which clearly follows the classic recipe for a sour.

The Daiquiri is a rum version of the traditional sour, although these days many people will unfortunately confuse it with the blended frozen version, which, unless properly made, can be too reminiscent of "slushee" drinks from childhood.

It is fairly certain that the name of this drink comes from the similarly named town on the east coast of Cuba. While the commonly told story says that it was an American by the name of Jennings Cox who was living in Daiquiri who invented the drink, it is more likely that this was just a commonly served drink and that Americans who came to visit Mr. Cox and were served this drink began referring to it as "that Daiquiri drink." While the Margarita uses Cointreau as its sweetening ingredient, the Daiquiri uses just plain sugar or simple syrup for the task. However, it too is a sour.

The first appearance of the Sidecar recipe is found in *Cocktails: How to Mix Them*, by Robert Vermeire, published in 1922. It is debated whether this drink originated in Paris or London, but it is generally accepted that it was created in Europe at just about the same time that American Prohibition began. Over the years, the proportions have changed a bit to make a less tart drink.

For all of these cocktails it has become overly common for bars to use a "sour mix" to make them, often just combining a premade sour mix with the base spirit in order to quickly and efficiently churn out drinks. This approach, however, is not one that should be followed by a quality bar, any more than a quality restaurant would premake all of their meals and simply reheat them in the microwave.

☐ MARGARITA

For glass: Lime wedge, coarse (kosher) salt
1½ oz. blanco tequila
¾ oz. Cointreau or triple sec
¾ oz. fresh lime juice

Rim chilled cocktail glass with lime and salt. Shake remaining ingredients with ice and strain into glass.

℉ DAIQUIRI

2 oz. light rum
¾ oz. fresh lime juice
¾ oz. simple syrup

Shake with ice and strain into a chilled cocktail glass.

℉ SIDECAR

1 oz. Cognac
1 oz. triple sec
½ oz. fresh lemon juice

Shake with ice and strain into a chilled cocktail glass.

While each of these cocktails follows the same basic approach of spirit plus sweet plus sour, the actual ratios being used for each of them are listed differently. Because of the variation among spirits brands and the even greater variation in things like natural citrus, you should be prepared to adjust your recipes for balance. These recipes are merely a starting point.

THE MAI-TAI

Just as America was coming out of Prohibition, Donn Beach was setting up shop with his Polynesian-themed restaurants, which became known as "Don the Beachcomber." In the 1940s Victor Bergeron threw his hat in the ring and started the Trader Vic's chain. These two franchises specifically ushered in a new era, not only in restaurant culture, but in the cocktails they produced as well. This was the time of the "tiki craze," and there were many similarly themed restaurants that sprang up during this time in order to provide the American public with a much-needed vacation, one sip at a time. Rum was the prominent spirit, with various, often exotic, juices and syrups being used as flavoring agents. Actually, rum is Caribbean, not Polynesian, but when something tastes as good as well-made tiki drink, why split hairs?

Competition between these restaurants was often fierce, with their various cocktail recipes being closely guarded. Bartenders would have to guess at the ingredients of these tropical libations, creating many false recipes. With the casual proliferation of such a variety of different recipes for a cocktail with a single name, it is difficult to identify which is the original drink. One of the most popular drinks during this time was the Mai-Tai, and because of this it probably ended up with the highest number of variations. Fortunately, the version that started its popularity, which is referred to as the original Mai-Tai, was recorded by Victor "Trader Vic" Bergeron in 1944. There was apparently a similarly named drink listed on an earlier "Don the Beachcomber" menu, but its recipe was so radically different (and unpopular) that the Trader Vic recipe is clearly a different drink entirely.

As recorded by Mr. Bergeron himself, the original recipe for the Mai-Tai was as follows:

☐ MAI-TAI (TRADER VIC'S)

    2 oz. 17-year-old J. Wray and Nephew Ltd. rum
    ½ oz. French Garnier orgeat
    ½ oz. Holland DeKuyper orange Curaçao
    ¼ oz. rock candy syrup
    Juice from one fresh lime
    Garnish: ½ lime shell, fresh mint sprig

Hand shake and garnish with half of the lime shell inside the drink and float a sprig of fresh mint at the edge of the glass.

J. Wray and Nephew Ltd. now make a 21-year-old rum, but any aged Jamaican rum will be fine. Garnier is no longer in business, so use the oregeat of your choice. You can make a good Mai-Tai with any brand of curaçao. Rock candy syrup is made from crystallized sugar, but simple syrup is a fine stand-in.

This drink is served at other bars across the country with ingredients as far-reaching as pineapple juice, grenadine, passion fruit syrup, orange juice, amaretto, and even cherry brandy. Sometimes the resultant drink may be quite good indeed, but technically it is not a Mai-Tai and would be better to take an original name than to wear the guise of this classic. See page 125 for a contemporary, but classic, Mai-Tai.

BLOODY MARY

The Bloody Mary is an interesting cocktail, with ingredients more commonly found in the kitchen than behind the bar. The most credible story is that it was invented by Fernand Petiot of Harry's American Bar in Paris in the 1920s. When it traveled to America, for many years it was known as a Red Snapper. Its storied past has even inspired drinks-expert Jeff Pogash (full disclosure: father of editor) to write a book titled *The Quest for the Bloody Mary* (2011, Thorn Willow Press).

A vodka-based cocktail, the Bloody Mary owes its flavor to the other ingredients, as vodka does not impart much taste on its own.

The basic Bloody Mary recipe:

♆ BLOODY MARY

1½ oz. vodka
3 oz. tomato juice
¼ oz. fresh lemon juice
4 dashes Worcestershire sauce
2–3 drops hot red pepper sauce
Freshly ground black pepper
Garnish: Lime wedge, 3 green olives

Roll with ice between both halves of Boston shaker. Strain into ice-filled old-fashioned glass. Garnish with lime and olives.

The above is essentially the "mother" recipe from which different offspring arise. The vodka and tomato juice are the core ingredients, but as for the rest, anything goes as long as you arrive at a spicy and savory drink with a rich and robust flavor.

Among the creative ingredients that have found their way into the Bloody Mary are celery salt, wasabi, horseradish, cumin, chili powder, liquid smoke, steak sauce, sherry, beef broth, clam juice, and countless others. The Bloody Mary has essentially become the "meat loaf" of cocktails. Almost anything goes as long as it's recognizable in the end. The same can be said for the garnish, which can be as simple as a celery stick or as complex as steamed shrimp.

Historical Cocktail Names

Throughout this book, you will see the same cocktail names appear again and again—Bishop, Cobbler, Rickey, and more. Knowing the characteristics of a given cocktail is one way to keep track of the various recipes. The basic recipes for many of these drinks are in the Brandy chapter on pages 45–64. Simply substitute the base spirit of choice (vodka, gin, whiskey, or what have you) as desired. Here are some the most common cocktails, most of which have been in service for decades, if not centuries.

Bishop A red wine–based drink, sweetened with citrus and sugar and sometimes spiced.

Buck Usually made with gin, this is a tall drink with ginger ale and a generous squeeze of fresh lemon juice.

Cobbler Shaved or cracked ice is a key element in a cobbler, with the addition of a base liquor and a generous topping of seasonal fresh fruit.

Collins Originally made with gin, but now most often with vodka, the Collins is a thirst-quenching drink of base liquor, lemon juice, and sugar, topped off with soda water.

Crusta The two identifying marks of a Crusta are a sugar-rimmed serving glass (the "crust" that gives the cocktail its name) and a long spiral of citrus zest to garnish and flavor the drink.

Daisy Similar to a Sour (base spirit, lemon juice, and sugar) but with a dose of grenadine or fruit syrup, and served over ice. Some versions have a splash of soda water.

Fix Another tall, tart drink with base spirit, lemon juice, and sugar, always served over lots of ice, sometimes shaved ice.

Fizz A shaken cocktail comprised of base spirit (usually gin), citrus juice, sugar, and sometimes cream, it gets its bubbles from soda water. Some Fizzes include egg (whole, white, or yolk) to encourage a good froth.

Flip On the sweet side, this rich cocktail is always shaken with an egg.

Highball One of the most popular cocktails, this is simply a base spirit with a carbonated liquid, usually soda. Americans like it with ice, which British drinkers traditionally omit.

Julep A symbol of Southern hospitality, the word comes from the Arabic *julāb* ("rose water"), which originally meant a sweetened medicine. Today, it is a base spirit (almost always bourbon), sweetened with sugar and served with a profusion of fresh mint, traditionally over shaved ice in a silver cup.

Pousse-Café The name of this drink type ("coffee pusher" in French) identifies it as a beverage to be served after dinner or even after dessert. It consists of carefully layered liqueurs (and sometimes other ingredients) in a tall, but small, glass.

Rickey Related to the Collins, but without sugar.

Sangaree The name is derived from the Spanish *sangria*, showing how the original version featured fortified wine from the Mediterranean (such as port). It often has a topping of grated nutmeg.

Sling A tall cocktail along the lines of a Collins, but with fruit brandy as a main flavoring, these drinks are usually related to the original Singapore Sling (mixed with gin, cherry brandy, Bénédictine, and soda).

Smash A cousin of the Julep, in which flavoring ingredients (fruits, sugar, and/or mint) are muddled (that is, smashed) and mixed with a base liquor.

Sour Actually, this kind of cocktail is more sweet-and-sour, as simple syrup is used to balance the sour ingredient (commonly lemon or lime juice). A sour can be made with just about any base spirit, although whiskey is the most familiar.

Swizzle The drinks in this cocktail family are all mixed with a barspoon (standing in for a branch of a swizzle bush) that is twirled between the bartender's palms.

Toddy These days, a toddy is a warming drink of spirits and hot water (and sometimes spices). In Colonial America, it could have been any alcoholic drink that combined liquor and water of any temperature.

BRANDY

BRANDY TAKES ITS NAME from the Dutch word *brandewijn*, or "burned wine," which refers to the process of heating the wine during distillation. Brandy as a category embodies a dizzying number of subcategories, including fruit brandy, grappa, marc, pomace, and eau de vie, to name only a few. The most generic definition for this spirit is that it is distilled from fermented fruit; it is sometimes aged in oak casks or barrels; and it usually clocks in at around 80 proof. While it is often considered an after-dinner sipping spirit, brandy is also widely used in cocktails.

Generally, fruit brandies and eaux de vie can legally be made from practically any fruit, including apples, pears, apricots, blackberries, and cherries. At the high end of the brandy spectrum, you'll find Calvados from the north of France, cognac and Armagnac from southwest France, and Solera Gran Reserva under the Brandy de Jerez imprimatur from the south of Spain. Artisanal brandies are also being made here in the United States, with many of the best hailing from California and Oregon.

In cocktails, cognac plays a leading role in a number of recipes dating back to the birth of the cocktail in Antoine Peychaud's apothecary shop in New Orleans. Indeed, the original juleps were made with cognac, not whiskey.

Armagnac, cognac's rustic cousin, has a distinctly stronger flavor than cognac and is employed as a substitute to enhance the brandy presence in a cocktail. Calvados, made with apples, is naturally used to ratchet up the quality of any cocktail calling for mere apple brandy. New Jersey's applejack gets its due in the Jack Rose and other classics. Pisco, a South American brandy, has found its way into many drinks beyond the Pisco Sour and Pisco Punch.

⅄ ACCOUTREMENT

Created by CHRIS HANNAH,
New Orleans, LA

1½ oz. Calvados
½ oz. Strega
¼ oz. orange-flavored liqueur,
  preferably Creole Shrubb
½ oz. fresh lemon juice
2 dashes Peychaud's bitters
Garnish: Italian cherry in syrup

*Shake with ice and strain
into chilled cocktail glass.
Add cherry.*

☐ ALABAZAM

2 oz. Armagnac
¾ oz. fresh lemon juice
½ oz. orange curaçao
½ oz. simple syrup
2 dashes Angostura bitters
2 dashes Peychaud's bitters
Garnish: Orange twist, flamed
  (see Note)

*Shake with ice and strain
into ice-filled old-fashioned
glass. Flame orange twist
and add.*

Note: To flame citrus, ignite a match and hold in one hand. Bend orange twist in other hand to express oil into flame; oil will spark slightly.

♈ AMERICAN BEAUTY COCKTAIL

½ oz. brandy
½ oz. dry vermouth
½ oz. fresh orange juice
½ oz. grenadine
1 dash white crème de menthe
1 dash port

Shake first five ingredients with ice and strain into chilled cocktail glass. Top with port.

♈ B & B

½ oz. brandy
½ oz. Bénédictine

Combine ingredients in cordial glass.

♈ BABBIE'S SPECIAL COCKTAIL

1½ oz. apricot-flavored brandy
½ oz. gin
½ oz. half-and-half

Shake with ice and strain into chilled cocktail glass.

♈ BEE STINGER

1½ oz. blackberry brandy
½ oz. white crème de menthe

Shake with ice and strain into chilled cocktail glass.

♈ BISTRO SIDECAR

Created by KATHY CASEY, Seattle, WA

For glass: Tangerine wedge, superfine sugar
1½ oz. brandy
½ oz. Tuaca
½ oz. hazelnut liqueur, such as Frangelico
½ oz. fresh tangerine juice
¼ oz. fresh lemon juice
¼ oz. simple syrup
Garnish: Roasted hazelnut

Rim chilled cocktail glass with tangerine and sugar. Shake ingredients with ice. Strain into glass. Add hazelnut.

Y BOMBAY COCKTAIL

Harry Craddock, an American
bartender who landed
at London's Savoy after
Prohibition, chronicled many of
his creations in his 1930 *Savoy
Cocktail Book.* You'll see some
of his recipes in this book.

1 oz. brandy
½ oz. dry vermouth
½ oz. sweet vermouth
¼ oz. triple sec
¼ tsp. anisette

*Stir with ice and strain into
chilled cocktail glass.*

Y BRANDY ALEXANDER NO. 1

¾ oz. brandy
¾ oz. dark crème de cacao
¾ oz. heavy cream
Garnish: Freshly grated nutmeg

*Shake well with ice and
strain into chilled cocktail
glass. Top with nutmeg.*

Y BRANDY ALEXANDER NO. 2

1 oz. brandy
1 oz. white crème de cacao
1 oz. half-and-half
Garnish: Freshly grated
    nutmeg

*Shake with ice and strain
into chilled cocktail glass. Top
with nutmeg.*

Y BRANDY CASSIS

1½ oz. brandy
1 oz. fresh lemon juice
½ oz. crème de cassis
Garnish: Lemon twist

*Shake with ice and strain
into chilled cocktail glass.
Add lemon twist.*

℧ BRANDY COBBLER

2 oz. brandy
1 tsp. simple syrup
2 oz. soda water
Garnish: Fresh seasonal
    fruit

*Combine brandy, syrup, and
soda water in red-wine glass.
Fill glass with shaved ice.
Garnish with fruit. Serve
with straws.*

▭ BRANDY COLLINS

2 oz. brandy
¾ oz. fresh lemon juice
¾ oz. simple syrup
Soda water
Garnish: Orange or lemon
    wheel, maraschino cherry

*Shake brandy, lemon juice,
and syrup and strain into ice-
filled Collins glass. Fill with
soda water and stir. Garnish
with citrus and cherry. Serve
with straws.*

▽ BRANDY CRUSTA

One of the oldest cocktails,
appearing in the first
bartenders' guide by
"Professor" Jerry Thomas
in 1862, this drink is
distinguished by its sugared
rim and a curled lemon zest
almost filling the glass.

For glass: Lemon wedge,
    superfine sugar
Long, wide spiral of lemon zest
2 oz. brandy
½ oz. triple sec
1 tsp. maraschino liqueur
1 tsp. fresh lemon juice
1 dash Angostura bitters
Garnish: Orange wheel

*Rim chilled cocktail glass
with lemon and sugar. Curl
the zest spiral on its side in
glass. Stir ingredients with
ice and strain into glass.
Garnish with orange.*

🍺 BRANDY DAISY

2 oz. brandy
1 oz. fresh lemon juice
1 tsp. simple syrup
¼ oz. raspberry syrup or
    grenadine
Garnish: Fresh seasonal fruit

*Shake with ice and strain
into beer mug or 8-oz. metal
cup. Add ice. Garnish with
fruit.*

🍺 BRANDY FIX

2½ oz. brandy
¾ oz. fresh lemon juice
¾ oz. simple syrup
Garnish: Lemon wheel

*Stir brandy, lemon juice, and
syrup in shaved ice–filled
highball glass. Add lemon.
Serve with straws.*

🍺 BRANDY FIZZ

2 oz. brandy
¾ oz. fresh lemon juice
¾ oz. simple syrup
Soda water

*Shake brandy, lemon juice,
and syrup with ice and
strain into ice-filled highball
glass. Fill with soda water
and stir.*

🍺 BRANDY HIGHBALL

2 oz. brandy
Ginger ale or soda water
Garnish: Lemon twist

*Pour brandy into ice-filled
highball glass. Fill with ginger ale or soda water. Add
lemon twist and stir gently.*

🍺 BRANDY JULEP

2½ oz. brandy
½ oz. simple syrup
5–6 fresh mint leaves
Garnishes: Pineapple, orange,
    or lemon slice; maraschino
    cherry

*Stir brandy, syrup, and mint
in Collins glass. Fill with
shaved ice and stir until
mint rises to top, being careful not to bruise leaves. (Do
not hold sides of glass while
stirring to frost exterior.)
Garnish with fruit. Serve
with straws.*

◻ BRANDY SANGAREE

2 oz. brandy
½ oz. simple syrup
Soda water
½ oz. port
Garnish: Freshly grated nutmeg

Add brandy and syrup to highball glass. Add ice, fill with soda water, and stir. Float port (see page 12) on top and top with nutmeg.

◻ BRANDY SLING

2 oz. brandy
¾ oz. fresh lemon juice
¾ oz. cherry-flavored brandy
Garnish: Lemon twist

Stir in old-fashioned glass. Fill with ice and stir again. Add lemon twist.

◻ BRANDY SMASH

1 sugar cube
1 oz. soda water
4 fresh mint leaves
2 oz. brandy
Garnish: Lemon twist, orange wheel, maraschino cherry

Muddle sugar with soda water and mint in old-fashioned glass. Add brandy and ice. Stir and add lemon twist. Garnish with orange and cherry.

▽ BRANDY SOUR

2 oz. brandy
¾ oz. fresh lemon juice
¾ oz. simple syrup
Garnish: Lemon half-wheel, maraschino cherry

Shake with ice and strain into chilled cocktail glass. Garnish with lemon and cherry.

◻ BRANDY SWIZZLE

2 oz. brandy
¾ oz. fresh lime juice
¾ oz. simple syrup
2 dashes Angostura bitters
Soda water

Stir brandy, lime juice, syrup, and bitters in Collins glass. Add ice and enough soda to fill glass ¾ full. Swizzle with barspoon to frost glass. Add more ice and soda as needed. Serve with swizzle stick.

◻ BRANDY TODDY

2 oz. brandy
1 tsp. simple syrup
Garnish: Lemon twist

Stir brandy and syrup in old-fashioned glass. Add 1 ice cube and lemon twist.

BULLDOG COCKTAIL

1½ oz. cherry-flavored brandy
¾ oz. gin
½ oz. fresh lime juice

Shake with ice and strain into chilled cocktail glass.

BULL'S EYE

1 oz. brandy
2 oz. hard cider
Ginger ale

Stir brandy and hard cider in highball glass. Add ice, fill with ginger ale, and stir again.

CALVADOS COCKTAIL

1½ oz. Calvados
1½ oz. fresh orange juice
¾ oz. triple sec
1 dash orange bitters

Shake with ice and strain into chilled cocktail glass.

CARA SPOSA

1 oz. coffee-flavored brandy
¾ oz. triple sec
½ oz. half-and-half

Shake with ice and strain into chilled cocktail glass.

CHAMPS ÉLYSÉES COCKTAIL

Here's another contribution from Harry Craddock's *Savoy Cocktail Book.*

1 oz. brandy
½ oz. yellow Chartreuse
½ oz. fresh lemon juice
1 tsp. simple syrup
1 dash Angostura bitters

Shake with ice and strain into chilled cocktail glass.

CHERRY BLOSSOM

For glass: Cherry-flavored brandy, superfine sugar
1½ oz. brandy
½ oz. cherry-flavored brandy
½ oz. fresh lemon juice
¼ oz. triple sec
¼ oz. grenadine
Garnish: Maraschino cherry

Rim chilled cocktail glass with brandy and sugar. Shake ingredients with ice and strain into glass. Add cherry.

▢ CHICAGO COCKTAIL

For glass: Lemon wedge,
    superfine sugar
2 oz. brandy
¼ oz. triple sec
1 dash Angostura bitters

*Rim chilled old-fashioned
glass with lemon and sugar.
Stir remaining ingredients
with ice and strain into
glass.*

▢ COFFEE GRASSHOPPER

¾ oz. coffee-flavored brandy
¾ oz. white crème de menthe
¾ oz. half-and-half

*Shake with ice and strain
into ice-filled old-fashioned
glass.*

▽ COLD DECK COCKTAIL

1 oz. brandy
½ oz. sweet vermouth
1 tsp. white crème de menthe

*Stir with ice and strain into
chilled cocktail glass.*

▽ CORPSE REVIVER NO. 1

The Corpse Reviver No. 2 is a
gin drink, but Cognac fans like
this one, which is sure to bring
you around.

2 oz. cognac
1 oz. Calvados, apple brandy,
    or applejack
1 oz. sweet vermouth

*Stir with ice and strain into
a chilled cocktail glass.*

▢ CRÈME DE CAFÉ

1 oz. coffee-flavored brandy
½ oz. light rum
½ oz. anisette
1 oz. half-and-half

*Shake with ice and strain
into chilled old-fashioned
glass.*

▽ THE CRUX

¾ oz. Dubonnet
¾ oz. triple sec
¾ oz. brandy
¾ oz. fresh lemon juice
Garnish: Orange twist

*Stir with ice and strain into
chilled cocktail glass. Add
orange twist.*

▽ CUBAN COCKTAIL NO. 2

1½ oz. brandy
½ oz. light rum
½ oz. apricot-flavored brandy
½ oz fresh lime juice

*Shake with ice and strain
into chilled cocktail glass.*

❢ D'ARTAGNAN

1 tsp. Armagnac
1 tsp. Grand Marnier
1 tsp. simple syrup
½ oz. fresh orange juice
3 oz. chilled Champagne
Garnish: 3 long, thin strips of
    orange zest (use channel
    tool)

*Shake first four ingredients
with ice and strain into
champagne flute. Top with
Champagne and insert
orange zest strips to extend
the length of the glass.*

▽ DEAUVILLE COCKTAIL

½ oz. brandy
½ oz. apple brandy
½ oz. triple sec
½ oz. fresh lemon juice

*Shake with ice and strain
into chilled cocktail glass.*

▽ EAST INDIA COCKTAIL NO. 1

1½ oz. brandy
½ oz. Jamaican rum
½ oz. triple sec
½ oz. pineapple juice
1 dash Angostura bitters
Garnish: Lemon twist,
    maraschino cherry

*Shake with ice and strain
into chilled cocktail glass.
Add lemon twist and cherry.*

▢ EL PROFESOR

Created by ENRIQUE
SANCHEZ, San Francisco, CA

1 oz. pisco
½ oz. Punt e Mes
½ oz. Bénédictine
2 dashes aromatic bitters,
    such as Fee's
Garnish: Lemon twist

*Stir with ice and strain into
chilled old-fashioned glass.
Add lemon twist.*

FALLEN LEAVES

¾ oz. Calvados
¾ oz. sweet vermouth
¼ oz. dry vermouth
1 dash brandy
Garnish: Lemon twist

Stir with ice and strain into chilled cocktail glass. Add lemon twist.

FANCY BRANDY

2 oz. brandy
¼ oz. triple sec
¼ oz. simple syrup
1 dash Angostura bitters
Garnish: Lemon twist

Shake with ice and strain into chilled cocktail glass. Add lemon twist.

FONTAINEBLEAU SPECIAL

1 oz. brandy
1 oz. anisette
½ oz. dry vermouth

Shake with ice and strain into chilled cocktail glass.

FRENCH QUARTER

2½ oz. brandy
¾ oz. Lillet Blanc
Garnish: Lemon quarter-wheel

Stir with ice and strain into chilled cocktail glass. Garnish with lemon.

GOAT'S DELIGHT

1½ oz. brandy
1½ oz. kirschwasser
¼ oz. half-and-half
1 dash orgeat or almond syrup
1 dash absinthe or pastis

Shake with ice and strain into chilled cocktail glass.

GOLDEN DAWN

1 oz. apple brandy
½ oz. apricot-flavored brandy
½ oz. gin
1 oz. fresh orange juice
1 tsp. grenadine

Shake first four ingredients with ice and strain into ice-filled old-fashioned glass. Add grenadine.

☒ HARVARD COCKTAIL

1½ oz. brandy
¾ oz. sweet vermouth
½ oz fresh lemon juice
1 tsp. grenadine
1 dash Angostura bitters

Shake with ice and strain into chilled cocktail glass.

☒ JACK-IN-THE-BOX

1 oz. applejack
1 oz. pineapple juice
1 dash Angostura bitters

Shake with ice and strain into chilled cocktail glass.

☒ JACK MAPLES

2 oz. applejack
1 tsp. maple syrup (grade B or medium-amber)
1 dash aromatic bitters, such as Fee's
Garnish: Cinnamon stick

Stir with ice and strain into cocktail glass. Garnish with cinnamon stick.

☒ JACK ROSE COCKTAIL

Was this drink named for a notorious gangster? Probably not. Jack is a nickname for New Jersey applejack, and grenadine gives the drink a pink tinge, so that may provide the simplest, if dullest, answer.

1½ oz. applejack
½ oz. fresh lime juice
¼ oz. grenadine

Shake with ice and strain into chilled cocktail glass.

☒ JAPANESE

2 oz. brandy
½ oz. orgeat or almond syrup
2 dashes Angostura bitters
Garnish: Lemon twist

Stir with ice and strain into chilled cocktail glass. Add lemon twist.

☒ JERSEY LIGHTNING

1½ oz. applejack
½ oz. sweet vermouth
1 oz. fresh lime juice

Shake with ice and strain into chilled cocktail glass.

🍷 JOHNNY APPLESEED

Created by JONATHAN POGASH, New York, NY

2 slices Fuji apple, chopped
½ oz. fresh lemon juice
½ oz. simple syrup
1 oz. cognac
½ oz. cherry-flavored brandy
1 oz. unfiltered apple juice
Garnish: 1 Fuji apple slice

Muddle first 3 ingredients in mixing glass. Add remaining ingredients and shake with ice. Strain through wire sieve into ice-filled wine glass. Garnish with apple slice.

🍷 JACK RABBIT PUNCH

Created by JONATHAN POGASH, New York, NY

1½ oz. applejack
¾ oz. pear liqueur
¼ oz. allspice liqueur (pimento dram)
¾ oz. fresh lemon juice
½ oz. maple syrup
2 oz. sparkling wine
Garnish: Freshly grated nutmeg, cinnamon stick, sliced pear

Shake ingredients, except for sparkling wine, with ice and strain into ice-filled brandy snifter. Top with sparkling wine. Add garnishes.

KUMQUAT COOLER

Created by JIM MEEHAN,
New York, NY

3 kumquats, sliced
1½ oz. cognac
½ oz. Strega
½ oz. fresh lemon juice
¼ oz. dark rum
¼ oz. simple syrup
Garnish: Kumquat slice and
   lemon wheel, speared on
   toothpick

*Muddle kumquats in mixing
glass. Add remaining ingredients and ice and shake.
Strain into crushed ice–filled
Collins glass. Garnish with
kumquat and lemon.*

LA JOLLA

1½ oz. brandy
½ oz. crème de banana
½ oz. fresh lemon juice
1 tsp. fresh orange juice

*Shake with ice and strain
into chilled cocktail glass.*

LIBERTY COCKTAIL

1½ oz. apple brandy
¾ oz. light rum
1 tsp. simple syrup

*Stir with ice and strain into
chilled cocktail glass.*

LUXURY COCKTAIL

1 oz. brandy
2 dashes orange bitters
3 oz. chilled Champagne

*Gently fold ingredients with
ice, so as not to remove bubbles, then strain into chilled
champagne flute.*

METROPOLE

1½ oz. brandy
1½ oz. dry vermouth
2 dashes orange bitters
1 dash Peychaud's bitters
Garnish: Maraschino cherry

*Stir with ice and strain into
chilled cocktail glass. Garnish
with cherry.*

MIDNIGHT COCKTAIL

1 oz. apricot-flavored brandy
½ oz. triple sec
½ oz. fresh lemon juice

*Shake with ice and strain
into chilled cocktail glass.*

☕ MON SHERRY

Created by HAL WOLIN,
New York, NY

1½ oz. cognac
¾ oz. pear liqueur
½ oz. medium-dry sherry, such
   as amontillado
2 dashes orange bitters
Garnish: Italian preserved
   cherry, freshly grated
   nutmeg

*Shake with ice and strain
into chilled cocktail glass.
Add cherry and top with
nutmeg.*

☕ NICKY FINN

1 oz. brandy
1 oz. triple sec
1 oz. fresh lemon juice
1 dash absinthe or pastis
Garnish: Maraschino cherry or
   lemon twist

*Shake with ice and strain
into chilled cocktail glass.
Garnish with cherry or
lemon twist.*

☐ NIGHT & DAY

Created by PETER CHASE,
New York, NY

¾ oz. cognac
¾ oz. rye whiskey
¾ oz. dry vermouth
½ oz. maple syrup
1 dash Peychaud's bitters
1 dash Angostura bitters
Garnish: Orange and lemon
   twists

*Shake with ice and strain
into ice-filled old-fashioned
glass. Add orange and lemon
twists.*

☕ THE NORMANDY

1½ oz. Calvados
1½ oz. Dubonnet
1 oz. apple cider
¼ oz. fresh lime juice
Garnish: Red apple slice

*Shake with ice and strain
into chilled cocktail glass.
Garnish with apple slice.*

☕ OLYMPIC COCKTAIL

¾ oz. brandy
¾ oz. triple sec
¾ oz. fresh orange juice

*Shake with ice and strain
into chilled cocktail glass.*

▽ PARADISE COCKTAIL

1 oz. apricot-flavored brandy
¾ oz. gin
1 oz. fresh orange juice

Shake with ice and strain into chilled cocktail glass.

▢ PISCO PUNCH

The drink of the Gold Rush in San Francisco, as the most readily available brandy was Peruvian. This is an adaptation of the original, invented at The Bank Exchange bar.

2 oz. pisco
¾ oz. pineapple juice
½ oz. simple syrup
½ oz. fresh lemon juice

Shake with ice and strain into ice-filled old-fashioned glass.

▽ PISCO SOUR

2 oz. pisco
¾ oz. fresh lime juice
¼ oz. simple syrup
½ egg white
Garnish: 1 dash Angostura bitters

Shake without ice. Add ice and shake again. Strain into chilled champagne flute or cocktail glass. Top with bitters.

▽ PLAZA PUNCH

Created by JONATHAN POGASH, New York, NY

1½ oz. pisco
¾ oz. orange liqueur
¼ oz. amaro
¾ oz. pineapple juice
½ oz. fresh lime juice
1 tsp. agave nectar
2 dashes Peychaud's bitters
Garnish: Freshly grated nutmeg

Shake with ice and strain into ice-filled brandy snifter. Top with nutmeg.

▽ PRESTO COCKTAIL

1 splash anisette
1½ oz. brandy
½ oz. sweet vermouth
½ oz. fresh orange juice

Pour anisette into chilled cocktail glass, swirl to coat inside; discard remaining anisette. Shake remaining ingredients with ice and strain into glass.

RENAISSANCE

2 oz. brandy
1 oz. sweet vermouth
½ oz. limoncello
2 dashes peach bitters
Garnish: Lemon twist

Stir with ice and strain into chilled cocktail glass. Add lemon twist.

ST. CHARLES PUNCH

"Professor" Jerry Thomas spent some time bartending in New Orleans. This drink appears in his book, and could be named for the St. Charles Hotel in that city.

1 oz. brandy
½ oz. triple sec
1 oz. fresh lemon juice
½ oz. simple syrup
3 oz. tawny port
Garnish: Lemon wheel, maraschino cherry

Shake first four ingredients with ice. Strain into ice-filled Collins glass. Top with port. Garnish with lemon and cherry.

SARATOGA COCKTAIL (JOHNSON VERSION)

Harry Johnson was another superstar of bartending's Golden Age during the late nineteenth century. His salute to New York State's horse-crazy resort town has fruity flavors.

2 oz. brandy
1 tsp. fresh lemon juice
1 tsp. pineapple juice
½ tsp. maraschino liqueur
2 dashes Angostura bitters

Shake with ice and strain into chilled cocktail glass.

SARATOGA COCKTAIL (THOMAS VERSION)

Saratoga Springs also inspired Professor Jerry Thomas to create a cocktail, but his has more alcohol heft.

¾ oz. brandy
¾ oz. rye whiskey
¾ oz. dry vermouth
2 dashes Angostura bitters
Garnish: Lemon wedge

Shake with ice and strain into chilled cocktail glass. Garnish with lemon.

♀ SEVILLA 75

1 oz. Spanish brandy
½ oz. fresh lemon juice
1 tsp. simple syrup
2 oz. Spanish sparkling wine
(cava)

*Shake first three ingredients
and strain into chilled red-wine
glass. Top with sparkling wine.*

▽ SHRINER COCKTAIL

1½ oz. brandy
1½ oz. sloe gin
1 tsp. simple syrup
2 dashes Angostura bitters
Garnish: Lemon twist

*Stir with ice and strain into
chilled cocktail glass. Add
lemon twist.*

▽ SIDECAR COCKTAIL

An American military officer,
who arrived at his favorite
Parisian bar in a motorcycle
sidecar, loved this drink, and
soon everyone in Paris was
drinking it.
For glass: Lemon wedge,
superfine sugar
1 oz. brandy
1 oz. triple sec
½ oz. fresh lemon juice

*Rim chilled cocktail glass
with lemon and sugar. Shake
remaining ingredients with
ice and strain into glass.*

▽ SLOPPY JOE'S COCKTAIL NO. 2

¾ oz. brandy
¾ oz. tawny port
¾ oz. pineapple juice
¼ oz. triple sec
¼ oz. grenadine

*Shake with ice and strain
into chilled cocktail glass.*

▢ SOMBRERO

1½ oz. coffee-flavored brandy
1 oz. half-and-half

*Pour brandy into ice-filled
old-fashioned glass. Float
half-and-half on top.*

☿ SOOTHER COCKTAIL

½ oz. brandy
½ oz. apple brandy
½ oz. triple sec
½ oz. fresh lemon juice
½ oz. simple syrup

Shake with ice and strain into chilled cocktail glass.

☿ STINGER

Reginald Claypool Vanderbilt, the millionaire equestrian, loved his brandy stingers.

1½ oz. brandy
½ oz. white crème de menthe

Shake with ice and strain into chilled cocktail glass.

☿ THE TANTRIS SIDECAR

Created by AUDREY SAUNDERS, New York, NY

For glass: Lemon wedge, superfine sugar
1 oz. VS cognac
½ oz. Calvados or apple brandy
½ oz. triple sec
½ oz. fresh lemon juice
½ oz. simple syrup
¼ oz. pineapple juice
¼ oz. green Chartreuse
Garnish: Lemon twist

Rim chilled cocktail glass with lemon and sugar. Shake remaining ingredients with ice and strain into glass. Add lemon twist.

☝ TULIP COCKTAIL

¾ oz. apple brandy
¾ oz. sweet vermouth
¼ oz. fresh lemon juice
¼ oz. apricot-flavored brandy

*Shake with ice and strain
into chilled cocktail glass.*

☝ VALENCIA COCKTAIL

1½ oz. apricot-flavored brandy
½ oz. fresh orange juice
2 dashes orange bitters

*Shake with ice and strain
into chilled cocktail glass.*

☝ WIDOW'S KISS

The Hoffman House ran one
of the premier bars during
New York's Gaslight Era, and
this ladylike drink probably
debuted there.

1½ oz. Calvados or apple
      brandy
¾ oz. yellow Chartreuse
¾ oz. Bénédictine
1 dash Angostura bitters

*Stir with ice and strain into
chilled cocktail glass.*

GIN

GIN WAS CREATED OVER 300 years ago by a Dutch chemist named Dr. Franciscus Sylvius in an attempt to enhance the therapeutic properties of juniper in a medicinal beverage. He called it *genièvre*, French for "juniper," a term that was anglicized by English soldiers fighting in the Netherlands, who also nicknamed it "Dutch courage." The popularity of gin in England became such that the "London dry" style evolved into the benchmark of quality. The clear spirit is made from a mash of cereal grain (primarily corn, rye, barley, and wheat) that is flavored with botanicals (primarily juniper), which gives it its unique taste. Other botanicals employed in top-secret recipes include coriander, lemon and orange peel, cassia root, anise, and fennel seeds, to name only a few.

Gin, like many other spirits, changed in character in the early nineteenth century, when advances made in distilling equipment revolutionized the way it was made. Today, it's changing again. A new international style called "New Western dry" has emerged in the past decade; it's lighter and more balanced, meant to be sipped as well as mixed into cocktails. Historical styles of gin are making a comeback too, such as "Old Tom" (a sweeter version of London dry) and the lower-proof Dutch original genever, which is distilled from malted grain mash similar to whiskey and aged in oak casks. Unless otherwise designated, the recipes in this book use London dry gin.

Regardless of the classification, probably the best way to compare gins is to mix them with tonic or vermouth and imagine the myriad possibilities.

ABBEY COCKTAIL

1½ oz. gin
1 oz. fresh orange juice
1 dash orange bitters
Garnish: Maraschino cherry

Shake with ice and strain into chilled cocktail glass. Add cherry.

A CURRANT AFFAIR

Created by ERYN REECE,
New York, NY

1½ oz. gin
½ oz. crème de cassis
½ oz. cream sherry
Garnish: Lemon wheel
    wrapped around 3 fresh
    black currants and
    skewered

Shake with ice and strain through wire sieve into chilled cocktail glass. Garnish with lemon and currants.

ALBEMARLE FIZZ

2 oz. gin
¾ oz. fresh lemon juice
1 tsp. raspberry syrup
¼ oz. simple syrup
Soda water

Shake first four ingredients with ice and strain into ice-filled highball glass. Fill with soda water.

⅄ ALEXANDER COCKTAIL NO. 1 (GIN)

Creamy and lush, the Brandy Alexander is a now-familiar after-dinner drink. However, you might want to get to know the original version, made with gin.

1 oz. gin
1 oz. white crème de cacao
1 oz. half-and-half
Garnish: Freshly grated nutmeg

Shake with ice and strain into chilled cocktail glass. Top with nutmeg.

⅄ THE APOLLO

Created by MOSES LABOY, New York, NY

1 (1-inch) piece fresh ginger, sliced
7 fresh sage leaves
1½ oz. gin
1 egg white
¾ oz. simple syrup
½ oz. fresh lemon juice
Garnish: 1 dash Angostura bitters, fresh sage leaf

Muddle ginger and 7 sage leaves in mixing glass. Add remaining ingredients and shake without ice. Add ice and shake again. Strain into chilled cocktail glass. Top with bitters and single sage leaf.

⅄ ARCHANGEL

1 cucumber slice
2¼ oz. gin
¾ oz. Aperol
Garnish: Lemon twist

Muddle cucumber in mixing glass. Add gin and Aperol with ice, stir, and strain into chilled cocktail glass. Add lemon twist.

⅄ ASTORIA BIANCO

Created by JIM MEEHAN, New York, NY

2 oz. gin
¾ oz. dry vermouth
2 dashes orange bitters
Garnish: Orange twist

Stir with ice and strain into chilled cocktail glass. Add orange twist.

⅄ AUDREY FANNING

2½ oz. gin
1 oz. sweet vermouth
½ oz. Cherry Heering
2 dashes Peychaud's bitters

Stir with ice and strain into chilled cocktail glass.

⅋ AVIATION

The crème de violette will turn the cocktail a color similar to the wild blue yonder, but if you don't have a bottle in your collection, leave it out.

2 oz. gin
½ oz. maraschino liqueur
¼ oz. fresh lemon juice
¼ oz. crème de violette or Crème Yvette (optional)
Garnish: Fresh or maraschino cherry

Shake with ice and strain into chilled cocktail glass. Garnish with cherry.

⬚ BAD-HUMORED OLD-FASHIONED

2 oz. genever
¼ oz. maple syrup
2 dashes Angostura bitters
Garnish: Lemon twist

Stir with ice and strain into chilled old-fashioned glass. Add lemon twist.

⅋ BASIL'S BITE

3 fresh basil leaves
2 oz. gin
1 tsp. Cynar
¾ oz. Aperol
Garnish: Small fresh basil leaf

Muddle basil leaves in mixing glass. Shake with remaining ingredients and ice. Strain into chilled cocktail glass. Garnish with basil leaf.

⅋ BEAUTY-SPOT COCKTAIL

1 dash grenadine
1 oz. gin
½ oz. sweet vermouth
½ oz. dry vermouth
½ oz. fresh orange juice

Dash grenadine into bottom of chilled cocktail glass. Shake remaining ingredients with ice. Strain into glass.

♈ BEE'S KNEES

This cocktail has "Prohibition era" written all over it. "Bee's knees" is a phrase from the Jazz Age meaning "the best," and the use of honey would sweeten and mask the rough taste of the gin.

2 oz. gin
½ oz. fresh lemon juice
¾ oz. Honey Syrup (page 21)

Shake with ice and strain into chilled champagne coupe.

♈ BEE STING

2 oz. gln
¾ oz. fresh lemon juice
¾ oz. Honey Syrup (page 21)
1 tsp. absinthe or pastis
Garnish: Star anise pod

Shake with ice and strain into chilled cocktail glass. Garnish with star anise.

♈ BELMONT COCKTAIL

2 oz. gin
¾ oz. half-and-half
¼ oz. raspberry syrup

Shake with ice and strain into chilled cocktail glass.

♈ BERLINER

For glass: Superfine sugar, coarsely ground caraway seed, lemon wedge
1½ oz. gin
½ oz. dry vermouth
½ oz. kümmel
½ oz. fresh lemon juice
Garnish: Lemon twist

Mix sugar and caraway seed. Rim chilled cocktail glass with lemon and sugar mixture. Shake next four ingredients with ice and pour into glass. Add lemon twist.

▯ BERMUDA BOUQUET

1½ oz. gin
¾ oz. apricot-flavored brandy
¾ oz. fresh orange juice
¾ oz. fresh lemon juice
¼ oz. simple syrup
1 tsp. grenadine
1 tsp. triple sec

Shake with ice and strain into ice-filled highball glass.

BLACK CAT

Created by NICHOLAS JARRETT, New York, NY

1 grapefruit twist
1 tsp. simple syrup
1 oz. Old Tom gin
1 oz. mezcal
¾ oz. Punt e Mes
¾ oz. amontillado sherry
Garnish: Grapefruit twist

Muddle grapefruit twist and syrup in mixing glass. Add other ingredients and stir with ice. Strain into chilled cocktail glass. Add grapefruit twist.

BLOOD ORANGE

1½ oz. gin
½ oz. Campari
½ oz. amaro, such as Ramazzotti or Averna
1 oz. fresh orange juice

Shake with ice and strain into chilled cocktail glass.

BLOOMSBURY

2 oz. gin
½ oz. Licor 43
½ oz. Lillet Blanc
2 dashes Peychaud's bitters
Garnish: Lemon twist

Stir with ice and strain into chilled cocktail glass. Add lemon twist.

BLUE MOON COCKTAIL

1½ oz. gin
¾ oz. blue curaçao
Garnish: Lemon twist

Stir with ice and strain into chilled cocktail glass. Add lemon twist.

BOBBO'S BRIDE

1 oz. gin
1 oz. vodka
½ oz. peach liqueur
½ oz. Campari
Garnish: Fresh peach slice

Stir with ice and strain into chilled cocktail glass. Garnish with peach.

BRONX COCKTAIL

It is clear that this is a Perfect Martini with some orange juice in it. The drink's history is not so apparent, and it may be another creation of the Waldorf-Astoria, or the invention of a homesick Bronx-born restaurateur who lived in Philadelphia.

1 oz. gin
½ oz. dry vermouth
½ oz. sweet vermouth
1 oz. fresh orange juice
Garnish: Orange wheel

Shake with ice and strain into chilled cocktail glass. Add orange wheel.

BROOKLYN WANDERER

Created by HAL WOLIN, New York, NY

2 oz. genever
½ oz. allspice liqueur (pimento dram)
½ oz. mezcal
½ oz. pineapple juice
½ oz. orgeat syrup
½ oz. fresh lime juice
½ oz. Cinnamon Syrup (page 20)
2 dashes Angostura bitters
Garnish: Fresh mint leaf

Shake without ice. Strain into ice-filled pilsner glass. Swizzle with barspoon. Garnish with mint.

THE BROTHERS PERRYMAN

Created by RYAN MAYBEE, Kansas City, MO

1½ oz. Plymouth gin
¾ oz. Campari
¾ oz. elderflower liqueur
Garnish: Orange twist, flamed (see page 46)

Stir well with ice and strain into ice-filled old-fashioned glass. Flame orange twist and add.

☐ CANDIED APPLE MARTINI

Created by JONATHAN POGASH, New York, NY

1 oz. Plymouth gin
½ oz. Grand Marnier
¼ oz. Cinnamon Syrup (page 20)
½ oz. fresh lemon juice
¾ oz. apple cider
Garnish: Red apple slice

Shake with ice and strain into chilled cocktail glass. Garnish with apple.

☐ CAPRICIOUS

1½ oz. gin
½ oz. dry vermouth
½ oz. elderflower liqueur
2 dashes Peychaud's bitters

Stir with ice and strain into chilled cocktail glass.

☐ THE CARICATURE COCKTAIL

1½ oz. gin
¾ oz. triple sec
½ oz. sweet vermouth
½ oz. Campari
½ oz. fresh grapefruit juice
Garnish: Orange twist

Shake with ice and strain into chilled cocktail glass. Add orange twist.

☐ CASINO COCKTAIL

2 oz. gin
¼ tsp. maraschino liqueur
¼ tsp. fresh lemon juice
2 dashes orange bitters
Garnish: Maraschino cherry

Shake with ice and strain into chilled cocktail glass. Add cherry.

☐ CHIN UP

1 (½-inch-thick) cucumber slice, peeled
2 oz. gin
½ oz. Cynar
½ oz. dry vermouth
1 small pinch salt
Garnish: Paper-thin cucumber slice

Muddle thick cucumber slice in mixing glass. Add remaining ingredients and ice, and stir well. Strain into chilled cocktail glass. Garnish with thin cucumber slice.

☐ CHOCOLATE ITALIAN

1½ oz. gin
¾ oz. Campari
¾ oz. Punt e Mes
¾ oz. white crème de cacao
Garnish: Orange twist

Stir with ice and strain into ice-filled old-fashioned glass. Add orange twist.

♈ CLARIDGE COCKTAIL

Dating back to Harry McElhone's 1927 book *Barflies and Cocktails* (he was the Harry of Harry's New York Bar in Paris), this cocktail is an artful blend of herbal and fruit flavors.

1 oz. gin
¾ oz. dry vermouth
½ oz. apricot-flavored brandy
¼ oz. triple sec

Stir with ice and strain into chilled cocktail glass.

♈ CLOISTER

1½ oz. gin
½ oz. yellow Chartreuse
½ oz. fresh grapefruit juice
¼ oz. fresh lemon juice
¼ oz. simple syrup
Garnish: Grapefruit twist

Shake with ice and strain into chilled cocktail glass. Add grapefruit twist.

♈ CLOVER CLUB

The Clover Club is an august business organization in Philadelphia, but the drink that bears its name is a frothy, pink diversion.

1½ oz. gin
¾ oz. fresh lemon juice
½ oz. sweet vermouth
¼ oz. grenadine or raspberry syrup
1 egg white

Shake without ice. Add ice and shake again. Strain into chilled red-wine glass.

☿ THE COLONIAL COOLER

1½ oz. gin
1½ oz. sweet vermouth
¼ oz. triple sec
1 dash Angostura bitters
Soda water
Garnish: Mint sprig, pineapple
    wedge

*Pour first four ingredients
into ice-filled Collins glass.
Fill with soda water. Garnish
with mint and pineapple.*

☿ CORNWALL NEGRONI

2 oz. gin
½ oz. Punt e Mes
½ oz. sweet vermouth
½ oz. Campari
Garnish: Orange twist, flamed
    (see page 46)

*Stir with ice and strain into
chilled cocktail glass. Flame
orange twist and add.*

☿ CORPSE REVIVER NO. 2

There was an entire group of
"morning-after" drinks, each
called a Corpse Reviver. See
page 53 for the cognac version.
¾ oz. gin
¾ oz. fresh lemon juice
¾ oz. triple sec
¾ oz. Lillet Blanc
1 dash absinthe or pastis

*Shake with ice and strain
into chilled cocktail glass.*

☿ THE CORRECT COCKTAIL

1½ oz. gin
½ oz. ginger liqueur
½ oz. triple sec
½ oz. fresh lemon juice
2 dashes orange bitters
Garnish: Lemon twist

*Shake with ice and strain
into chilled champagne flute.
Add lemon twist.*

☐ CREAM FIZZ

2 oz. gin
¾ oz. fresh lemon juice
¾ oz. simple syrup
¾ oz. half-and-half
Soda water

Shake first four ingredients with ice and strain into ice-filled highball glass. Fill with soda water and stir.

☐ CRIMSON COCKTAIL

1½ oz. gin
½ oz. fresh lemon juice
¼ oz. grenadine
¾ oz. tawny port

Shake first three ingredients with ice and strain into chilled cocktail glass. Float port (see page 12) on top.

☐ CRYSTAL SLIPPER COCKTAIL

1½ oz. gin
½ oz. blue curaçao
2 dashes orange bitters

Stir with ice and strain into chilled cocktail glass.

☐ CUCUMBER-APPLE FIZZ

Created by KENTA GOTA, New York, NY

1 apple slice
1 cucumber slice
¾ oz. fresh lemon juice
¾ oz. simple syrup
1½ oz. gin
¾ oz. Cynar
Soda water
Garnish: Apple and cucumber slices

Muddle apple and cucumber with lemon juice and syrup in mixing glass. Add gin and Cynar and shake with ice. Strain into ice-filled highball glass. Top with soda water. Garnish with apple and cucumber slices.

CUCUMBER CANTALOUPE SOUR

2 cucumber slices, chopped
2 oz. Cantaloupe Juice (recipe follows)
1½ oz. gin
¾ oz. fresh lemon juice
½ oz. Honey Syrup (page 21)
Garnish: Cucumber slice

Muddle chopped cucumber in mixing glass. Add remaining ingredients and shake with ice. Strain into chilled cocktail glass. Garnish with cucumber slice.

CANTALOUPE JUICE

Puree about ½ c. peeled, diced, and seeded cantaloupe in blender. Strain through cheesecloth-lined sieve.

THE DEEP BLUE SEA

2 oz. gin
¾ oz. Lillet Blanc
¼ oz. crème de violette
1 dash orange bitters
Garnish: Lemon twist

Stir with ice and strain into chilled cocktail glass. Add lemon twist.

DIVA QUARANTA

1½ oz. gin
1 oz. pomegranate juice
½ oz. simple syrup
½ oz. Campari
Garnish: Orange twist

Shake first three ingredients with ice and strain into chilled cocktail glass. Top with Campari. Add orange twist.

DOC DANEEKA ROYALE

2 oz. gin
½ oz. fresh lemon juice
½ oz. maple syrup
Chilled Champagne
Garnish: Grapefruit twist

Shake first three ingredients and strain into chilled cocktail glass. Top with Champagne. Add grapefruit twist.

☙ DOFF YOUR HAT

Created by DAVID WILLHITE,
Chicago, IL

1 oz. genever
¾ oz. Cynar
¾ oz. sweet vermouth
½ oz. Grand Marnier
1 dash orange bitters
Garnish: Orange twist

*Stir with ice and strain into
chilled cocktail glass. Twist
orange twist over drink, then
discard zest.*

☙ DUTCH AND BUTTERSCOTCH

1½ oz. genever
½ oz. butterscotch liqueur
2 dashes Angostura bitters
Garnish: Orange twist, flamed
    (see page 46)

*Stir with ice and strain into
chilled cocktail glass. Flame
orange twist and add.*

☙ EARL GREY MAR-TEA-NI

Created by AUDREY SAUNDERS,
New York, NY

For glass: Lemon wedge,
    superfine sugar
1½ oz. Earl Grey Gin (recipe
    follows)
1 oz. simple syrup
¾ oz. fresh lemon juice
1 egg white
Garnish: Freshly grated lemon
    zest, lemon twist

*Rim chilled cocktail glass
with lemon and sugar. Shake
remaining ingredients without ice. Add ice and shake
again. Strain into glass.
Grate lemon zest on top and
add lemon twist.*

EARL GREY GIN
*Shake 1 Tbs. loose-leaf Earl
Grey tea with 8 oz. gin in jar
and let stand 2 hours. Stir
and strain.*

ᒌ EASTSIDE

3 slices cucumber
6–8 fresh mint leaves
1 oz. fresh lime juice
¾ oz. simple syrup
2 oz. gin
Garnish: Cucumber slice

Muddle 3 cucumber slices and mint with lime juice and syrup. Add gin and ice and shake. Strain into chilled cocktail glass. Garnish with cucumber.

ᒌ EASY LIKE SUNDAY MORNING COCKTAIL

1½ oz. gin
1¼ oz. pineapple juice
¾ oz. simple syrup
½ oz. fresh lemon juice
1 dash Angostura bitters

Shake first four ingredients with ice and strain into ice-filled Collins glass. Add bitters and stir.

ᒌ EDEN

2 oz. gin
½ oz. fresh lemon juice
½ oz. rose syrup
¼ oz. Campari
Garnish: Lemon twist

Shake with ice and strain into ice-filled old-fashioned glass. Add lemon twist.

ᒌ THE ELDER STATESMAN

Created by RICK RODGERS, Maplewood, NJ

1 lime wedge
4 raspberries
1½ ounces gin
½ oz. elderberry liqueur
Garnish: Lime twist

Rim chilled cocktail glass with lime wedge. Muddle raspberries and lime wedge in mixer glass. Add gin and elderberry liqueur and shake with ice. Double-strain into glass. Add lime twist.

ᒌ EMERSON

1½ oz. gin
1 oz. sweet vermouth
½ oz. fresh lime juice
1 tsp. maraschino liqueur

Shake with ice and strain into chilled cocktail glass.

∀ THE ENGLISH CHANNEL

Created by JONATHAN POGASH, New York, NY

The gin is British, and the ginger liqueur is French, and they are symbolically separated by the English Channel, hence this cocktail's name.

2 large fresh basil leaves
1½ oz. gin
½ oz. ginger liqueur
½ oz. simple syrup
½ oz. fresh lemon juice
1 oz. peach puree
1 bay leaf
Garnish: Fresh basil leaf

Smack 2 basil leaves between the palms of your hands to release the aroma, then add to mixing glass. Add remaining ingredients with ice and shake. Strain into chilled cocktail glass. Garnish with basil.

∀ ENGLISH ROSE COCKTAIL

For glass: Lemon wedge, granulated sugar
1½ oz. gin
¾ oz. apricot-flavored brandy
¾ oz. dry vermouth
½ oz. fresh lemon juice
¼ oz. grenadine
Garnish: Maraschino cherry

Rim chilled cocktail glass with lemon and sugar. Shake next five ingredients with ice and strain into glass. Add cherry.

∀ FANCY GIN

2 oz. gin
½ oz. simple syrup
¼ oz. triple sec
1 dash Angostura bitters
Garnish: Lemon twist

Shake with ice and strain into chilled cocktail glass. Add lemon twist.

∀ FIFTY-FIFTY MARTINI

1½ oz. gin
1½ oz. dry vermouth

Stir with ice and strain into chilled cocktail glass.

Y FINO MARTINI

2 oz. gin
½ oz. fino sherry
Garnish: Lemon twist

Stir gin and sherry with ice in mixing glass. Strain into chilled cocktail glass. Add lemon twist.

▢ FITZGERALD

1½ oz. gin
1 oz. simple syrup
¾ oz. fresh lemon juice
2 dashes Angostura bitters
Garnish: Lemon wedge

Shake with ice and strain into chilled old-fashioned glass. Add lemon wedge.

Y FLAMINGO COCKTAIL

1½ oz. gin
½ oz. apricot-flavored brandy
½ oz. fresh lime juice
¼ oz. grenadine

Shake with ice and strain into chilled cocktail glass.

Y FLORIDA

1½ oz. gin
1 tsp. kirschwasser
1 tsp. triple sec
¾ oz. fresh orange juice
¼ oz. fresh lemon juice

Shake with ice and strain into chilled cocktail glass.

Y FRENCH "75"

The 75mm French howitzer model 1897 was a small but powerful gun. Harry's New York Bar felt that this drink packed a similar punch, and christened the cocktail after the artillery in 1915.
1½ oz. gin
¾ oz. fresh lemon juice
½ oz. simple syrup
Chilled Champagne

Shake first three ingredients with ice. Strain into chilled champagne flute and top with Champagne.

🍸 GARNET

1½ oz. gin
¾ oz. triple sec
¾ oz. pomegranate juice
¾ oz. fresh grapefruit juice
Garnish: Orange twist,
    flamed (see page 46)

*Shake with ice and strain
into chilled cocktail glass.
Flame orange twist and add.*

🍸 GERSHWIN

2 oz. gin
½ oz. ginger liqueur
½ oz. simple syrup
¾ oz. fresh lemon juice
3 drops rose water

*Shake with ice and strain
into chilled cocktail glass.*

🍸 GIBSON (GIN)

2½ oz. gin
½ oz. dry vermouth
Garnish: Cocktail onion

*Stir with ice and strain into
chilled cocktail glass. Add
onion.*

🍸 GIMLET (GIN)

2 oz. gin
¾ oz. fresh lime juice
¾ oz. simple syrup

*Shake with ice and strain
into chilled cocktail glass.*

*Note: If desired, substitute
1 oz. Rose's Sweetened Lime
Juice for the fresh lime juice
and simple syrup.*

🍸 GIN ALOHA

2 oz. gin
½ oz. triple sec
¾ oz. pineapple juice
1 dash orange bitters

*Shake with ice and strain
into chilled cocktail glass.*

🍸 GIN AND BITTERS

½ tsp. Angostura bitters
3 oz. gin

*Pour bitters into cocktail
glass and swirl the glass until
it is entirely coated with the
bitters. Add gin. (No ice is
used in this drink.)*

☐ GIN BUCK

1½ oz. gin
1 oz. fresh lemon juice
Ginger ale

*Pour gin and lemon juice into
ice-filled old-fashioned glass.
Fill with ginger ale and stir.*

☐ GIN GIN MULE

An antecedent to the Moscow
Mule (page 166). Audrey
Saunders, owner of Pegu Club
in New York City, makes this
version with gin and refreshing
notes of mint and lime.

6–8 mint sprigs
1 oz. simple syrup
¾ oz. fresh lime juice
1½ oz. gin

*Muddle mint with syrup and
lime juice in mixing glass. Add
gin and ice and shake well.
Strain into ice-filled highball
glass. Fill with ginger beer.*

☐ GIN AND SIN

1½ oz. gin
½ oz. fresh lemon juice
½ oz. fresh orange juice
¼ oz. grenadine

*Shake with ice and strain
into chilled cocktail glass.*

☐ GIN AND SIP

1 splash absinthe
2½ oz. gin
½ oz. amaro, such as
    Ramazzotti or Averna

*Swirl absinthe in chilled old-
fashioned glass to coat inside;
discard excess absinthe. Stir
gin and amaro with ice and
strain into glass.*

☐ GIN SQUIRT

1½ oz. gin
1 tsp. simple syrup
1 tsp. grenadine
Soda water
Garnish: Pineapple cubes,
    whole strawberries

*Stir first three ingredients
with ice and strain into
ice-filled highball glass. Fill
with soda water and stir.
Garnish with pineapple and
strawberries.*

☐ GIN THING

1½ oz. gin
½ oz. fresh lime juice
Ginger ale

*Pour gin and lime juice into
ice-filled highball glass and
fill with ginger ale.*

⬜ GIN AND TONIC

2 oz. gin
Tonic water
Garnish: Lime wedge (optional)

Pour gin into ice-filled highball glass and fill with tonic water. Stir. Add lime wedge, if desired.

⬜ GIRL FROM CADIZ

Created by RYAN MAYBEE,
Kansas City, MO

1 tsp. dried juniper berries
½ oz. simple syrup
1½ oz. Plymouth gin
1½ oz. fino sherry
½ oz. fresh lemon juice
4 fresh mint leaves
Garnish: Lemongrass stalk

Muddle juniper berries with simple syrup in mixing glass. Add gin, sherry, lemon juice, and mint and shake well with ice. Strain through wire sieve into ice-filled Collins glass. Garnish with lemongrass.

🍸 GOLDEN DAZE

1½ oz. gin
½ oz. peach-flavored brandy
1 oz. fresh orange juice

Shake with ice and strain into chilled cocktail glass.

🍸 GOLF COCKTAIL

1½ oz. gin
¾ oz. dry vermouth
2 dashes Angostura bitters

Stir with ice and strain into chilled cocktail glass.

⬜ GRAND ROYAL FIZZ

2 oz. gin
¾ oz. fresh orange juice
½ oz. fresh lemon juice
½ oz. half-and-half
½ oz. simple syrup
1 tsp. maraschino liqueur
Soda water

Shake first six ingredients with ice. Strain into ice-filled highball glass. Fill with soda water and stir.

🍸 GREEN DRAGON

1½ oz. gin
1 oz. fresh lemon juice
½ oz. kümmel
½ oz. green crème de menthe
4 dashes orange bitters

Shake with ice and strain into chilled cocktail glass.

⬜ GREYHOUND (GIN)

1½ oz. gin
5 oz. fresh grapefruit juice

Pour into ice-filled highball glass. Stir well.

☐ HAYS FIZZ

½ tsp. absinthe or pastis
2 oz. gin
¾ oz. fresh lemon juice
¾ oz. simple syrup
Soda water
Garnish: Cherry/orange flag

*Add pastis to Collins glass
and swirl to coat inside
of glass. Shake remaining
ingredients with ice. Strain
into ice-filled glass. Fill with
soda water. Garnish with
cherry/orange flag.*

☐ HOFFMAN HOUSE MARTINI

This venerable hotel,
demolished in 1915, served a
drink that is a dead ringer for a
wet Martini.

1½ oz. gin
¾ oz. dry vermouth
2 dashes orange bitters
Garnish: Orange twist

*Stir with ice and strain into
chilled cocktail glass. Add
orange twist.*

☐ HOKKAIDO COCKTAIL

1½ oz. gin
1 oz. sake
½ oz. triple sec

*Shake with ice and strain
into chilled cocktail glass.*

☐ HOMESTEAD COCKTAIL

1½ oz. gin
¾ oz. sweet vermouth
Garnish: Orange wheel

*Stir with ice and strain
into chilled cocktail glass.
Garnish with orange wheel.*

☐ HONOLULU COCKTAIL NO. 1

1½ oz. gin
½ oz. simple syrup
¼ oz. fresh orange juice
¼ oz. pineapple juice
¼ oz. fresh lemon juice
1 dash orange bitters

*Shake with ice and strain
into chilled cocktail glass.*

☐ HONOLULU COCKTAIL NO. 2

¾ oz. gin
¾ oz. maraschino liqueur
¾ oz. Bénédictine

*Stir with ice and strain into
chilled cocktail glass.*

☒ HOSKINS

2 oz. gin
¾ oz. Amer Picon or Torani Amer
¾ oz. maraschino liqueur
¼ oz. triple sec
1 dash orange bitters
Garnish: Orange twist, flamed (see page 46)

Stir with ice and strain into chilled cocktail glass. Flame orange twist and add.

☒ HUDSON BAY

1 oz. gin
½ oz. cherry-flavored brandy
½ oz. fresh orange juice
¼ oz. 151-proof rum
¼ oz. fresh lime juice

Shake with ice and strain into chilled cocktail glass.

☒ HUMMINGBIRD DOWN

2 oz. gin
¾ oz. fresh lemon juice
¾ oz. Honey Syrup (page 21)
¼ oz. green Chartreuse
Garnish: Fresh mint leaf

Shake with ice and strain into chilled cocktail glass. Add mint leaf.

☒ IDEAL COCKTAIL

1 oz. gin
1 oz. dry vermouth
¼ oz. maraschino liqueur
¼ oz. fresh grapefruit or lemon juice
Garnish: Maraschino cherry

Shake with ice and strain into chilled cocktail glass. Add cherry.

☒ IMPERIAL COCKTAIL

1½ oz. gin
1½ oz. dry vermouth
1 tsp. maraschino liqueur
1 dash Angostura bitters
Garnish: Maraschino cherry

Stir with ice and strain into chilled cocktail glass. Add cherry.

☒ THE INSCRIPTION

Created by TED HENWOOD, New York, NY

Dash of absinthe
2½ oz. gin
1 oz. elderflower liqueur
Garnish: Orange twist

Swirl absinthe in chilled cocktail glass to coat inside; discard excess absinthe. Stir gin and elderflower liqueur with ice and strain into glass. Add orange twist.

JAMAICA GLOW

1 oz. gin
½ oz. Jamaican rum
¾ oz. fresh orange juice
½ oz. red wine

Shake with ice and strain into chilled cocktail glass.

JASMINE

¾ oz. Campari
1½ oz. gin
1 oz. triple sec
½ oz. fresh lemon juice

Shake with ice and strain into chilled cocktail glass.

JOCKEY CLUB COCKTAIL

1½ oz. gin
½ oz. fresh lemon juice
½ oz. white crème de cacao
1 dash Angostura bitters

Shake with ice and strain into chilled cocktail glass.

THE JOLLITY BUILDING

1½ oz. gin
½ oz. amaro, such as Ramazzotti or Averna
¼ oz. maraschino liqueur
1 dash orange bitters
Garnish: Orange twist

Stir with ice and strain into chilled cocktail glass. Add orange twist.

JOULOUVILLE

1 oz. gin
½ oz. apple brandy
½ oz. fresh lemon juice
¼ oz. sweet vermouth
¼ oz. grenadine

Shake with ice and strain into chilled cocktail glass.

JUDGETTE COCKTAIL

¾ oz. peach-flavored brandy
¾ oz. gin
¾ oz. dry vermouth
¼ oz. fresh lime juice
Garnish: Maraschino cherry

Shake with ice and strain into chilled cocktail glass. Add cherry.

▽ JUNIPER BREEZE NO. 1

Created by JULIE REINER,
New York, NY

Use nonalcoholic elderflower
cordial, not liqueur, for this
cocktail.

1½ oz. gin
¾ oz. fresh grapefruit juice
½ oz. cranberry juice
½ oz. elderflower cordial
¼ oz. fresh lime juice
Garnish: Orange twist

*Roll with ice in shaker. Pour
into chilled cocktail glass.
Add orange twist.*

▽ JUPITER

2 oz. gin
1 oz. dry vermouth
1 tsp. fresh orange juice
1 tsp. crème de violette, Crème
    Yvette, or Grand Marnier

*Shake with ice and strain
into chilled cocktail glass.*

▽ LA BICYCLETTE

2 oz. gin
¾ oz. sweet vermouth
½ oz. elderflower liqueur
2 dashes peach bitters

*Stir with ice and strain into
chilled cocktail glass.*

▽ LA CAMPANILE COCKTAIL

Created by CHRIS PATINO,
New York, NY

2 oz. Plymouth gin
¾ oz. ruby port
1 oz. fresh orange juice
¼ oz. Fernet-Branca
Garnish: Orange twist

*Shake with ice and strain
into chilled cocktail glass.
Add orange twist.*

▽ LA LOUCHE

1½ oz. gin
½ oz. Lillet Rouge
¼ oz. yellow Chartreuse
¼ oz. fresh lime juice
Garnish: Lime twist

*Shake with ice and strain
into chilled cocktail glass.
Add lime twist.*

⬚ LA TAZZA D`EVA

6 fresh mint leaves
1 oz. amaro, such as
    Ramazzotti or Averna
1 oz. gin
1 oz. apple juice
1 oz. tonic water
Garnish: Apple slice, rosemary
    sprig

*Muddle mint in highball
glass. Add ice and remaining
ingredients and stir.
Garnish with apple and
rosemary.*

⅄ LADY FINGER

1 oz. gin
1 oz. cherry-flavored brandy
½ oz. kirschwasser

*Shake with ice and strain
into chilled cocktail glass.*

⅄ LEAVE-IT-TO-ME COCKTAIL NO. 1

1 oz. gin
½ oz. apricot-flavored
    brandy
½ oz. dry vermouth
¼ oz. fresh lemon juice
¼ oz. grenadine

*Shake with ice and strain
into chilled cocktail glass.*

⅄ LEAVE-IT-TO-ME COCKTAIL NO. 2

1½ oz. gin
1 tsp. raspberry syrup
1 tsp. fresh lemon juice
1 tsp. maraschino liqueur

*Stir with ice and strain into
chilled cocktail glass.*

⬚ LEO DE JANEIRO

2 oz. gin
2 oz. pineapple juice
4 dashes Angostura bitters
Garnish: Pineapple wedge

*Shake with ice and strain
into ice-filled Collins glass.
Garnish with the pineapple
wedge on the glass rim.*

⅄ LIGHT AND DAY

2 oz. gin
½ oz. yellow Chartreuse
¼ oz. maraschino liqueur
¼ oz. fresh orange juice
3 dashes Peychaud's bitters

*Stir with ice and strain into
chilled cocktail glass.*

☿ LONDON COCKTAIL

2 oz. gin
½ oz. simple syrup
1 tsp. maraschino liqueur
2 dashes orange bitters
Garnish: Lemon twist

Stir with ice and strain into chilled cocktail glass. Add lemon twist.

☿ THE LONDONER

2 oz. gin
½ oz. Grand Marnier
½ oz. sweet vermouth
1 dash orange bitters
Garnish: Orange twist, flamed

Shake with ice and strain into chilled cocktail glass. Flame orange twist and add.

▯ MAJOR BAILEY

12 fresh mint leaves
¼ oz. fresh lime juice
¼ oz. fresh lemon juice
½ oz. simple syrup
2 oz. gin
Garnish: Mint sprig

Muddle first four ingredients in Collins glass. Add gin and ice and stir until glass is frosted. Add mint sprig and serve with straws.

☿ MARLOWE

Raymond Chandler's iconic detective, Philip Marlowe, liked his Gimlets heavy on the Rose's.

1½ oz. gin
1½ oz. Rose's Sweetened Lime Juice

Shake with ice and strain into chilled cocktail glass.

☿ MARTINEZ COCKTAIL

This is a modern-day version of the cocktail that may or may not have become the Martini. Read more on the subject on page 30.

1½ oz. Old Tom gin
½ oz. sweet vermouth
1 tsp. maraschino liqueur
1 dash orange bitters

Stir with ice and strain into chilled cocktail glass.

☿ MARTINI (TRADITIONAL 2-TO-1)

1½ oz. gin
¾ oz. dry vermouth
Garnish: Lemon twist or green olive

Stir with ice and strain into chilled cocktail glass. Add lemon twist or olive.

▼ MARTINI (DRY 4-TO-1)

2 oz. gin
½ oz. dry vermouth
Garnish: Lemon twist or green olive

Stir with ice and strain into chilled cocktail glass. Add lemon twist or olive.

▼ MARTINI (EXTRA DRY 8-TO-1)

1 splash dry vermouth
2 oz. gin
Garnish: Lemon twist or green olive

Swirl vermouth in chilled cocktail glass to coat inside; discard excess vermouth. Stir gin with ice and strain into glass. Add lemon twist or olive.

▼ MARTINI (PERFECT)

1½ oz. gin
½ oz. dry vermouth
½ oz. sweet vermouth
Garnish: Lemon twist or green olive

Stir with ice and strain into chilled cocktail glass. Add lemon twist or olive.

▼ MARTINI (SWEET)

1 oz. gin
1 oz. sweet vermouth
Garnish: Lemon twist

Stir with ice and strain into chilled cocktail glass. Add lemon twist.

▼ MAURICE COCKTAIL

1 oz. gin
1 oz. fresh orange juice
½ oz. sweet vermouth
½ oz. dry vermouth
1 dash Angostura bitters

Shake with ice and strain into chilled cocktail glass.

▢ MAXWELL'S RETURN

15 fresh rosemary leaves
2 oz. gin
1 oz. pineapple juice
½ oz. simple syrup
½ oz. fresh lime juice
¼ oz. green Chartreuse
Garnish: Rosemary sprig

Muddle rosemary leaves in mixing glass. Add remaining ingredients. Shake with ice and double-strain into ice-filled old-fashioned glass. Garnish with rosemary sprig.

☐ MELON STAND

4 (1-inch) chunks peeled
    watermelon
2 oz. gin
½ oz. Aperol
½ oz. simple syrup
¾ oz. fresh lemon juice
Garnish: Watermelon cube
    or ball

*Muddle melon chunks in
mixing glass. Add remaining ingredients. Shake with
ice and strain into Collins
glass filled with crushed ice.
Garnish with watermelon.*

☐ MERCY, MERCY

2 oz. gin
½ oz. Aperol
½ oz. Lillet Blanc
1 dash Angostura bitters
Garnish: Orange twist

*Stir with ice and strain into
chilled cocktail glass. Add
orange twist.*

☐ MONARCH

7 fresh mint leaves
2 oz. gin
¾ oz. fresh lemon juice
¾ oz. elderflower liqueur
½ oz. simple syrup
Garnish: Grapefruit twist

*Smack mint leaves between
palms and drop into mixing glass. Add remaining
ingredients and ice. Shake
and double-strain into chilled
cocktail glass. Add grapefruit
twist.*

☐ THE MONEYPENNY

For glass: Lemon wedge,
    Demerara sugar
1 oz. gin
1 oz. fresh grapefruit juice
½ oz. Lillet Blanc
½ oz. fresh lemon juice
1 dash grapefruit bitters
Garnish: Grapefruit twist

*Rim chilled cocktail glass
with lemon and sugar. Shake
remaining ingredients with
ice and strain into glass. Add
grapefruit twist.*

Y MONKEY GLAND

In the 1920s, there was a popular youth rejuvenation process that involved monkey hormones, which lent its name to this invigorating cocktail.

2 oz. gin
1 oz. fresh orange juice
¼ oz. grenadine
1 dash absinthe
Garnish: Orange twist

Shake with ice and strain into chilled cocktail glass. Add orange twist.

Y MORRO

For glass: Lemon wedge, superfine sugar
1 oz. gin
½ oz. dark rum
½ oz. pineapple juice
½ oz. fresh lime juice
1 tsp. simple syrup

Rim chilled cocktail glass with lemon and sugar. Shake remaining ingredients with ice and strain into glass.

Y NEGRONI

The story goes that bartender Fosco Scarselli of Florence, Italy, concocted this *molto Italiano* cocktail for Count Camillo Negroni in 1919.

¾ oz. gin
¾ oz. Campari
¾ oz. sweet vermouth
Garnish: Orange twist

Stir with ice and strain into chilled cocktail glass or ice-filled old-fashioned glass. Add orange twist.

Y NEW AMSTERDAM

2 oz. genever
1 oz. kirschwasser
1 tsp. simple syrup
2 dashes Peychaud's bitters
Garnish: Lemon twist

Stir with ice and strain into chilled cocktail glass. Add lemon twist.

Y NON CI CREDO

2 oz. gin
¾ oz. Aperol
¾ oz. fresh lemon juice
¼ oz. simple syrup
1 egg white
3 dashes peach bitters

Shake without ice. Add ice, shake again, and strain into chilled cocktail glass.

Y NOVARA

1½ oz. gin
½ oz. Campari
½ oz. passion fruit juice
½ oz. fresh lemon juice

Shake with ice and strain into chilled cocktail glass.

Y OBITUARY COCKTAIL

2 oz. gin
¼ oz. dry vermouth
¼ oz. absinthe

Stir with ice and strain into chilled cocktail glass.

☐ THE OLD GOAT

1½ oz. genever
¾ oz. crème de cassis
Ginger ale
Garnish: Lime wedge

Combine gin and crème de cassis in ice-filled Collins glass. Top with ginger ale and stir. Squeeze and add lime wedge.

Y OPERA

2 oz. gin
½ oz. Dubonnet
¼ oz. maraschino liqueur
1 dash orange bitters
Garnish: Lemon twist

Stir with ice and strain into chilled cocktail glass. Add lemon twist.

Y ORANGE BLOSSOM

1½ oz. gin
¾ oz. fresh orange juice
¼ oz. simple syrup

Shake with ice and strain into chilled cocktail glass.

🍸 ORIENT EXPRESS

2 oz. gin
1 oz. sake
½ oz. Lemongrass Syrup
  (page 21)
Garnish: Thin green apple
  slice

*Stir with ice and strain into
chilled cocktail glass. Garnish
with apple.*

🥃 THE OUTSIDER

2 oz. gin
1 oz. apple cider
1 oz. fresh lemon juice
¾ oz. simple syrup
1 splash ginger ale
Garnish: Thin red apple
  slice

*Shake first four ingredients
with ice and strain into
ice-filled Collins glass. Add
ginger ale. Garnish with
apple slice.*

🍸 PALM BEACH COCKTAIL

1½ oz. gin
¼ oz. sweet vermouth
¼ oz. fresh grapefruit juice

*Shake with ice and strain
into chilled cocktail glass.*

🥃 PAPAYA SLING

1½ oz. gin
1 oz. fresh lime juice
½ oz. papaya-flavored syrup
1 dash Angostura bitters
Soda water
Garnish: Skewered pineapple
  chunks

*Shake first four ingredients
with ice and strain into
ice-filled Collins glass. Fill
with soda water and stir.
Garnish with skewered
pineapple.*

🥃 PARCHMENT FIZZ

Created by DAMON DYER,
New York, NY

1½ oz. Plymouth gin
¾ oz. fresh lime juice
½ oz. dry vermouth
½ oz. simple syrup
½ oz. pear eau-de-vie
2 dashes Peychaud's bitters
1 dash absinthe
Soda water
Garnish: Pear slice

*Shake first seven ingredi-
ents with ice. Strain into
ice-filled highball glass. Top
with soda water. Garnish
with pear.*

⅄ PARISIAN

1 oz. gin
1 oz. dry vermouth
¼ oz. crème de cassis

Shake with ice and strain into chilled cocktail glass.

⅄ PARK AVENUE

1½ oz. gin
½ oz. pineapple juice
¼ oz. sweet vermouth

Stir with ice and strain into chilled cocktail glass.

⅄ PEGU CLUB

This drink hails from the 1920s. The Pegu Club in New York City pays homage to the original in Rangoon, Burma.

2 oz. gin
½ oz. orange curaçao
½ oz. fresh lime juice
1 dash Angostura bitters

Stir with ice and strain into chilled cocktail glass.

⅄ PERFECT COCKTAIL

1½ oz. gin
¼ oz. dry vermouth
¼ oz. sweet vermouth
1 dash Angostura bitters

Stir with ice and strain into chilled cocktail glass.

⅄ PERFECT 10

1 oz. gin
½ oz. triple sec
½ oz. Campari
¼ oz. fresh lemon juice
¼ oz. simple syrup
Garnish: Lemon twist

Shake with ice and strain into chilled cocktail glass. Add lemon twist.

⅄ PINK GIN

1½ oz. gin
3–4 dashes Angostura bitters

Stir with ice and strain into chilled cocktail glass.

⅄ PINK LADY

1½ oz. gin
¾ oz. fresh lemon juice
½ oz. applejack
¼ oz. grenadine
1 egg white

Shake without ice. Add ice and shake again. Strain into chilled red-wine glass.

POLLYANNA

3 orange wheels
3 pineapple chunks
2 oz. gin
½ oz. sweet vermouth
¼ oz. grenadine

Muddle orange and pineapple. Add remaining ingredients, shake with ice, and strain into chilled cocktail glass.

POLO COCKTAIL

1½ oz. gin
½ oz. fresh lemon juice
½ oz. fresh orange juice

Shake with ice and strain into chilled cocktail glass.

POMPANO

1 oz. gin
1 oz. fresh grapefruit juice
½ oz. dry vermouth

Shake with ice and strain into chilled cocktail glass.

PRINCETON COCKTAIL

1 oz. gin
1 oz. dry vermouth
½ oz. fresh lime juice

Shake with ice and strain into chilled cocktail glass.

PROHIBITION COCKTAIL

1½ oz. gin
1½ oz. Lillet Blanc
¼ oz. apricot-flavored brandy
¼ oz. fresh orange juice
Garnish: Lemon twist

Shake and strain into cocktail glass. Add lemon twist.

THE PULITZER

Created by JONATHAN POGASH, New York, NY

1¼ oz. Plymouth gin
½ oz. elderflower liqueur
¼ oz. Fernet-Branca
¼ oz. fresh lemon juice
1 tsp. agave nectar
Garnish: Fresh mint sprig

Shake with ice and strain into chilled cocktail glass. Garnish with mint.

⬚ RAMOS GIN FIZZ

The invention of Harry Ramos, a nineteenth-century New Orleans bartender, this drink is still a *de rigueur* brunch cocktail in the Crescent City as well as in San Francisco. For a while, the cocktail was so popular that Ramos had to hire an entire battalion of bartenders to keep up with the shaking.

1½ oz. gin
1 oz. heavy cream
½ oz. simple syrup
½ oz. fresh lemon juice
½ oz. fresh lime juice
1 egg white
3–4 dashes orange blossom
    water
1 oz. soda water

Shake all ingredients except soda water without ice well until foamy. Add ice and shake well until chilled. Strain into chilled highball glass. Top with soda water and stir.

⬚ REMSEN COOLER

Similar to a Gin Cooler, but a bit sweeter, thanks to the Old Tom gin.

2 oz. Old Tom gin
1 tsp. simple syrup
Soda water or ginger ale
Garnish: Lemon and/or orange
    zest spiral

Stir gin and syrup in Collins glass. Add ice, fill with soda water or ginger ale, and stir again. Insert citrus spiral(s) and dangle end(s) over rim of glass.

⬚ ROBERT E. LEE COOLER

2 oz. gin
2 oz. soda water
½ oz. fresh lime juice
1 tsp. simple syrup
¼ tsp. anisette
Ginger ale
Garnish: Orange and/or lemon
    zest spiral

Pour first five ingredients into ice-filled Collins glass. Top with ginger ale and stir. Add citrus spiral(s) and dangle end(s) over rim.

ROSE COCKTAIL (ENGLISH)

For glass: Lemon wedge,
    superfine sugar
1 oz. gin
½ oz. apricot-flavored brandy
½ oz. dry vermouth
¼ oz. fresh lemon juice
¼ oz. grenadine

*Rim chilled cocktail glass
with lemon and sugar. Shake
remaining ingredients with
ice and strain into glass.*

ROSE COCKTAIL (FRENCH)

1½ oz. gin
½ oz. cherry-flavored brandy
½ oz. dry vermouth

*Stir with ice and strain into
chilled cocktail glass.*

SALTY DOG (GIN)

One could substitute vodka for
the gin, but this is the most
flavorful version.

For glass: Lemon wedge,
    kosher salt
1½ oz. gin
5 oz. fresh grapefruit juice

*Rim highball glass with
lemon and salt. Fill with ice.
Pour in gin and grapefruit
juice and stir well.*

SAN MARTIN COCKTAIL

Another cocktail named for a
person, this one is probably
an eponym for José de San
Martín, the Latin American
patriot.

1½ oz. gin
1½ oz. sweet vermouth
1 tsp. green or yellow
    Chartreuse

*Stir with ice and strain into
chilled cocktail glass.*

SAN SEBASTIAN

1 oz. gin
½ oz. fresh grapefruit juice
½ oz. fresh lemon juice
¼ oz. light rum
¼ oz. triple sec

*Shake with ice and strain
into chilled cocktail glass.*

SATAN'S WHISKERS

¾ oz. gin
¾ oz. dry vermouth
¾ oz. sweet vermouth
½ oz. Grand Marnier
½ oz. fresh orange juice
1 dash orange bitters

*Shake with ice and strain into
chilled cocktail glass.*

Y THE SHIPROCK

Created by TED HENWOOD,
New York, NY

3 fresh sage leaves
2½ oz. Plymouth gin
½ oz. Ginger Syrup (page 21)
½ oz. fresh lemon juice
1 drop orange blossom water
Garnish: Orange twist

Muddle sage leaves in mixing glass. Add gin, ginger syrup, lemon juice, and orange blossom water and shake with ice. Strain into chilled cocktail glass. Add orange twist.

Y SILVER BULLET

1 oz. gin
1 oz. kümmel
½ oz. fresh lemon juice

Shake with ice and strain into chilled cocktail glass.

▯ SILVER KING FIZZ

2 oz. gin
¾ oz. fresh lemon juice
¾ oz. simple syrup
1 egg white
4 dashes orange bitters
Soda water
Garnish: Orange wheel

Shake first five ingredients very well without ice until foamy. Add ice and shake again. Strain into ice-filled highball glass. Top with soda water. Garnish with orange.

Y SILVER STAR DAISY

1 oz. gin
1 oz. fresh lemon juice
½ oz. apple brandy
½ oz. orange curaçao
½ oz. simple syrup
1 egg white
Soda water
1 dash orange bitters

Shake all but bitters very well without ice. Add ice and shake again. Strain into ice-filled highball glass. Top with soda, then dash with bitters.

⅋ SMOKEY HOLLANDER

Created by CHRIS HANNAH, New Orleans, LA

1½ oz. genever
½ oz. mezcal
½ oz. fresh lemon juice
½ oz. agave nectar
Garnish: Lemon twist

Shake with ice and strain into chilled cocktail glass. Add lemon twist.

⅋ SO CUE

1 oz. gin
1 oz. soju (Korean liqueur)
1 oz. dry vermouth
¾ oz. simple syrup
½ oz. fresh lime juice
Garnish: Cucumber slice

Stir with ice and strain into chilled cocktail glass. Garnish with cucumber slice.

⅋ SORRISO

Created by FRANCESCO LAFRANCONI, Las Vegas, NV

1 oz. Plymouth gin
1 oz. pear-flavored vodka
½ oz. oloroso sherry
½ oz. cherry-flavored brandy
2 dashes Angostura bitters
Garnish: Orange and lemon twists, Italian preserved cherry

Stir with ice and strain into chilled cocktail glass. Garnish with lemon and orange twists and cherry.

⅋ SOUTH-SIDE COCKTAIL

8–10 fresh mint leaves
1½ oz. gin
¾ oz. fresh lemon juice
¾ oz. simple syrup
Garnish: Fresh mint sprig

Muddle mint leaves gently in mixing glass. Add remaining ingredients and shake with ice. Strain into chilled cocktail glass. Add the mint sprig.

☐ SOUTH-SIDE FIZZ

8–10 fresh mint leaves
2 oz. gin
¾ oz. fresh lemon juice
¾ oz. simple syrup
Soda water
Garnish: Fresh mint sprig

*Muddle mint leaves gently in
mixing glass. Add gin, lemon
juice, and syrup and shake
with ice. Strain into ice-filled
highball glass. Fill with soda
water and stir. Add mint sprig.*

☐ THE STANDARD

Created by JAMES MENITE,
New York City, NY

1¼ oz. gin
½ oz. yellow Chartreuse
1¼ oz. fresh ruby red
    grapefruit juice
¾ oz. fresh lemon juice
Garnish: Orange twist, flamed
    (see page 46)

*Shake with ice and strain
into cocktail glass. Flame
orange twist and add.*

☐ STAR DAISY

1 oz. gin
1 oz. apple brandy
1 oz. fresh lemon juice
1 tsp. grenadine
1 tsp. simple syrup
Garnish: Fresh seasonal fruit

*Shake with ice. Strain into
ice-filled beer mug or metal
cup. Garnish with fruit.*

☐ STRAITS SLING

2 oz. gin
1 oz. fresh lemon juice
½ oz. Cherry Heering
½ oz. Bénédictine
2 dashes orange bitters
2 dashes Angostura bitters
Soda water

*Shake first six ingredients
with ice. Strain into ice-filled
Collins glass. Fill with soda
water and stir.*

☐ SUMMER CABINET

1 oz. gin
¾ oz. oloroso sherry
½ oz. fresh lemon juice
½ oz. apricot liqueur, such as
    barack pálinka
1 dash lemon bitters

*Shake with ice and strain
into chilled cocktail glass.*

⬜ THE SUN ALSO RISES

Created by JONATHAN POGASH,
New York, NY

4 raspberries
¼ oz. fresh lime juice
¼ oz. fresh lemon juice
½ oz. simple syrup
1¼ oz. Peach Tea–Infused Gin
　(recipe follows)
¼ oz. Grand Marnier
Garnish: Fresh mint sprig

*Muddle raspberries with lime
and lemon juices and syrup.
Add gin and Grand Marnier
and shake with ice. Strain
through wire sieve into ice-
filled old-fashioned glass.
Garnish with mint.*

PEACH TEA–INFUSED GIN

*Pour 1 c. gin into bowl.
Add 1 peach tea bag.
Let stand for 20 minutes.
Strain into another bowl,
pressing hard on tea bag.
Funnel into covered jar,
pressing hard on peach bag.
Store, refrigerated, for up
to 3 weeks.*

⅄ SWEET BASIL MARTINI

3 fresh basil leaves
1 lemon wedge
1½ oz. gin
¾ oz. Lillet Blanc
½ oz. simple syrup
Garnish: Lemon wheel

*Muddle the basil and lemon
wedge in mixing glass. Add
remaining ingredients and
shake with ice. Strain into
chilled cocktail glass. Garnish
with lemon.*

⬜ THE TART GIN COOLER

2 oz. gin
2 oz. fresh pink grapefruit juice
2 oz. tonic water
1 dash Peychaud's bitters

*Pour first three ingredients
into ice-filled Collins glass.
Top with bitters.*

☐ TILLICUM

Robert Hess (www.drinkboy
.com) is the creator of this
smoked salmon–garnished
variation on the Martini
theme.

2¼ oz. gin
¾ oz. dry vermouth
2 dashes Peychaud's
    bitters
Garnish: 1 slice smoked
    salmon, skewered on a
    toothpick

*Stir with ice and strain into
chilled cocktail glass. Garnish
with salmon.*

☐ TOM COLLINS

In the 1870s, a practical
joke made the rounds where
the instigator insisted that
the victim knew their mutual
(and fictional) good friend
"Tom Collins" to the point that
fisticuffs often occurred. That
is just one tale of how this
cocktail was named.

2 oz. gin
1 oz. fresh lemon juice
1 oz. simple syrup
Soda water
Garnish: Orange and lemon
    wheels, maraschino cherry

*Shake gin, lemon juice, and
syrup with ice and strain
into Collins glass. Add several ice cubes, fill with soda
water, and stir. Garnish with
orange, lemon, and cherry.
Serve with a straw.*

🥤 TROPICAL SPECIAL

2 oz. fresh grapefruit juice
1½ oz. gin
1 oz. fresh orange juice
1 oz. fresh lime juice
½ oz. triple sec
Garnish: Fresh tropical fruit
 slices, maraschino cherry

*Shake with ice and strain
into ice-filled highball glass.
Garnish with tropical fruits
and cherry.*

🍸 TURF COCKTAIL

There are three distinct
cocktails named for a horse
lover's hangout. Our favorite
version hails from the old
Waldorf-Astoria Hotel's bar of
the late nineteenth century.

2 oz. genever
1 oz. sweet vermouth
1 dash Angostura bitters
Garnish: Lemon twist

*Stir with ice and strain into
chilled cocktail glass. Add
lemon twist.*

🍸 TUXEDO COCKTAIL

Again, we owe thanks to Harry
Johnson's 1882 *Bartender's
Manual* for a timeless libation.

1 oz. Old Tom gin
1 oz. dry vermouth
1 tsp. absinthe
1 tsp. maraschino liqueur
2 dashes orange bitters
Garnish: Maraschino cherry

*Stir with ice and strain into
chilled cocktail glass. Add the
cherry.*

🍸 UNION COCKTAIL

1½ oz. gin
¾ oz. sloe gin
1 tsp. grenadine

*Shake with ice and strain
into chilled cocktail glass.*

🍸 UNION JACK

2 oz. gin
½ oz. Pimm's No. 1
½ oz. crème de violette or
 Crème Yvette
2 dashes orange bitters
Garnish: Orange twist

*Stir with ice and strain into
chilled cocktail glass. Add
orange twist.*

⅄ VESPER

James Bond's favorite cocktail, as described in Ian Fleming's book *Casino Royale*, named for Vesper Lynd, the novel's female character. We suggest stirring, not shaking, the drink, but it's hard to argue with 007.

3 oz. gin
1 oz. vodka
½ oz. Cocchi Americano
Garnish: Large lemon twist

Shake with ice. Strain into chilled Champagne or cocktail glass. Add lemon twist.

⅄ VIEUX MOT

1½ oz. gin
¾ oz. fresh lemon juice
½ oz. elderflower liqueur
½ oz. simple syrup

Shake with ice and strain into chilled cocktail glass.

⅄ VOW OF SILENCE

1½ oz. gin
¾ oz. fresh grapefruit juice
½ oz. fresh lime juice
½ oz. yellow Chartreuse
¼ oz. amaro, such as Averna
¼ oz. simple syrup

Shake with ice and strain into chilled cocktail glass.

⅄ WAIKIKI BEACHCOMBER

¾ oz. gin
¾ oz. triple sec
½ oz. pineapple juice

Shake with ice and strain into chilled cocktail glass.

⅄ WALLICK COCKTAIL

The Hotel Wallick was another old-time New York hostelry with a famous bar. This cocktail consists of a recognizable blend of gin, vermouth, and a sweetener.

1½ oz. gin
1½ oz. dry vermouth
1 tsp. triple sec

Stir with ice and strain into chilled cocktail glass.

▯ WALLIS BLUE COCKTAIL

To color this cocktail blue, substitute blue curaçao for the triple sec.

For glass: Lime wedge, superfine sugar
1 oz. gin
1 oz. triple sec
1 oz. fresh lime juice

Rim old-fashioned glass with lime and sugar. Fill with ice. Shake remaining ingredients with ice and strain into glass.

♉ WATER LILY

¾ oz. gin
¾ oz. triple sec
¾ oz. crème de violette
¾ oz. fresh lemon juice
Garnish: Orange twist

Shake with ice and strain into chilled cocktail glass. Add orange twist.

♉ WESTERN ROSE

1 oz. gin
½ oz. dry vermouth
½ oz. apricot-flavored brandy
1 tsp. fresh lemon juice

Shake with ice and strain into chilled cocktail glass.

♉ WHITE LADY

1½ oz. gin
¾ oz. triple sec
½ oz. fresh lemon juice

Shake with ice and strain into chilled cocktail glass.

♉ WHITE SPIDER

1 oz. gin
¾ oz. fresh lemon juice
½ oz. triple sec
¼ oz. simple syrup

Shake with ice and strain into chilled cocktail glass.

♉ THE WINKLE

3 fresh sage leaves
2 oz. gin
1 oz. fresh lime juice
½ oz. limoncello
½ oz. simple syrup
4 raspberries
Garnish: Lemon twist

Muddle sage in mixing glass. Add remaining ingredients. Shake with ice and double-strain into chilled cocktail glass. Add lemon twist.

♉ WOODSTOCK

1½ oz. gin
1 oz. fresh lemon juice
1½ tsp. maple syrup
1 dash orange bitters

Shake with ice and strain into chilled cocktail glass.

♉ YOKAHAMA ROMANCE

2½ oz. sake
1 oz. gin
¼ oz. maraschino liqueur
Garnish: 1 unsprayed rose petal

Stir with ice and strain into chilled cocktail glass. Add rose petal.

RUM

RUM WAS FIRST PRODUCED in Brazil, Barbados, and Jamaica after Columbus introduced sugarcane to the West Indies in the late fifteenth century; within two centuries it was the favorite spirit of New England. Today this spirit, created from molasses, sugarcane juice, or syrup made by reducing the free-run juice of sugarcane, is among the most popular in the United States.

Rums can be divided into three stylistic types: Light rums, sometimes called white or silver, are traditionally produced in southern Caribbean islands (like Puerto Rico, Trinidad, and Barbados) and aged up to a year in barrels. Medium rums, sometimes called gold or amber, are smoother as a result of either congeners (organic compounds produced during fermentation), the addition of caramel, or occasionally through aging in wood barrels. Dark rums, which take their color from being aged anywhere from 3 to 12 years (and in some cases from the addition of caramel), are produced in the tropics: Jamaica, Haiti, and Martinique. And speaking of the French island of Martinique, if you see the words "rhum agricole" on a bottle or menu it refers to how pure-cane rum is known there. Brazilians call their pure-cane spirit "cachaça," which is synonymous with Caipirinha cocktails.

Subcategories of rum include spiced or flavored rums, which are infused with spices or aromatics while being distilled. There are also 151-proof rums, also called high-proof rums, which are often added to complete a mixed drink, or used in desserts or dessert cocktails that call for flaming—literally igniting the spirit. (Obviously, one should be very careful when playing with fire and high-proof rum!)

A DAY AT THE BEACH

1 oz. coconut-flavored rum
½ oz. amaretto
4 oz. fresh orange juice
½ oz. grenadine
Garnish: Pineapple wedge, strawberry

Shake rum, amaretto, and orange juice with ice and pour into ice-filled highball glass. Top with grenadine. Garnish with pineapple and strawberry.

AGRICOLE RUM PUNCH

2 oz. aged rhum agricole
1 oz. fresh lime juice
1 oz. simple syrup
2 dashes Angostura bitters
¼ oz. allspice liqueur (pimento dram)
Garnish: Freshly ground nutmeg

Shake with ice and strain into ice-filled Collins glass. Top with nutmeg.

AIR MAIL

1 oz. light rum
½ oz. fresh lime juice
½ oz. Honey Syrup (page 21)
1 splash chilled Champagne

Shake rum, lime juice, and syrup with ice. Strain into chilled champagne flute. Top with Champagne.

☐ ANCIENT MARINER

1 oz. aged rum
1 oz. dark rum
¾ oz. fresh lime juice
½ oz. fresh grapefruit juice
½ oz. simple syrup
¼ oz. allspice liqueur
  (pimento dram)
Garnish: Lime wedge, fresh
  mint sprig

*Shake with ice and strain
into old-fashioned glass filled
with crushed ice. Garnish
with lime and mint.*

☐ BAHAMA MAMA

½ oz. dark rum
½ oz. coconut liqueur
¼ oz. 151-proof rum
¼ oz. coffee liqueur
½ oz. fresh lemon juice
4 oz. pineapple juice
Garnish: Strawberry or
  maraschino cherry

*Shake with ice and strain
into ice-filled highball glass.
Garnish with strawberry or
cherry.*

☐ BAJITO

4 fresh mint leaves
4 fresh basil leaves
5 slices fresh lime
1 oz. simple syrup
3 oz. dark rum
Garnish: 1 fresh basil leaf

*Muddle mint, 4 basil leaves,
and lime with syrup in mixing glass. Add ice and rum.
Shake well and strain into
ice-filled old-fashioned glass.
Garnish with basil leaf.*

☐ THE BEACHBUM

1 oz. light rum
1 oz. dark rum
½ oz. apricot-flavored brandy
1 oz. pineapple juice
¾ oz. fresh lime juice
½ oz. almond or orgeat syrup
Garnish: Orange/cherry flag

*Shake with ice and strain
into ice-filled Collins glass.
Garnish with orange/cherry
flag.*

▽ THE BEAUTY BENEATH

2 oz. dark rum
½ oz. sweet vermouth
½ oz. Campari
½ oz. triple sec
1 dash Angostura bitters
Garnish: Orange twist

Shake with ice and strain into chilled cocktail glass. Add orange twist.

▽ BEE'S KISS

1½ oz. light rum
1 oz. heavy cream
¾ oz. Honey Syrup (page 21)

Shake and strain into a chilled champagne flute.

▢ BERMUDA RUM SWIZZLE

2 oz. dark rum
1 oz. fresh lime juice
1 oz. pineapple juice
1 oz. fresh orange juice
¼ oz. falernum
Soda water
Garnish: Orange wheel, maraschino cherry

Combine first five ingredients in ice-filled Collins glass. With barspoon between your palms, move hands back and forth and up and down to quickly rotate and lift spoon, until glass is frosted. Top with soda water. Garnish with orange and cherry. Serve with a swizzle stick.

▢ BERMUDA TRIANGLE

1 oz. peach schnapps
½ oz. spiced rum
3 oz. fresh orange juice

Pour ingredients into ice-filled old-fashioned glass.

▯ BITCHES' BREW

1 oz. dark rum
1 oz. rhum agricole
1 oz. fresh lime juice
½ oz. simple syrup
½ oz. allspice liqueur (pimento dram)
1 egg
Garnish: Freshly grated nutmeg

Shake without ice. Shake with ice and strain into highball glass. Top with nutmeg.

▯ THE BITTER, DARK & STORMY

Created by TED HENWOOD, New York, NY

2½ oz. dark rum
5 dashes orange bitters
Ginger beer
Garnish: Lime wedge

Pour rum and bitters into ice-filled highball glass. Top with ginger beer and stir. Squeeze lime into glass and add wedge.

▯ BITTERLY DARK

1½ oz. dark rum
1 oz. amaro, such as Ramazzotti or Averna
1 oz. fresh blood orange juice
¼ oz. crème de cassis
Garnish: Blood orange wheel

Shake and strain into chilled cocktail glass. Garnish with orange wheel.

▯ BLACK MARIA

2 oz. light rum
2 oz. coffee-flavored brandy
½ oz. simple syrup
4 oz. hot strong brewed coffee

Stir in prewarmed Irish coffee glass.

▯ BLACK WIDOW

3 oz. dark rum
1 oz. white crème de menthe

Shake with ice and strain into ice-filled old-fashioned glass.

🍸 BLOOD AND SAMBA

¾ oz. cachaça
¾ oz. sweet vermouth
¾ oz. Cherry Heering
¾ oz. fresh orange juice
2 dashes Peychaud's bitters
Garnish: Orange twist,
    flamed

*Shake with ice and strain
into chilled cocktail
glass. Flame orange twist
and add.*

🍸 BLUE HAWAIIAN

A tiki drink with impeccable
heritage, it was created in
1957 by Harry Yee, head
bartender at the Hilton
Hawaiian Village, in Waikiki,
Hawaii.

1 oz. light rum
1 oz. blue curaçao
1 oz. cream of coconut
2 oz. pineapple juice
Garnish: Pineapple wedge,
    maraschino cherry

*Combine ingredients with
1 c. crushed ice in blender on
high speed. Pour into chilled
highball glass. Garnish with
pineapple and cherry.*

🍸 BORINQUEN

1½ oz. light rum
1 oz. fresh lime juice
1 oz. fresh orange juice
½ oz. passion fruit syrup
1 tsp. 151-proof rum

*Process with ½ c. crushed ice
in blender on low
speed. Pour into chilled
old-fashioned glass.*

🍸 BOSSA NOVA SPECIAL COCKTAIL

1 oz. dark rum
1 oz. Galliano
¼ oz. apricot-flavored brandy
2 oz. pineapple juice
¼ oz. fresh lemon juice
1 egg white
Garnish: Maraschino cherry

*Shake without ice. Shake
with ice and strain into ice-
filled highball glass. Garnish
with cherry.*

🍸 BUCCANEER

1½ oz. spiced rum
½ oz. white crème de cacao
¾ oz. fresh lime juice
¾ oz. pineapple juice
½ oz. falernum
1 dash Angostura bitters
Garnish: Freshly grated nutmeg

*Shake with ice and strain
into chilled cocktail glass. Top
with nutmeg.*

🍸 CABLE CAR

This drink is a specialty of star
mixologist Tony Abou-Ganim.

For glass: Lemon wedge,
    Cinnamon Sugar (recipe
    follows)
2 oz. spiced rum
¾ oz. triple sec
¾ oz. fresh lemon juice
½ oz. simple syrup
Garnish: Lemon twist, ground
    cinnamon

*Rim chilled cocktail glass with
lemon wedge and cinnamon
sugar. Shake remaining ingredients with ice and strain into
glass. Add lemon twist and top
with a sprinkle of cinnamon.*

CINNAMON SUGAR

*Mix equal parts superfine
sugar and ground cinnamon.*

☐ CAIPIRINHA

The national drink of Brazil,
the name means "country
bumpkin."

1 whole lime, cut into quarters
½ oz. simple syrup
2 oz. cachaça

*Muddle lime and syrup in
old-fashioned glass. Add
cachaça and stir. Fill with ice
and stir again.*

☐ CANADO SALUDO

1½ oz. light rum
1 oz. fresh orange juice
1 oz. pineapple juice
½ oz. fresh lemon juice
½ oz. grenadine
5 dashes Angostura bitters
Garnish: Pineapple wedge,
    orange wheel, maraschino
    cherry

*Pour ingredients into ice-
filled highball glass and stir
well. Garnish with pineapple,
orange, and cherry.*

� CAPTAIN'S BLOOD

1½ oz. dark rum
¼ oz. fresh lime juice
¼ oz. simple syrup
¼ oz. falernum
2 dashes Angostura bitters
Garnish: Lemon zest spiral

*Shake with ice and strain
into chilled cocktail glass.
Add lemon spiral.*

Y CARIBBEAN GINGER

Created by RAFAEL REYES,
New York, NY

To obtain fresh ginger juice,
shred fresh ginger (no need
to peel) on the large holes
of a box grater, wrap in a
clean bar towel, and wring
into a bowl.

2 oz. dark rum
1 oz. pineapple juice
½ oz. Demerara Syrup
(page 20)
½ oz. fresh lime juice
½ oz. fresh ginger juice
Garnish: Ground cinnamon

*Shake well with ice and
strain into chilled cocktail
glass. Top with cinnamon.*

Y CHANTILLY COCKTAIL

For glass: Lemon wedge,
Cinnamon Sugar (page 113)
1½ oz. dark rum
¾ oz. apricot-flavored brandy
1 oz. fresh lemon juice
1 oz. simple syrup
2 dashes peach bitters
Garnish: Cinnamon stick
wrapped with orange zest
spiral

*Rim chilled cocktail glass
with lemon and cinnamon
sugar. Shake remaining ingredients with ice and strain
into glass. Add cinnamon-
orange garnish.*

☐ CHET BAKER

1 sugar cube
2 dashes Angostura bitters
2 oz. dark rum
¼ oz. Punt e Mes
¼ oz. Honey Syrup (page 21)
Garnish: Lemon twist

*Muddle sugar cube with
bitters in mixing glass. Add
ice, then other ingredients,
and stir briefly. Strain into
ice-filled old-fashioned glass.
Garnish with lemon twist.*

☐ CHOCOLATE RUM

1 oz. light rum
½ oz. dark crème de cacao
½ oz. white crème de menthe
1 tsp. 151-proof rum
¼ oz. half-and-half

Shake with ice and strain into ice-filled old-fashioned glass.

☐ COFFEY PARK SWIZZLE

1 oz. dark rum
1 oz. amontillado sherry
¾ oz. ginger liqueur
¾ oz. fresh lime juice
¼ oz. falernum
4 dashes Angostura bitters
Garnish: Mint sprig

Pour ingredients into crushed ice-filled Collins glass. With barspoon between your palms, move hands back and forth and up and down to quickly rotate and lift spoon until glass is frosted. Add mint.

COLADAS

☐ LEMON-COCONUT COLADA

1½ oz. citrus-flavored rum
1½ oz. coconut-flavored rum
2 oz. cream of coconut
1 oz. heavy cream
4 oz. pineapple juice
½ oz. fresh lemon juice
Garnish: Freshly grated lemon zest or toasted coconut

Shake with ice and strain into ice-filled hurricane glass. Top with lemon zest or coconut.

▢ PIÑA COLADA

Another rum drink with a murky history, it was probably the invention of Ramon "Monchito" Marrero at the Caribe Hilton's Beachcomber Bar in San Juan, PR, in 1954, at the time when cream of coconut was just hitting the marketplace.

3 oz. light rum
3 oz. pineapple juice
1½ oz. cream of coconut
Garnish: Pineapple wedge, maraschino cherry

Combine ingredients with 2 c. of crushed ice in blender on high speed. Pour into chilled Collins glass. Garnish with pineapple and cherry and serve with a straw.

▽ CONCRETE JUNGLE

Created by HAL WOLIN, New York, NY

1½ oz. dark rum
½ oz. Calvados
½ oz. Amaro Nonino
½ oz. sweet vermouth
1 dash absinthe
1 dash orange bitters

Stir with ice and strain into chilled cocktail glass.

▽ CREOLE CLUB COCKTAIL

2 oz. aged rhum agricole
1 oz. Creole Shrubb (rum-based orange liqueur)
¾ oz. fresh lime juice
1 dash Angostura bitters
1 dash orange bitters
Garnish: Freshly grated nutmeg, star anise pod

Shake with ice and strain into chilled cocktail glass. Top with nutmeg and add star anise.

▢ CUBA LIBRE

Coca-Cola was introduced to Cuba in 1900, and this cocktail was born almost immediately thereafter. "¡Cuba libre! (Free Cuba!)" was a battle cry during the Cuban War of Independence, which ended just two years before.

2 oz. rum
Cola
Garnish: Lime wedge

Pour rum into ice-filled high-ball glass. Fill with cola and stir. Squeeze lime into glass and add wedge.

🍸 CUBAN SPECIAL

1 oz. light rum
½ oz. pineapple juice
½ oz. fresh lime juice
¼ oz. triple sec
Garnish: Pineapple wedge,
  maraschino cherry

Shake with ice and strain into chilled cocktail glass. Garnish with pineapple and cherry.

🍸 THE CURE AND THE CAUSE

Created by ANDRES SANCHEZ, Philadelphia, PA

You will find jars of wild hibiscus flowers in rose syrup at specialty stores. See page 303 for online resources.

12 blueberries
½ oz. syrup from wild hibiscus flowers in rose syrup
1½ oz. cachaça
¾ oz. açai berry liqueur
1 oz. fresh lime juice
Garnish: Fresh blueberries

Muddle 12 blueberries and syrup in mixing glass. Add remaining ingredients and shake with ice. Strain into ice-filled highball glass. Garnish with blueberries.

DAIQUIRIS

🍸 CLASSIC DAIQUIRI

This is the original cocktail and not the frozen version, which can be found on page 241.

2 oz. light rum
¾ oz. fresh lime juice
¾ oz. simple syrup

Shake with ice and strain into chilled cocktail glass.

🍸 DERBY DAIQUIRI

1½ oz. light rum
1 oz. fresh orange juice
½ oz. fresh lime juice
½ oz. simple syrup

Combine ingredients with ½ c. cracked ice in blender and blend on low speed until smooth. Pour into champagne flute.

⅄ HEMINGWAY DAIQUIRI

Papa liked his Daiquiris with grapefruit juice and sweetness provided by maraschino. A double of this drink is called a Papa Doble, and Hemingway was certainly a two-fisted drinker.

2 oz. light rum
¾ oz. fresh grapefruit juice
½ oz. fresh lime juice
¼ oz. maraschino liqueur

Shake with ice and strain into ice-filled cocktail glass.

⅄ PASSION DAIQUIRI

1½ oz. light rum
1 oz. fresh lime juice
½ oz. passion fruit juice or puree
½ oz. simple syrup

Shake with ice and strain into chilled cocktail glass.

⅄ STRAWBERRY DAIQUIRI

2 strawberries, chopped
1 oz. fresh lime juice
½ oz. simple syrup
1 oz. light rum
½ oz. strawberry schnapps

Muddle strawberries, lime juice, and syrup in mixing glass. Add rum and schnapps. Shake with ice and strain into chilled cocktail glass.

⅄ DAISY DE SANTIAGO

2 oz. dark rum
¾ oz. fresh lime juice
¾ oz. simple syrup
1 oz. yellow Chartreuse
Garnish: Fresh mint sprig

Shake first three ingredients with ice and strain into ice-filled red-wine glass. Carefully float Chartreuse (see page 12) on top. Add mint.

☐ DARK 'N STORMY

The national drink of Bermuda requires just two Bermudian products, ginger beer and dark rum. Dark 'n Stormy® is a registered trademark of Gosling Brothers Limited, Hamilton, Bermuda.

Ginger beer
2 oz. Gosling's dark rum

Pour ginger beer into an ice-filled old-fashioned glass. Float rum (see page 12) on top.

☐ DOCTOR FUNK NO. 2

The real Doctor Funk was Robert Louis Stevenson's physician in the South Seas. Some versions of this drink go heavy on the absinthe, so add more if you wish.

1½ oz. dark rum
½ oz. falernum
½ oz. grenadine
¾ oz. fresh lime juice
1 dash absinthe
1 dash Angostura bitters
Soda water
Garnish: Lime wedge

Shake first six ingredients with ice and strain into hurricane glass. Fill with soda water. Add lime.

☐ EL PRESIDENTE COCKTAIL NO. 1

It is said that this was the drink that Cuban president Carmen Menocal tried to serve to President Calvin Coolidge during a state visit. As the meeting occurred during Prohibition, Coolidge reportedly declined.

1½ oz. light rum
¾ oz. fresh lime juice
1 tsp. pineapple juice
1 tsp. grenadine

Shake with ice and strain into chilled cocktail glass.

☐ EL PRESIDENTE COCKTAIL NO. 2

1½ oz. light rum
¾ oz. dry vermouth
1 dash Angostura bitters

Stir with ice and strain into chilled cocktail glass.

♈ FLORIDITA NO. 1

1½ oz. light rum
½ oz. fresh lime juice
½ oz. sweet vermouth
1 tsp. white crème de cacao
1 tsp. grenadine
Garnish: Lime twist

Shake with ice and strain into chilled cocktail glass. Add lime twist.

♈ FLORIDITA NO. 3

2 oz. light rum
¾ oz. fresh lime juice
½ oz. fresh grapefruit juice
½ oz. maraschino liqueur
½ oz. simple syrup
Garnish: Lime wheel

Shake with ice and strain into chilled champagne flute. Garnish with lime wheel.

▢ FOG CUTTER

1½ oz. light rum
½ oz. brandy
½ oz. gin
1½ oz. fresh lemon juice
1 oz. fresh orange juice
1½ tsp. almond or orgeat syrup
1 tsp. sweet sherry

Shake first six ingredients with ice and strain into ice-filled Collins glass. Top with sherry.

▢ GINGER GRAPEFRUIT RICKEY

2 oz. light rum
2 oz. fresh grapefruit juice
1 oz. ginger liqueur
½ oz. fresh lime juice
Soda water

Shake first four ingredients with ice. Strain into ice-filled highball glass and top with soda water.

♈ GOLDEN ECLIPSE

Created by CHARLES H. STEADMAN, Palm Beach, FL

1½ oz. dark rum
¼ oz. amaro, such as Ramazzotti or Averna
½ oz. fresh lemon juice
1 dash orange bitters
3 oz. sparkling apple cider
Garnish: Golden Delicious apple wedge

Shake first four ingredients with ice. Strain into chilled cocktail glass. Top with cider. Garnish with apple wedge perched on glass rim.

HAI KARATE

2 oz. dark rum
1 oz. fresh lime juice
1 oz. pineapple juice
1 oz. fresh orange juice
1 tsp. maple syrup
1 dash Angostura bitters
Garnish: Cherry/orange flag

Shake with ice and strain into ice-filled Collins glass. Garnish with cherry/orange flag.

HARVEST NECTAR

1½ oz. light rum
1 oz. pineapple juice
1 oz. cranberry juice
1 oz. fresh orange juice
1 oz. lemon-lime soda

Shake with ice and strain into ice-filled beer mug.

HEMINGWAY'S NOG

Created by ALEX STRAUS, Hollywood, CA

1½ oz. dark rum
¾ oz. vanilla liqueur
¼ oz simple syrup
1 oz. crème fraîche
3 dashes tiki bitters, such as Bittermen's 'Elemakule
Garnish: Freshly grated nutmeg

Shake with ice and strain into chilled cocktail glass. Top with nutmeg.

THE HOLY ROLLER

Created by TREVOR EASTER, San Francisco, CA

1½ oz. cachaça
¾ oz. fresh lime juice
½ oz. Honey Syrup (page 21)
6–8 fresh mint leaves
2 dashes Angostura bitters
½ oz. Champagne or sparkling wine
Garnish: Fresh mint sprig

Shake first five ingredients with ice. Strain into chilled cocktail glass. Top with Champagne or sparkling wine. Garnish with mint.

☐ HURRICANE

The specialty cocktail of Pat O'Brien's in New Orleans. You can buy Hurricane mix, but this from-scratch version is even better.

1½ oz. dark rum
1½ oz. light rum
1 oz. passion fruit syrup
1 oz. lime juice
¾ oz. fresh orange juice
½ oz. simple syrup
½ oz. grenadine
Garnish: Orange half-wheel, maraschino cherry

Shake with ice and strain into ice-filled hurricane glass. Garnish with orange and cherry.

☐ HURRICANE LEAH

¼ oz. light rum
¼ oz. gin
¼ oz. vodka
¼ oz. blanco tequila
¼ oz. blue curaçao
1 dash cherry-flavored brandy
1½ oz. simple syrup
1½ oz. fresh lemon juice
3 oz. fresh orange juice
Garnish: Orange wheel

Pour ingredients, in order given, into ice-filled hurricane glass and stir. Garnish with orange wheel.

☐ HUSH AND WONDER

1 splash crème de violette
2 oz. light rum
¾ oz. fresh lime juice
¾ oz. simple syrup
3 dashes grapefruit bitters

Pour crème de violette into chilled cocktail glass and swirl to coat; discard excess liqueur. Shake remaining ingredients with ice and strain into glass.

⬜ JACK SPARROW FLIP

2 oz. dark rum
¾ oz. madeira
¾ oz. simple syrup
1 egg
2 dashes Angostura bitters
Garnish: Freshly grated nutmeg

Shake without ice. Then shake with ice and strain into highball glass. Top with nutmeg.

⬜ JAMAICAN GINGER

1½ oz. light rum
1 oz. dark rum
½ oz. falernum
½ oz. fresh lime juice
4 dashes Angostura bitters
Ginger ale
Garnish: Lime wheel

Stir first five ingredients in ice-filled Collins glass. Top with ginger ale. Garnish with lime.

⬜ KNICKERBOCKER SPECIAL COCKTAIL

2 oz. light rum
½ tsp. triple sec
1 tsp. fresh lemon juice
1 tsp. fresh orange juice
1 tsp. raspberry syrup
Garnish: Small pineapple slice

Shake with ice and strain into chilled cocktail glass. Garnish with pineapple.

⬜ KO ADANG

2 oz. dark rum
1 oz. coconut rum
½ oz. ginger liqueur
½ oz. mango nectar
½ oz. cream of coconut
½ oz. fresh lime juice
Garnish: Lime wheel

Shake with ice and strain into ice-filled Collins glass. Garnish with lime.

🍸 LA VITA DULCE

Created by ABIGAIL GULLO,
New York City, NY

1½ oz. spiced rum
¾ oz. mezcal
¾ oz. fresh lime juice
¾ oz. simple syrup
Garnish: Ground cinnamon

*Shake with ice and strain
into chilled cocktail glass. Top
with cinnamon.*

🍷 LEVELHEADED COCKTAIL

1½ oz. aged rhum agricole
1 oz. cold brewed coffee
½ oz. allspice liqueur (pimento
   dram)
¼ oz. simple syrup
2 dashes Angostura bitters

*Shake with ice and strain
into snifter.*

🥃 LOOK OUT BELOW

1½ oz. 151-proof rum
½ oz. fresh lime juice
¼ oz. grenadine

*Shake with ice and strain
into ice-filled old-fashioned
glass.*

🥃 LOUNGE LIZARD

1 oz. dark rum
½ oz. amaretto
Cola
Garnish: Lime wedge

*Pour rum and amaretto into
ice-filled Collins glass. Fill
with cola and stir. Garnish
with lime.*

🍸 LUMINATION

2 slices fresh ginger
1 oz. simple syrup
2 oz. dark rum
1 oz. VS Cognac
1 oz. fresh lemon juice
1 dash Angostura bitters
Garnish: Lemon twist

*Muddle ginger in syrup in
mixing glass. Add remain-
ing ingredients and ice and
shake. Strain into chilled
champagne flute. Add lemon
twist.*

⬜ MAI-TAI (TRADER VIC VERSION)

2 oz. dark rum, preferably Jamaican
½ oz. orange curaçao
1 oz. fresh lime juice (reserve ½ lime shell for garnish)
½ oz. orgeat syrup
¼ oz. rock candy syrup or simple syrup
Garnish: Fresh mint sprig; pineapple wedge skewered with maraschino cherry

Shake ingredients without ice. Strain into ice-filled old-fashioned glass. Garnish with lime shell, mint, and skewered pineapple and cherry.

🍸 MARTINIQUE ROSE

2 oz. aged rhum agricole
½ oz. amaretto
¾ oz. fresh lime juice
¾ oz. fresh grapefruit juice
½ oz. orgeat or almond syrup

Shake with ice and strain into chilled cocktail glass.

⬜ MOJITO

This Cuban drink has attained cocktail immortality. Some believe that its history is as long as rum itself, even if it has only recently gained popularity in the U.S.

3 lime wedges
8–10 fresh mint leaves
¾ oz. simple syrup
2 oz. light rum
Soda water
Garnish: Fresh mint sprig

Muddle the limes, mint, and syrup in a Collins glass. Add the rum with ice and stir well. Top with soda water. Garnish with mint.

⬜ MONKEY WRENCH

1½ oz. light rum
Fresh grapefruit juice

Pour rum into ice-filled Collins glass. Fill with grapefruit juice and stir.

☐ NEVADA COCKTAIL

1½ oz. light rum
1 oz. fresh grapefruit juice
¾ oz. fresh lime juice
¾ oz. simple syrup
1 dash Angostura bitters

Shake with ice and strain into chilled cocktail glass.

☐ NEW ORLEANS BUCK

1½ oz. light rum
1 oz. fresh orange juice
½ oz. fresh lemon juice
Ginger ale

Shake first three ingredients with ice and strain into ice-filled Collins glass. Fill with ginger ale and stir.

☐ NIGHT CAP

Whiskey or brandy make fine nightcaps, too.

2 oz. light rum
½ oz. simple syrup
Warm milk
Garnish: Freshly grated
    nutmeg

Pour rum and syrup in pre-warmed Irish coffee glass, fill with warm milk, and stir. Top with nutmeg.

☐ THE OLD CUBAN

This recipe is a specialty of Audrey Saunders, owner of Pegu Club, New York, NY

6 fresh mint leaves
1 oz. simple syrup
¾ oz. fresh lime juice
1½ oz. dark rum
2 dashes Angostura bitters
2 oz. Champagne
Garnish: Chopped fresh mint

Muddle mint leaves, syrup, and lime juice in mixing glass. Add rum, bitters, and ice and shake well. Strain into chilled cocktail glass and top with Champagne. Garnish with chopped mint.

☐ PADDINGTON

1 splash absinthe
1½ oz. light rum
½ oz. Lillet Blanc
½ oz. fresh grapefruit juice
½ oz. fresh lemon juice
1 tsp. orange marmalade
Garnish: Grapefruit twist

Pour absinthe into chilled cocktail glass, swirl to coat inside, and discard excess. Shake remaining ingredients with ice and strain into glass. Add grapefruit twist.

⚗ PARIS WHEN IT SIZZLES

2 oz. dark rum
¾ oz. elderflower liqueur
½ oz. fresh lime juice
1 dash Angostura bitters
Garnish: Lime wedge

Shake with ice and strain into chilled cocktail glass. Garnish with lime.

⚗ PEARL BUTTON

2 oz. cachaça (Brazilian rum)
¾ oz. Lillet Blanc
½ oz. fresh lime juice
Lemon-lime soda
Garnish: Pineapple wedge, maraschino cherry

Shake first three ingredients with ice and strain into ice-filled Collins glass. Top with soda. Garnish with pineapple and cherry.

⚗ PINEAPPLE FIZZ

2 oz. light rum
1 oz. pineapple juice
1 tsp. simple syrup
Soda water

Shake rum, pineapple juice, and syrup with ice and strain into chilled highball glass over 2 ice cubes. Fill with soda water and stir.

⚗ PINK PARADISE

1½ oz. coconut-flavored rum
1 oz. amaretto
3 oz. cranberry juice
1½ oz. pineapple juice
Garnish: Pineapple wedge, maraschino cherry

Stir ingredients in ice-filled hurricane glass. Garnish with pineapple and cherry.

⚗ PLANTER'S COCKTAIL

1½ oz. Jamaican rum
½ oz. fresh lemon juice
1 tsp. simple syrup

Shake with ice and strain into chilled cocktail glass.

☐ PLANTER'S PUNCH NO. 1

2½ oz. light rum
2 oz. fresh lime juice
½ oz. simple syrup
2 oz. soda water
1 dash grenadine
Garnish: Lemon, orange,
   and pineapple slices;
   maraschino cherry

Stir rum, lime juice, syrup, and bitters in ice-filled Collins glass until glass is frosted. Fill with soda water and top with grenadine. Garnish with the fruit. Serve with a straw.

☐ PLANTER'S PUNCH NO. 2

2 oz. light rum
2 oz. fresh orange juice
1 oz. fresh lime juice
½ oz. pineapple juice
¼ oz. fresh lemon juice
1 oz. Jamaican rum
¼ oz. triple sec
1 dash grenadine
Garnish: Lemon, orange,
   and pineapple slices;
   maraschino cherry; fresh
   mint sprig dipped in sugar

Stir first five ingredients in ice-filled Collins glass until glass is frosted. Add Jamaican rum, stir, and top with triple sec and grenadine. Garnish with fruit and mint. Serve with a straw.

♀ PROHIBITION PUNCH

Created by Hospitality
Holdings, New York, NY

1½ oz. dark rum
¾ oz. Grand Marnier
1 oz. passion fruit juice
1 oz. cranberry juice
¼ oz. fresh lemon juice
2 oz. Champagne

Shake first five ingredients with ice. Strain into ice-filled snifter. Top with Champagne.

▽ PUERTO RICAN RUM DAISY

1½ oz. dark rum
¼ oz. orange curaçao
¾ oz. fresh lemon juice
½ oz. fresh orange juice
½ oz. simple syrup
1 dash Angostura bitters
Garnish: Freshly grated
    nutmeg, orange wheel

*Shake with ice and strain
into chilled cocktail glass.
Top with nutmeg and garnish
with orange.*

▽ QUAKER'S COCKTAIL

¾ oz. light rum
¾ oz. brandy
½ oz. fresh lemon juice
¼ oz. raspberry syrup

*Shake with ice and strain
into chilled cocktail glass.*

▽ RESTLESS NATIVE

2 oz. coconut rum
¾ oz. white crème de cacao
1½ oz. fresh lime juice
Garnish: Lime zest spiral

*Shake with ice and strain
into chilled cocktail glass.
Garnish with lime spiral.*

▽ RIO FIX

1 splash absinthe or pastis
1½ oz. cachaça
½ oz. maraschino liqueur
¾ oz. fresh lime juice
½ oz. pineapple juice

*Pour pastis into chilled
champagne flute and swirl to
coat inside. Shake remaining ingredients with ice and
strain into glass.*

▽ ROBSON COCKTAIL

1½ oz. Jamaican rum
½ oz. fresh lemon juice
½ oz. fresh orange juice
¼ oz. grenadine

*Shake with ice and strain
into chilled cocktail glass.*

▢ RUM OLD-FASHIONED

1½ oz. light rum
1 tsp. 151-proof rum
1 tsp. simple syrup
1 dash Angostura bitters
Garnish: Lemon twist

*Stir in ice-filled old-fashioned
glass. Add lemon twist.*

🍸 RUM RELAXER

1½ oz. light rum
1 oz. pineapple juice
½ oz. grenadine
Lemon-lime soda
Garnish: Orange wheel,
    maraschino cherry

*Shake first three ingredients
with ice and pour with ice
into hurricane or parfait
glass. Fill glass with lemon-
lime soda. Garnish with
orange and cherry.*

🥃 RUM SCREWDRIVER

1½ oz. light rum
5 oz. fresh orange juice

*Stir rum and orange juice in
ice-filled highball glass.*

🥃 RUM SWIZZLE

2 oz. light or dark rum
1 oz. fresh lime juice
½ oz. simple syrup
2 dashes Angostura bitters
Soda water

*Combine first four ingredients
in ice-filled Collins glass. With
bar spoon between your palms,
move hands back and forth
and up and down to quickly
rotate and lift spoon, until glass
is frosted. Top with soda water.
Serve with a swizzle stick.*

🍸 SAINT LUCY BRACER

2 oz. dark rum
½ oz. butterscotch schnapps
½ oz. sweet vermouth
2 dashes Angostura bitters
Garnish: Edible flower, such as
    nasturtium

*Stir with ice and strain into
chilled cocktail glass. Garnish
with flower.*

🍸 SANTIAGO COCKTAIL

1½ oz. light rum
1 oz. fresh lime juice
½ oz. simple syrup
½ oz. grenadine

*Shake with ice and strain
into chilled cocktail glass.*

🍸 SARGASSO

2 oz. aged rhum agricole
¾ oz. dry sherry
½ oz. Aperol
2 dashes Angostura bitters
Garnish: Orange twist

*Stir with ice and strain into
chilled cocktail glass. Garnish
with orange twist.*

⅄ SAXON COCKTAIL

1¾ oz. light rum
½ oz. fresh lime juice
½ tsp. grenadine
Garnish: Orange twist

*Shake with ice and strain
into chilled cocktail glass.
Add orange twist.*

⅄ SIR WALTER COCKTAIL

¾ oz. light rum
¾ oz. brandy
1 tsp. grenadine
1 tsp. triple sec
1 tsp. fresh lemon juice

*Shake with ice and
strain into chilled cocktail
glass.*

⅄ SLOPPY JOE'S COCKTAIL NO. 1

¾ oz. light rum
¾ oz. dry vermouth
½ oz. triple sec
1 oz. fresh lime juice
½ oz. grenadine

*Shake with ice and strain
into chilled cocktail glass.*

⅄ SPANISH TOWN COCKTAIL

2 oz. light rum
½ oz. triple sec

*Stir with ice and strain into
chilled cocktail glass.*

▯ STONE WALL

3 thin slices peeled fresh
 ginger
¾ oz. Demerara Syrup (page 20)
1½ oz. fresh apple cider
1½ oz. light rum
Jamaican ginger beer
Garnish: Green apple slice,
 lime wedge

*Muddle ginger and syrup in
mixing glass. Add cider and
rum and shake with ice. Strain
into ice-filled old-fashioned
glass and fill with ginger
beer. Add apple and lime.*

▯ STORMY COLADA

2 oz. dark rum
2 oz. pineapple juice
Ginger beer
Garnish: Skewered pineapple
 wedge, mint sprig, candied
 ginger slice

*Add rum and pineapple juice
to ice-filled highball glass. Fill
with ginger beer and stir. Add
skewered garnish.*

☟ SUNSET AT GOWANUS

2 oz. dark rum
¾ oz. fresh lime juice
½ oz. maple syrup
¼ oz. brandy
¼ oz. yellow Chartreuse

*Shake with ice and strain
into chilled cocktail glass.*

☐ SUSIE TAYLOR

2 oz. light rum
½ oz. fresh lime juice
Ginger ale

*Pour rum and lime juice into
ice-filled Collins glass. Fill
with ginger ale and stir.*

☐ TAHITI CLUB

2 oz. light rum
½ oz. fresh lemon juice
½ oz. fresh lime juice
½ oz. pineapple juice
¼ oz. maraschino liqueur
Garnish: Lemon wheel

*Shake with ice and strain
into ice-filled old-fashioned
glass. Add lemon.*

☟ TOMATO DAIQUIRI

3 fresh cherry tomatoes
2 oz. dark rum
1 oz. fresh lime juice
1 oz. simple syrup
1 dash Angostura bitters

*Muddle tomatoes in mixing
glass. Add remaining ingredients. Shake with ice and
strain into chilled cocktail
glass.*

☟ TORRIDORA
COCKTAIL

1½ oz. light rum
½ oz. coffee-flavored brandy
1½ tsp. half-and-half
1 tsp. 151-proof rum

*Shake first three ingredients
with ice and strain into
chilled cocktail glass. Float
151-proof rum (see page 12)
on top.*

☐ TROPICA COCKTAIL

2 oz. light rum
3 oz. pineapple juice
1 oz. fresh grapefruit juice
1 dash grenadine
Garnish: Pineapple wedge

*Mix ingredients in ice-filled
Collins glass. Add pineapple
wedge.*

🍸 URBAN ANXIETY

Created by AARON DEFEO,
Tucson, AZ

1 oz. cachaça
1 oz. sweet vermouth
¾ oz. Cynar
2 dashes Angostura bitters
Garnish: Grapefruit twist,
    flamed (see page 46)

Stir with ice and strain into chilled cocktail glass. Flame grapefruit twist and add.

▯ VAN VLEET

3 oz. light rum
1 oz. maple syrup
1 oz. fresh lemon juice

Shake with ice and strain into ice-filled old-fashioned glass.

🍸 VIRGINIA DARE

2 slices ripe pear
2 oz. dark rum
½ oz. Bénédictine
2 dashes Angostura bitters

Muddle 1 pear slice in mixing glass. Add remaining ingredients. Shake with ice and strain through a fine wire sieve into chilled cocktail glass. Garnish with remaining pear slice.

🍸 WHITE LILY COCKTAIL

¾ oz. light rum
¾ oz. triple sec
¾ oz. gin
1 dash anisette

Shake with ice and strain into chilled cocktail glass.

🍸 WHITE LION COCKTAIL

1½ oz. light rum
1 oz. fresh lemon juice
½ oz. simple syrup
1 tsp. grenadine
2 dashes Angostura bitters

Shake with ice and strain into chilled cocktail glass.

🍸 X.Y.Z. COCKTAIL

1 oz. light rum
½ oz. triple sec
½ oz. fresh lemon juice

Shake with ice and strain into chilled cocktail glass.

☐ ZOMBIE

The main addition to the
Polynesian drink canon by
Donn (Don the Beachcomber)
Beach. Here is a mash-up of
the many circulating recipes
for this fully loaded tiki classic.
The constants are copious
amounts of rum and fruit
juices.

1 oz. gold rum
1 oz. 151-proof rum
1 oz. light rum
1 oz. fresh lemon juice
1 oz. fresh lime juice
1 oz. pineapple juice
1 oz. passion fruit syrup
2 tsp. Demerara Syrup (page
   20)
1 dash tiki (such as
   Bittermen's 'Elemakule) or
   Angostura bitters (optional)
Garnish: Fresh mint sprig

*Shake with ice and pour into
chilled Collins glass. Garnish
with mint.*

TEQUILA

TEQUILA IS MADE FROM the blue agave plant, an aloe vera–like plant that takes between eight and ten years to mature. Then it can only be harvested once by stripping away its leaves and cooking what's left: a core that weighs on average forty to seventy pounds (and it takes fifteen pounds of core to produce only one quart of tequila). The cooked cores are fermented with yeast (which converts the sugar to alcohol), then distilled twice—the second time yielding what will become tequila.

Like Scotch and bourbon, tequila takes its name from its place of origin, in this case the town of Tequila in Mexico's state of Jalisco. By Mexican law, it can only be produced in this region under strict guidelines—though that doesn't stop less scrupulous producers from making it outside those boundaries with whatever they want. There are two kinds of tequila: 100 percent blue agave and *mixto*, the former made purely from agave, the latter distilled with a mixture of 60 percent blue agave plus "other sugars." Just look for "100 percent agave" and you're safe. Mezcal, similar to tequila but with a richer, smokier flavor, is made mostly in Oaxaca, from the maguey plant.

Finally, there are four official classifications for tequila, though some have confusing subtitles. At the first rung is *blanco* (also called "silver" or "white"), which is clear, transparent, and bottled immediately after distillation. Next comes *oro* ("gold," or "*joven*"), which is blanco blended with caramel and other additives to impart an aged appearance; then *reposado*, which is blanco actually aged in white oak barrels for up to one year. At the top there's *añejo*, which is blanco aged in white oak barrels for at least one year, though often much longer.

☐ ALAMO SPLASH

1½ oz. blanco tequila
1 oz. fresh orange juice
½ oz. pineapple juice
1 splash lemon-lime soda

Pour first three ingredients into ice-filled Collins glass. Top with lemon-lime soda and stir.

☐ AMANTE PICANTE

2 cucumber slices
2 fresh cilantro sprigs
2 oz. blanco tequila
1 oz. fresh lime juice
1 oz. simple syrup
2 dashes jalapeño hot pepper
    sauce
Garnish: Cucumber slice

Muddle 2 cucumber slices and cilantro in mixing glass. Add remaining ingredients. Shake with ice and double-strain into chilled cocktail glass. Garnish with cucumber.

☐ BRAVO

2 oz. añejo tequila
¼ oz. agave nectar
2 dashes Angostura bitters
1 dash orange bitters
Garnish: Grapefruit twist

Stir with ice and strain into chilled old-fashioned glass. Add grapefruit twist.

☐ BIG RED HOOTER

1 oz. blanco tequila
¾ oz. amaretto
2 oz. pineapple juice
½ oz. grenadine
Garnish: Maraschino
    cherry

Pour tequila and amaretto into ice-filled Collins glass. Fill with pineapple juice and top with grenadine. Add cherry. Serve with straw.

☐ BLOODY MARIA

1 oz. blanco tequila
2 oz. tomato juice
¼ oz. fresh lemon juice
1 dash hot red pepper
  sauce
1 pinch celery salt
Garnish: Lemon wheel

Stir with ice. Strain into ice-filled old-fashioned glass. Add lemon wheel.

⟨ BLUE MARGARITA

For glass: Lime juice, coarse
  salt
1½ oz. blanco tequila
½ oz. blue curaçao
1 oz. fresh lime juice

Rim chilled cocktail glass with lime juice and salt. Shake remaining ingredients with ice and strain into glass.

☐ BRAVE BULL

1½ oz. blanco tequila
1 oz. coffee liqueur
Garnish: Lemon twist

Pour into ice-filled old-fashioned glass and stir. Add lemon twist.

☐ BUM'S RUSH

1½ oz. blanco tequila
¾ oz. triple sec
¾ oz. honey liqueur
1 oz. fresh lime juice
1 oz. fresh apple cider
Garnish: Lime wedge

Shake with ice and strain into ice-filled Collins glass. Garnish with lime.

⟨ CACTUS BERRY

For glass: Lime wedge, coarse
  salt
1¼ oz. blanco tequila
1¼ oz. red wine
½ oz. triple sec
½ oz. simple syrup
¼ oz. fresh lemon juice
¼ oz. fresh lime juice
1 splash lemon-lime soda

Rim chilled cocktail glass with lime and salt. Shake remaining ingredients with ice and pour into glass.

🍸 CAMINO DEL RAY

Created by TED HENWOOD,
New York, NY

1¾ oz. añejo tequila
1 oz. oloroso sherry
½ oz. Drambuie
1 dash rhubarb bitters
Garnish: Lemon twist

Stir with ice and strain into chilled cocktail glass. Add lemon twist.

🍸 CATALINA MARGARITA

1½ oz. blanco tequila
1 oz. peach schnapps
1 oz. blue curaçao
2 oz. simple syrup
2 oz. fresh lemon juice

Shake with ice and strain into chilled cocktail glass.

🍷 CHAPALA

1½ oz. reposado tequila
1½ oz. fresh orange juice
¾ oz. fresh lemon juice
¼ oz. grenadine
Garnish: Orange blossoms
   (optional); orange wedge

Shake and strain into hurricane glass. Fill glass with crushed ice. Garnish with orange blossoms, if using, and orange wedge.

🍸 CHUPA CABRA

2 oz. blanco tequila
¾ oz. fresh grapefruit juice
½ oz. fresh lime juice
½ oz. Campari
½ oz. simple syrup
1 dash Angostura bitters
Garnish: Lime wheel

Shake with ice and strain into chilled cocktail glass. Garnish with lime.

🍸 COMPANY B

1 whole strawberry, hulled
1½ oz. blanco tequila
½ oz. Campari
½ oz. triple sec
½ oz. fresh lemon juice
¼ oz. agave nectar
Garnish: Strawberry slice

Muddle whole strawberry in mixing glass. Add remaining ingredients. Shake with ice and strain through fine wire sieve into chilled cocktail glass. Garnish with strawberry slice.

▯ COUNT CAMILLO'S PALOMA

Think of this as a tequila Negroni, just the way Count Camillo Negroni, the supposed namesake of the Italian cocktail, would have liked it—if he were Mexican instead of Italian.

¾ oz. blanco tequila
¾ oz. sweet vermouth
¾ oz. Campari
2 oz. grapefruit soda
Garnish: Rosemary sprig

Pour ingredients into Collins glass and stir briefly. Fill with ice. Garnish with rosemary.

▯ DIABLO

1½ oz. blanco tequila
¾ oz. crème de cassis
½ oz. fresh lime juice
Ginger ale
Garnish: Lime wheel

Shake first three ingredients with ice. Strain into ice-filled Collins glass. Top with ginger ale. Garnish with lime.

☌ DIRTY DAISY

Created by BLAIR FRODELIUS, Syracuse, NY

1½ oz. reposado tequila
1 oz. white curaçao
½ oz. olive brine
1 tsp. balsamic vinegar
1 tsp. fresh lime juice
Garnish: Lime wheel

Shake well with ice and strain into chilled cocktail glass. Garnish with lime wheel.

☌ EL MOLINO

Created by JIM MEEHAN, New York, NY

1½ oz. mezcal
¾ oz. palo cortado or oloroso sherry
¼ oz. allspice liqueur (pimento dram)
¼ oz. white crème de cacao

Stir with ice and strain into chilled cocktail glass.

☐ EL NIÑO

6 lime wedges
1 whole strawberry
¾ oz. simple syrup
2 oz. blanco tequila
5 drops rose water

Muddle lime, strawberry, and syrup in mixing glass. Add tequila and rose water and ice. Shake briefly and strain into ice-filled old-fashioned glass.

☐ EL OSO (THE BEAR)

Created by BRENDAN DORR, Washington, DC

1¾ oz. añejo tequila
¾ oz. honey liqueur
½ oz. maraschino liqueur
2 dashes The Bitter Truth's Jerry Thomas' Own Decanter Bitters
Garnish: Dehydrated Orange Wheel (recipe follows)

Stir with ice. Drop dehydrated orange wheel into old-fashioned glass and add ice. Strain cocktail into glass.

DEHYDRATED ORANGE WHEEL

Slice 1 large navel orange into $\frac{1}{16}$-inch-thick rounds. Arrange on baking sheet lined with silicone baking mat. Sift 3 tbsp. confectioners' sugar over oranges. Bake in preheated 225°F oven until dried, about 2¼ hours. Let cool completely. Store in airtight container at room temperature for up to 1 month. Makes about 1½ dozen.

♈ FLOWER POWER

2 oz. blanco tequila
1 oz. fresh grapefruit juice
½ oz. agave nectar
1 egg white
3 drops orange blossom
    water
2 dashes Peychaud's bitters

*Shake without ice. Then
shake with ice and strain into
chilled cocktail glass.*

♈ HIGH PLAINS DRIFTER NO. 1

1 splash Campari
2 oz. blanco tequila
¾ oz. fresh lime juice
¾ oz. Honey Syrup (page 21)
1 dash Angostura bitters

*Swirl Campari in chilled
cocktail glass to coat inside;
discard excess Campari.
Shake remaining ingredients
with ice and strain into
glass.*

▢ HOT PANTS

For glass: Lime wedge, coarse
    salt
1½ oz. blanco tequila
½ oz. peppermint schnapps
½ oz. fresh grapefruit juice
2 tsp. simple syrup

*Rim old-fashioned glass
with lime and salt. Fill
with ice. Shake remaining
ingredients with ice. Strain
into glass.*

♈ THE INTERESTING COCKTAIL

2 oz. blanco tequila
½ oz. Aperol
½ oz. dark crème de cacao
¾ oz. fresh lemon juice
Garnish: Grapefruit twist

*Shake with ice and strain
into chilled cocktail glass.
Add grapefruit twist.*

⅂ JINX COCKTAIL

Created by JAKE SHER,
White Plains, NY

1 oz. blanco tequila
¾ oz. blood orange liqueur
¾ oz. Becherovka (Czech
    digestif)
1 oz. fresh grapefruit juice
Garnish: Grapefruit twist,
    flamed (see page 46)

*Shake with ice and strain
into chilled cocktail glass.
Flame grapefruit twist
and add.*

⅂ LA BOMBA

For glass: Lime wedge,
    superfine sugar
1¼ oz. gold tequila
¾ oz. triple sec
1½ oz. pineapple juice
1½ oz. fresh orange juice
2 dashes grenadine
Garnish: Lime wheel

*Rim chilled cocktail glass
with lime wedge and sugar.
Combine next four ingre-
dients with ice and shake
briefly. Pour with ice into
glass. Add grenadine
and garnish with lime
wheel.*

⅂ LA ULTIMA PALABRA

¾ oz. blanco tequila
¾ oz. fresh grapefruit juice
¾ oz. fresh lime juice
¾ oz. yellow Chartreuse
¾ oz. maraschino liqueur
Garnish: Grapefruit twist

*Shake with ice and strain
into chilled cocktail glass.
Add grapefruit twist.*

⅂ MARGARITA

The story behind the Margarita
is on page 35. The rimming of
the glass is optional.

For glass: Lime wedge, coarse
    salt
1½ oz. blanco tequila
¾ oz. Cointreau triple sec
¾ oz. fresh lime juice

*Rim chilled cocktail glass
with lime and salt. Shake
remaining ingredients and ice
and strain into glass.*

*Note: To serve on-the-rocks,
strain into ice-filled, rimmed
old-fashioned glass.*

MEXICAN FIRING SQUAD

2 oz. blanco tequila
1 oz. simple syrup
¾ oz. fresh lime juice
1 tsp. pomegranate molasses (available at Middle Eastern grocers)
2 dashes Angostura bitters
Garnish: Lime wheel

Shake and strain into ice-filled highball glass. Garnish with lime.

MEXICAN MADRAS

1½ oz. blanco tequila
2 oz. cranberry juice
1 oz. fresh orange juice
¼ oz. fresh lime juice
Garnish: Orange wheel

Shake with ice and strain into old-fashioned glass. Garnish with orange.

MEXICAN MONK

Created by ERIC ALPERIN, Los Angeles, CA

2 oz. reposado tequila
½ oz. dry sherry
¼ oz. coffee liqueur
¼ oz. Bénédictine
Garnish: Lemon twist

Stir well with ice and strain into chilled cocktail glass. Add lemon twist.

MEXICOLA

2 oz. blanco tequila
½ oz. fresh lime juice
Cola

Pour tequila and lime juice into ice-filled Collins glass. Fill with cola and stir.

NO. 8

2 oz. reposado tequila
¾ oz. palo cortado or oloroso sherry
½ oz. honey liqueur
2 dashes orange bitters
Garnish: Lemon twist

Stir with ice and strain into chilled cocktail glass. Garnish with lemon twist.

☐ THE NOMAD SOUTH

**Created by TED HENWOOD,
New York, NY**

2 oz. blanco tequila
1 oz. fresh orange juice
½ oz. fresh blood orange juice
½ oz. agave nectar
½ oz. fresh lime juice
1 dash whiskey barrel bitters

*Shake well with ice and
strain into ice-filled old-
fashioned glass.*

☐ THE OAXACA OLD-FASHIONED

A modern-day classic, this
drink was invented by
New York bartender Phil Ward.

1½ oz. reposado tequila
½ oz. mezcal
¼ oz. agave nectar
2 dashes Angostura bitters
Garnish: Orange twist, flamed

*Stir with ice and strain
into chilled old-fashioned
glass. Flame orange twist
and add.*

☐ PALOMA

2 oz. blanco tequila
Grapefruit-flavored soda
Garnish: Lime wedge

*Pour tequila into ice-filled
Collins glass. Fill glass with
soda and stir briefly. Garnish
with lime wedge.*

☐ PALOMA (NATURAL)

2 oz. blanco tequila
2 oz. fresh white or ruby red
   grapefruit juice
Soda water
Garnish: Lime wedge

*Pour tequila and grapefruit
juice into ice-filled Collins
glass. Fill with soda water
and stir briefly. Garnish with
lime wedge.*

⅄ PIÑA AGAVE

2 cucumber slices
1½ oz. blanco tequila
1 oz. pineapple juice
¾ oz. fresh lemon juice
½ oz. agave nectar
Lemon-lime soda
Garnish: Cucumber slice

Muddle 2 cucumber slices in mixing glass. Add the next four ingredients. Shake with ice and strain into chilled cocktail glass. Top with soda and garnish with cucumber slice.

⅄ THE PONCHO

2 oz. reposado tequila
½ oz. dry vermouth
½ oz. maraschino liqueur
2 dashes Peychaud's bitters
Garnish: Maraschino cherry

Stir with ice and strain into chilled cocktail glass. Add cherry.

⅄ PURPLE PANCHO

For glass: Lime wedge,
    superfine sugar
1 oz. blanco tequila
½ oz. blue curaçao
½ oz. sloe gin
2 oz. fresh lime juice
1 oz. fresh lemon juice
1 oz. simple syrup
Garnish: Lime wheel

Rim chilled cocktail or margarita glass with lime wedge and sugar. Shake remaining ingredients with ice and pour with ice into glass. Garnish with lime wheel.

⅄ QUETZALCOATL

Created by JAKE SHER,
White Plains, NY

1 oz. blanco tequila
¾ oz. mezcal
½ oz. crème de pêche
½ oz. guava puree
½ oz. fresh grapefruit juice
Garnish: Grapefruit twist

Shake with ice and strain into cocktail glass. Add grapefruit twist.

☐ SANTANA SLING

1½ oz. reposado tequila
½ oz. Cherry Heering
¼ oz. Batavia arrack or light rum
½ oz. fresh lime juice
3 oz. ginger beer

Pour first four ingredients into ice-filled Collins glass and stir. Add ginger beer and stir again.

☐ SATIN SHEETS

1½ oz. blanco tequila
½ oz. falernum
½ oz. simple syrup
¾ oz. fresh lime juice
Garnish: Lime wheel

Shake with ice and strain into chilled cocktail glass. Garnish with lime.

☐ SEA OF CORTEZ

1½ oz. blanco tequila
1 oz. fresh lime juice
¾ oz. crème de cassis
¼ oz. orange curaçao

Shake with ice and strain into chilled cocktail glass.

☐ THE SFOZANDO

Created by ERYN REECE, New York, NY

1 oz. mezcal
¾ oz. rye whiskey
½ oz. dry vermouth
½ oz. Bénédictine
1 dash chocolate bitters
Garnish: Orange twist

Stir with ice and strain into cocktail glass. Add orange twist.

☐ SIDEWINDER

Created by BRENT BUTLER, San Francisco, CA

1½ oz. reposado tequila
½ oz. Campari
½ oz. vanilla syrup, preferably B.A. Reynold's
½ oz. fresh lime juice
¼ oz. mezcal
2 oz. ginger beer
1 pinch sea salt
Garnish: Fresh mint sprig

Fill Collins glass ¾ full with crushed ice. Add all ingredients. Swizzle with barspoon until glass is frosted. Fill to brim with additional ice. Garnish with mint.

🍸 SILK STOCKINGS

1½ oz. blanco tequila
1 oz. white crème de cacao
1½ oz. heavy cream
1 dash grenadine
Garnish: Ground cinnamon

Shake ingredients with ice and strain into chilled cocktail glass. Top with cinnamon.

🍸 SMOKED MARGARITA

½ tsp. smoky Scotch whisky, such as Islay or Skye
1 oz. reposado tequila
1 oz. triple sec
½ oz. fresh lemon juice
½ oz. fresh lime juice
Garnish: Lime wedge

Pour Scotch into old-fashioned glass and swirl to coat. Add ice. Shake remaining ingredients with ice and strain into glass. Add lime wedge.

🍸 SOUTH OF THE BORDER

1 oz. blanco tequila
¾ oz. coffee-flavored brandy
½ oz. fresh lime juice
Garnish: Lime wheel

Shake with ice and strain into chilled sour glass. Garnish with lime.

🍸 SPICE OF LIFE

Created by ADAM FRAGER, St. Louis, MO

3 cucumber slices
12 fresh mint leaves
¾ oz. simple syrup
2 oz. Jalapeño-Infused Tequila (recipe follows)
¾ oz. fresh lime juice
Garnish: Cucumber slice, fresh mint sprig

Muddle 3 cucumber slices, mint leaves, and syrup in mixing glass. Add tequila and lime juice with ice and shake. Double-strain into ice-filled old-fashioned glass. Garnish with cucumber slice and mint sprig.

JALAPEÑO-INFUSED TEQUILA

Combine 1 c. reposado tequila with ½ seeded and chopped jalapeño in bowl. Let stand at room temperature for 30 minutes. Strain to remove jalapeño, then funnel into bottle. Store in refrigerator for up to 2 weeks.

☐ STRAWBERRY MARGARITA

For glass: Lime wedge,
   superfine sugar or coarse
   salt (optional)
3 fresh strawberries, cut in
   half
¾ oz. strawberry schnapps
1½ oz. blanco tequila
¾ oz. triple sec
¾ oz. fresh lime juice
Garnish: Whole strawberry

*If desired, rim chilled cocktail
glass with lime and sugar or
salt. Muddle strawberries
with schnapps in mixing
glass. Add remaining ingredients and shake with ice.
Strain through fine wire sieve
into glass. Add strawberry.*

☐ SUNDAY CONFESSION

1 oz. blanco tequila
1 oz. limoncello
½ oz. fresh lemon juice
Ginger beer
Garnish: Lemon wedge

*Pour the first three ingredi-
ents into Collins glass and
stir briefly. Add ice and
top with ginger beer. Add
lemon.*

☐ TEQUILA CANYON

1½ oz. blanco tequila
¼ oz. triple sec
1 oz. cranberry juice
1 oz. pineapple juice
1 oz. fresh orange juice
Garnish: Lime wheel

*Pour into Collins glass and
stir. Add ice. Garnish with
lime. Serve with straw.*

☐ TEQUILA MATADOR

1½ oz. blanco tequila
2 oz. pineapple juice
½ oz. fresh lime juice

*Shake with ice and strain
into chilled champagne
flute.*

♈ TEQUILA MOCKINGBIRD

Created by JONATHAN POGASH, New York, NY

For glass: Lime wedge, coarse salt
¼ tsp. minced ginger
1¾ oz. blanco tequila
1½ tsp. agave nectar
1 oz. fresh lime juice
Garnish: Lime wheel

Rim one half of a chilled cocktail glass with lime and salt. Muddle ginger in mixing glass. Add remaining ingredients with ice and shake. Strain into glass. Garnish with lime wheel.

♈ TEQUILA PINK

1½ oz. blanco tequila
1 oz. dry vermouth
¼ oz. grenadine

Shake with ice and strain into chilled cocktail glass.

▯ TEQUILA SMASH

4 blueberries
4 Bing cherries
2 oz. blanco tequila
½ oz. maraschino liqueur
½ oz. fresh lime juice
Garnish: Lime wheel skewered with blueberry and Bing cherry

Muddle blueberries and cherries in mixing glass. Add remaining ingredients and shake. Double-strain into ice-filled old-fashioned glass. Garnish with skewered fruit.

▯ TEQUILA STRAIGHT

1 pinch coarse salt
1½ oz. blanco tequila
1 lime wedge

Put salt between thumb and index finger on back of one hand. Hold shot glass of tequila in same hand and lime wedge in other hand. Taste the salt, drink the tequila, and then suck the lime.

TEQUILA SUNRISE

2 oz. blanco tequila
4 oz. fresh orange juice
¾ oz. grenadine

*Pour tequila and orange juice
into ice-filled highball glass.
Stir and add ice. Slowly pour
in grenadine and allow to
settle at glass bottom. Before
drinking, stir to create the
"sunrise."*

TEQUONIC

2 oz. blanco tequila
¼ oz. fresh lemon or lime juice
Tonic water
Garnish: Lemon or lime wedge

*Pour tequila into ice-filled
old-fashioned glass. Add
juice, fill with tonic water,
and stir. Garnish with citrus
wedge.*

TÍA JUANATHAN

1½ oz. blanco tequila
½ oz. fresh lime juice
½ oz. Aperol
½ oz. yellow Chartreuse
Soda water
Garnish: Orange half-wheel

*Shake first four ingredients
with ice and strain into ice-
filled highball glass. Top with
soda water. Garnish with
orange.*

TIJUANA TAXI

2 oz. gold tequila
1 oz. blue curaçao
1 oz. tropical fruit schnapps
Lemon-lime soda
Garnish: Orange wheel,
    maraschino cherry

*Pour first three ingredients
into ice-filled large highball
glass. Fill with lemon-lime
soda. Garnish with orange
and cherry.*

TOREADOR

1½ oz. blanco tequila
½ oz. dark crème de cacao
½ oz. half-and-half
Garnish: Whipped cream, cocoa

Shake with ice. Strain into chilled cocktail glass. Top with whipped cream, sprinkle with cocoa.

VAGABUNDO

You'll need fresh celery juice to make this cocktail.

2 oz. reposado blanco tequila
1½ oz. pineapple juice
1½ oz. fresh celery juice
½ oz. fresh lime juice
Garnish: Lime wheel

Shake ingredients with ice. Strain into ice-filled hurricane glass. Garnish with lime wheel.

VIVA VILLA

For glass: Lime wedge, coarse salt
1½ oz. blanco tequila
1 oz. fresh lime juice
½ oz. simple syrup

Rim old-fashioned glass with lime and salt. Fill with ice. Shake remaining ingredients with ice and strain into glass.

WAITING ON SUMMER

Created by DANIEL BAUTISTA, Chicago, IL

3 cucumber slices
3 fresh sage leaves
½ oz. fresh lime juice
1½ oz. blanco tequila
¾ oz. simple syrup
3 oz. ginger ale
Garnish: Strawberry slice

Muddle cucumber, sage, and lime juice in mixing glass. Add tequila and syrup with ice and shake. Double-strain into ice-filled Collins glass. Top with ginger ale. Garnish with strawberry.

VODKA

ACCORDING TO U.S. LAW, vodkas produced in the country must be pure spirits with no additives except water; nonaged; and basically colorless, tasteless, and odorless. This description may sound lackluster, but it explains why vodka is one of today's most popular spirits: Because of its purity, vodka graciously assumes the characteristics of whatever it's mixed with.

Vodka is generally made from grain (corn, rye, or wheat) or potatoes, with grain accounting for nearly all the vodka available on the international market. It is a rectified spirit, meaning it's distilled at least three times, and then filtered—the most important step—typically through charcoal, although some distillers claim to employ diamond dust and even quartz crystals.

Stylistic differences between one vodka and another are subtle, even at the very high end, given that discernible flavor isn't a factor. Vodka is often described by its texture on the tongue or mouthfeel, ranging from clean and crisp to viscous and silky. Subtle sensations in the finish—after it's swallowed—can range from slightly sweet to medicinal. The finish could also reveal if a vodka is hot, rough, and raw (usually the mark of an inexpensive bulk vodka, or perhaps one with higher-than-normal 80 proof) or, conversely, if it is smooth, round, and rich (one made by a master distiller).

That said, the very best vodkas, the so-called super-premium brands (priced higher than $30 per bottle), are perfect when unadorned, say in a Martini, or for a chilled straight shot to accompany caviar. Flavored vodkas are used in many drinks, but they work best in tandem with actual fruit and other ingredients, as some of these vodkas can taste artificial.

🍸 ADMIRAL PERRY

Created by BLAIR FRODELIUS, Syracuse, NY

2 oz. pear-flavored vodka
1 oz. cinnamon schnapps
1 oz. dry vermouth
1 dash white crème de cacao
Garnish: Thin pear slice

Stir with ice and shake into chilled cocktail glass. Garnish with pear slice.

🍸 AQUEDUCT

1½ oz. vodka
¾ oz. fresh lime juice
½ oz. white curaçao or triple sec
½ oz. apricot-flavored brandy
Garnish: Orange twist

Shake with ice and strain into chilled cocktail glass. Add orange twist.

🥛 BASIL 8

3 fresh basil leaves
5 white grapes
1½ oz. vodka
¾ oz. fresh lime juice
1 oz. simple syrup
1 dash Angostura bitters
Ginger ale
Garnish: Fresh basil sprig, white grape

Muddle basil and 5 grapes in Collins glass. Add next four ingredients and stir. Add ice and top with ginger ale. Garnish with basil sprig and 1 white grape.

☐ BEER BUSTER

1½ oz. 100-proof vodka
Chilled beer or ale
2 dashes hot red pepper sauce

Pour vodka into highball glass and fill with beer or ale. Add hot sauce and stir lightly.

☐ BELLA FRAGOLIA

Created by ERICK CASTRO,
San Francisco, CA

1 strawberry, chopped
4 fresh basil leaves
2 oz. vodka
1 oz. fresh lemon juice
1 oz. simple syrup
Soda water
Garnish: Strawberry slice,
    fresh basil leaf

Muddle chopped strawberry and 4 basil leaves in mixing glass. Add vodka, lemon juice, and syrup with ice and shake well. Double-strain into ice-filled old-fashioned glass and top with soda water. Garnish with strawberry and basil.

☐ BIANCA

For glass: Lime wedge,
    superfine sugar
1½ oz. citrus-flavored vodka
2 oz. pomegranate juice
¼ oz. fresh lime juice
1 splash simple syrup
1 splash fresh lemon juice
Garnish: Lemon twist, fresh
    pomegranate seeds

Rim chilled cocktail glass with lime and sugar. Shake remaining ingredients with ice and strain into glass. Add lemon twist and pomegranate seeds.

☐ THE BIG CRUSH

1 oz. raspberry-flavored
    vodka
½ oz. triple sec
½ oz. raspberry-flavored
    liqueur
½ oz. fresh lime juice
Chilled Champagne
Garnish: Fresh blackberries
    and raspberries

Shake first four ingredients with ice. Strain into chilled cocktail glass and top with Champagne. Garnish with berries.

☐ BLACK RUSSIAN

1½ oz. vodka
¾ oz. coffee liqueur

*Pour into ice-filled
old-fashioned glass and
stir.*

☐ THE BLOOD ORANGE

2 oz. orange-flavored vodka
1 oz. Campari
Garnish: Blood or navel orange
    half-wheel

*Stir with ice and strain into
chilled cocktail glass. Garnish
with orange.*

☐ BLOODY BULL

1 oz. vodka
2 oz. tomato juice
2 oz. cold beef bouillon
Garnish: Lemon wedge, lime
    wheel

*Pour into ice-filled highball
glass. Stir. Squeeze and add
lemon. Garnish with lime
wheel.*

☐ BLOODY MARY

Entertainer Geroge Jessel
claimed to be the inventor of
this beloved morning cocktail.

1½ oz. vodka
3 oz. tomato juice
¼ oz. fresh lime juice
4 dashes Worcestershire sauce
2–3 drops hot red pepper sauce
Freshly ground black pepper
    to taste
Garnish: Lime wedge, celery
    stalk

*Roll with ice between both
halves of Boston shaker.
Strain into ice-filled old-
fashioned glass. Garnish with
lime and celery.*

☐ BLUE LAGOON

1 oz. vodka
1 oz. blue curaçao
½ oz. fresh lemon juice
½ oz. simple syrup
Garnish: Maraschino cherry

*Shake with ice and strain
into ice-filled highball glass.
Garnish with cherry.*

∇ BORDEAUX COCKTAIL

1½ oz. citrus-flavored vodka
½ oz. Lillet Blanc
Garnish: Lemon twist

Stir with ice and strain into chilled cocktail glass. Add lemon twist.

⬚ BULLFROG

1½ oz. vodka
5 oz. lemonade
Garnish: Lime wheel

Pour into ice-filled Collins glass and stir. Garnish with lime.

⬚ BULL SHOT

1½ oz. vodka
3 oz. cold beef bouillon
1 dash Worcestershire sauce
1 pinch salt
1 pinch freshly ground black pepper

Shake with ice and strain into chilled old-fashioned glass.

⬚ CAESAR

For glass: Lemon wedge, celery salt
1½ oz. vodka
4 oz. tomato-clam juice
½ tsp. prepared horseradish
1 dash Worcestershire sauce
1 pinch salt
1 pinch freshly ground black pepper
Garnish: Celery stalk, lemon wedge

Rim highball glass with lemon and celery salt, and then fill with ice. Shake ingredients with ice and strain into glass. Garnish with celery and lemon.

⬚ CAPE CODDER

1½ oz. vodka
5 oz. cranberry juice
Garnish: Lime wedge

Pour into ice-filled highball glass. Stir well. Garnish with lime.

▯ CASCO BAY LEMONADE

1½ oz. citrus-flavored
vodka
2 oz. simple syrup
2 oz. fresh lemon juice
1 splash cranberry juice
Lemon-lime soda
Garnish: Lemon wheel

*Shake first four ingredients
with ice. Pour into ice-filled
Collins glass. Fill glass with
lemon-lime soda. Float lemon
wheel on top.*

▯ THE CINQUECENTO

Created by FREDO CERASO,
Los Angeles, CA

1½ oz. bison grass vodka
(Zubrowka)
½ oz. Bénédictine
½ oz. Campari
¾ oz. fresh grapefruit juice
1 dash Angostura bitters
Garnish: Grapefruit twist

*Shake with ice. Strain through
wire sieve into chilled cocktail
glass. Add grapefruit twist.*

▯ CITRONELLA COOLER

1 oz. citrus-flavored vodka
1 dash fresh lime juice
2 oz. lemonade
1 oz. cranberry juice
Garnish: Lime wedge

*Stir in Collins glass. Add ice
and stir again. Squeeze and
add lime.*

▯ COSMOPOLITAN

The invention of the Cosmo,
which has passed the lips of
many a sophisticated lady
(and quite a few men, too), is
often credited to Cheryl Cook,
a bartender in South Beach,
FL. But it really took off when
master mixologist Dale DeGroff
served one to Madonna at
New York's late and lamented
Rainbow Room.

1½ oz. vodka
½ oz. fresh lime juice
½ oz. triple sec
½ oz. cranberry juice
Garnish: Lime wheel

*Shake well with ice and
strain into chilled cocktail
glass. Garnish with lime.*

CUBELTINI

3 cucumber slices
5–7 fresh mint leaves
1½ oz. simple syrup
2 oz. vodka
1 oz. fresh lime juice
Garnish: Fresh mint sprig

Muddle the cucumber, mint leaves, and syrup. Add vodka and lime juice. Shake and strain into chilled cocktail glass. Garnish with mint sprig.

DESERT SUNRISE

1¼ oz. vodka
1½ oz. fresh orange juice
1½ oz. pineapple juice
1 dash grenadine

Pour first three ingredients over crushed ice in Collins glass. Do not stir. Top with grenadine.

DREAMY DORINI SMOKING MARTINI

Created by AUDREY SAUNDERS, New York, NY

2 oz. vodka
½ oz. smoky Scotch, such as Laphroaig
4 drops pastis
Garnish: Lemon twist

Stir with ice and strain into a chilled cocktail glass. Add lemon twist.

FLATIRON MARTINI

Created by JULIE REINER, owner of Flatiron Lounge, New York, NY

1 splash triple sec
1½ oz. orange-flavored vodka
1½ oz. Lillet Blanc
Garnish: Orange wheel

Swirl triple sec in chilled cocktail glass to coat inside; discard excess triple sec. Stir vodka and Lillet with ice and strain into glass. Garnish with orange.

▢ FRISKY WITCH

1 oz. vodka
1 oz. Sambuca
Garnish: Black licorice stick

*Stir in old-fashioned glass.
Add ice and stir again.
Garnish with licorice.*

▢ GABLES COLLINS

1½ oz. vodka
1 oz. crème de noyaux
½ oz. fresh lemon juice
½ oz. pineapple juice
Soda water
Garnish: Lemon wheel,
    pineapple chunk

*Shake first four ingredients
with ice and strain into ice-
filled Collins glass. Fill with
soda water. Garnish with
lemon and pineapple.*

▢ GEORGIA MULE

1 peach slice, skinned
1½ oz. vodka
½ oz. fresh lemon juice
2 dashes peach bitters
Ginger beer
Garnish: Peach slice

*Muddle 1 peach slice in Collins
glass. Add vodka, lemon juice,
and bitters, then stir. Fill with
ice and ginger beer; stir again.
Garnish with peach slice.*

▢ GEORGIA PEACH

1½ oz. vodka
½ oz. peach schnapps
1 dash grenadine
Lemonade

*Stir first three ingredients in
Collins glass. Add ice and stir
again. Fill with lemonade.*

▢ GLASS TOWER

1 oz. vodka
1 oz. peach schnapps
1 oz. white rum
1 oz. triple sec
½ oz. sambuca
Lemon-lime soda
Garnish: Orange wheel,
    maraschino cherry

*Pour first five ingredients into
Collins glass. Add ice, then
fill with lemon-lime soda and
stir. Garnish with orange
and cherry.*

▽ GODCHILD

1 oz. vodka
1 oz. amaretto
1 oz. heavy cream

*Shake well with ice and
strain into chilled cocktail
glass.*

☐ GODMOTHER

1½ oz. vodka
¾ oz. amaretto

Combine in ice-filled old-fashioned glass.

☐ GRAPE NEHI

1 oz. vodka
1 oz. raspberry-flavored liqueur
1 oz. fresh lemon juice

Shake with ice and strain into chilled cocktail glass.

☐ THE GROUPIE

Created by ERIC TECOSKY,
Los Angeles, CA

3 lemon wedges
½ tsp. superfine sugar
2 oz. citrus-flavored vodka
Ginger beer

Muddle lemons and sugar in mixing glass. Add vodka and ice and shake. Strain into ice-filled old-fashioned glass and top with ginger beer.

☐ HANDBALL COOLER

1½ oz. vodka
Soda water
½ oz. fresh orange juice
Garnish: Lime wedge

Pour vodka into ice-filled highball glass. Fill almost to top with soda water. Top with orange juice and stir. Add lime.

☐ HARVEY WALLBANGER

In the 1970s, this golden-hued cocktail fueled virtually every Sunday brunch in America. The distinctive tall bottle of Galliano graced many a knotty pine–paneled home bar.

1 oz. vodka
4 oz. fresh orange juice
½ oz. Galliano

Stir vodka and orange juice in Collins glass. Add ice and stir again. Float Galliano (see page 12) on top.

℞ IBIZA

1 oz. orange-flavored vodka
½ oz. Campari
1 oz. fresh grapefruit juice
1 tsp. pomegranate molasses
1 dash peach schnapps
1 dash apple schnapps
Garnish: Grapefruit twist

*Shake with ice and strain
into chilled cocktail glass.
Add grapefruit twist.*

℞ ITALIAN SCREWDRIVER

For glass: Lime wedge,
  superfine sugar
1½ oz. citrus-flavored
  vodka
3 oz. fresh orange juice
2 oz. fresh grapefruit juice
1 splash ginger ale
Garnish: Lime wheel

*Rim hurricane glass with
lime wedge and sugar; fill
with ice. Shake remaining
ingredients with ice. Strain
into glass. Garnish with
lime.*

℞ JACKIE-O

You'll find pink sanding sugar at
cake decorating and specialty
food stores (page 303).

For glass: Lime wedge, pink
  sanding sugar
½ oz. citrus-flavored vodka
½ oz. orange-flavored vodka
½ oz. crème de cassis
1 oz. apricot nectar
½ oz. fresh lemon juice
½ oz. cranberry juice
Chilled Champagne
Garnish: Orange half-wheel,
  lime wheel

*Rim chilled large cocktail
glass with lime wedge and
pink sugar. Shake first six
ingredients with ice and
strain into glass. Top with
Champagne. Garnish with
orange and lime.*

▯ JUNGLE JUICE

1 oz. vodka
1 oz. light rum
½ oz. triple sec
1 oz. cranberry juice
1 oz. fresh orange juice
1 oz. pineapple juice
1 splash simple syrup
1 splash fresh lemon
    juice
Garnish: Orange wheel,
    maraschino cherry

*Shake with ice and pour
with ice into ice-filled Collins
glass. Garnish with orange
and cherry.*

▯ KATANA

3 cucumber slices
1½ oz. vodka
½ oz. sake
¾ oz. fresh lime juice
¾ oz. simple syrup
Garnish: 1 cucumber slice

*Muddle 3 cucumber slices
in mixing glass. Add
remaining ingredients.
Shake with ice. Double-
strain into chilled cocktail
glass. Garnish with
cucumber slice.*

▯ L.A. SUNRISE

1 oz. vodka
½ oz. crème de banana
2 oz. fresh orange juice
2 oz. pineapple juice
¼ oz. dark rum
Garnish: Lime wheel,
    maraschino cherry

*Shake first four ingredients
with ice. Strain into ice-filled
hurricane or parfait glass.
Float rum (see page 12) on
top. Garnish with lime and
cherry.*

▯ LEAVES OF GRASS

Created by NATASHA DAVID,
New York, NY

1½ oz. aquavit
½ oz. Old Tom gin
¼ oz. Demerara Syrup
    (page 20)
2 dashes orange bitters
1 dash absinthe
Garnish: Celery stick

*Stir with ice and strain into
ice-filled old-fashioned glass.
Add celery stick.*

⧖ LEMON DROP

Thanks to the arrival of lemon-flavored vodka on the scene, the Lemon Drop has become a modern classic.

For glass: Lemon wedge, superfine sugar
1½ oz. lemon-flavored vodka
¾ oz. fresh lemon juice
¼ oz. simple syrup
Garnish: Lemon wedge

Rim chilled cocktail glass with lemon and sugar. Shake ingredients with ice. Strain into glass. Squeeze lemon wedge and add.

⧖ LE PARADINI

1½ oz. vodka
½ oz. raspberry-flavored liqueur
½ oz. Grand Marnier
1 oz. chilled Champagne

Shake first three ingredients with ice and strain into chilled cocktail glass. Top with Champagne.

⧖ LIGHTS ON THE PLAZA

Created by JONATHAN POGASH, New York, NY

2 (½-inch-thick) cucumber slices, chopped
½ oz. fresh lemon juice
½ oz. simple syrup
1½ oz. açai berry–flavored vodka
½ oz. black raspberry liqueur
1 oz. sparkling wine
Garnish: 1 raspberry sandwiched between 2 thin cucumber slices, skewered

Muddle cucumbers, lemon juice, and syrup in mixing glass. Add vodka, raspberry liqueur, and ice and shake. Double-strain into chilled cocktail glass. Top with sparkling wine. Garnish with raspberry-cucumber skewer.

⧖ LIMONCELLO MANZANILLA MARMALADE SOUR

1½ oz. citrus-flavored vodka
¾ oz. limoncello
¾ oz. manzanilla sherry
¾ oz. fresh lemon juice
1 tsp. grapefruit marmalade
Garnish: Orange twist

Shake with ice and double-strain into chilled cocktail glass. Add orange twist.

◻ LONG ISLAND ICED TEA

If this drink makes you think of hot summer days in the Hamptons, you should know that it may have been invented in the 1920s in a community called Long Island near Kingsport, TN.

¾ oz. vodka
¾ oz. blanco tequila
¾ oz. gin
¾ oz. light rum
¾ oz. triple sec
½ oz. simple syrup
½ oz. fresh lemon juice
Cola, as needed
Garnish: Lemon wedge

Shake ingredients, except cola, with ice and pour with ice into highball glass. Add cola for color. Add lemon.

◻ THE LOOP

2 oz. black cherry–flavored vodka
½ oz. white crème de cacao
½ oz. Chile Syrup (page 20)
Garnish: Grated bittersweet chocolate

Shake ingredients with ice. Pour into chilled old-fashioned glass. Garnish with chocolate grated on top.

☖ LYCHEE LUCY

1½ oz. vodka
½ oz. lychee liqueur
½ oz. fresh orange juice
½ oz. pineapple juice
2 dashes Angostura bitters
Garnish: Canned pitted lychee nut stuffed with a small pineapple leaf

Shake with ice and strain into chilled cocktail glass. Add lychee-pineapple garnish.

◻ MADRAS

1½ oz. vodka
4 oz. cranberry juice
1 oz. fresh orange juice
Garnish: Lime wedge

Build in order given into ice-filled highball glass. Squeeze lime and add.

☖ MARTINI (VODKA)

If you insist on making your Martini with vodka, see the gin versions on page 89 and substitute the former for the latter.

☖ MISS JONES

1½ oz. vanilla-flavored
vodka
1 oz. fresh lemon juice
½ oz. butterscotch
schnapps
½ oz. limoncello
Garnish: Star anise pod

*Shake with ice and strain
into chilled cocktail glass.
Garnish with star anise.*

☖ MR. 404

1½ oz. vodka
¾ oz. elderflower liqueur
¾ oz. fresh lemon juice
½ oz. simple syrup
½ oz. Aperol
Garnish: Orange twist

*Shake with ice and strain
into chilled cocktail glass.
Add orange twist.*

☖ MOCHA EXPRESS

1½ oz. vodka
¾ oz. Irish cream liqueur
¾ oz. coffee liqueur
¾ oz. cold brewed espresso
coffee

*Shake with ice and strain
into chilled cocktail glass.*

☖ MOSCOW MULE

Many historians trace the
popularity of vodka in America
to this drink, invented in
Los Angeles in the early 1940s.
You can purchase authentic
Moscow Mule mugs at
www.amazon.com.

1½ oz. vodka
½ oz. fresh lime juice
Ginger beer
Garnish: Lime wedge

*Pour vodka and lime juice
into copper Moscow Mule
mug or standard beer mug.
Add ice cubes and fill with
ginger beer. Squeeze lime
wedge and add to glass.*

☖ PEACH ICED TEA

1½ oz. peach-flavored vodka
½ oz. orange curaçao
¾ oz. fresh lemon juice
½ oz. Honey Syrup (page 21)
2 oz. iced tea
Garnish: Peach slice, lemon
wheel

*Shake with ice and strain
into ice-filled Collins glass.
Garnish with peach and
lemon.*

🍸 PICKLED MARTINI

2 oz. vodka
¼ oz. dry vermouth
¾ oz. sweet pickle brine
Garnish: Sweet pickle slice

Stir with ice and strain into chilled cocktail glass. Garnish with pickle.

🍸 PICKLED PINK

Created by CHRIS PATINO, New York, NY

2 oz. vodka
1 oz. aquavit
½ oz. dill pickle brine
2 dashes Angostura bitters
Garnish: Dill sprig

Shake with ice and strain into cocktail glass. Garnish with dill.

🥃 PINK LEMONADE

1½ oz. citrus-flavored vodka
¼ oz. triple sec
¼ oz. fresh lime juice
¼ oz. fresh lemon juice
¼ oz. simple syrup
2 oz. cranberry juice
Garnish: Lemon wheel

Shake with ice and strain into ice-filled Collins glass. Garnish with lemon.

🍸 POLYNESIAN COCKTAIL

For glass: Lime wedge, superfine sugar
1½ oz. vodka
¾ oz. cherry-flavored brandy
¾ oz. fresh lime juice

Rim chilled cocktail glass with lime and sugar. Shake ingredients with ice and strain into glass.

🥃 PRETTY IN PINK

2 oz. vodka
½ oz. cranberry juice
¾ oz. crème de noyaux
¾ oz. fresh lemon juice
Soda water

Shake first four ingredients and strain into ice-filled Collins glass. Top with soda water.

🍸 PURPLE MASK

1 oz. vodka
1 oz. Concord grape juice
½ oz. white crème de cacao

Shake with ice and strain into chilled cocktail glass.

☐ PURPLE PASSION

1½ oz. vodka
2 oz. fresh grapefruit juice
2 oz. Concord grape juice
½ oz. simple syrup

Shake with ice. Pour with ice into Collins glass.

☐ PURPLE PASSION ICED TEA

½ oz. vodka
½ oz. light rum
½ oz. gin
½ oz. black raspberry liqueur
½ oz. simple syrup
¾ oz. fresh lemon juice
3 oz. lemon-lime soda
Garnish: Lemon twist

Pour ingredients into ice-filled highball glass in order listed and stir. Add lemon twist.

☐ PURPLE RUBY

1½ oz. vodka
1½ oz. pomegranate juice
½ oz. fresh grapefruit juice
¼ oz. fresh lime juice
¼ oz. Honey Syrup (page 21)
Garnish: Grapefruit twist

Shake with ice and strain into chilled cocktail glass. Add grapefruit twist.

☐ REDHEAD MARTINI

4 strawberries, cut into halves
¾ oz. fresh lemon juice
¾ oz. simple syrup
1½ oz. citrus-flavored vodka
1 splash chilled moscato d'Asti or sweet sparkling wine
Garnish: Strawberry

Muddle halved strawberries in mixing glass with lemon juice and syrup. Add vodka and ice and shake well. Strain into chilled cocktail glass. Add sparkling wine. Garnish with the strawberry.

ROSEMARY CLEMENTINE SPARKLE

Created by KATHY CASEY, Seattle, WA

¼ clementine or mandarin orange
1½ oz. vodka
¾ oz. fresh lemon juice
¾ oz. Honey Syrup (page 21)
1 fresh rosemary sprig
1 splash chilled sparkling wine or Champagne
Garnish: Fresh rosemary sprig

Squeeze clementine into mixing glass. Twist rind and add to glass. Add vodka, lemon juice, syrup, and rosemary sprig. Add ice and shake. Strain into chilled cocktail glass. Top with sparkling wine or Champagne. Garnish with remaining rosemary sprig.

ROUXBY RED

For glass: Lemon wedge, coarse salt
1½ oz. grapefruit-flavored vodka
¼ oz. fresh lemon juice
¾ oz. fresh grapefruit juice
½ oz. Campari
½ oz. simple syrup

Rim chilled cocktail glass with lemon and salt. Shake remaining ingredients with ice and strain into glass.

SAMPAN SHIPWRECK A

Created by JAKE SHER, White Plains, NY

1½ oz. vodka
½ oz. orange liqueur
½ oz. canned coconut milk
½ oz. cold brewed chai tea
½ oz. orgeat or almond syrup
Garnish: Pineapple wedge

Shake well with ice. Double-strain into chilled cocktail glass. Perch pineapple on rim of glass.

⬜ SALTY DOG (VODKA)

For glass: Lemon wedge,
    coarse salt
1½ oz. vodka
5 oz. fresh grapefruit juice

*Rim highball glass with
lemon and salt. Fill with ice.
Add vodka and grapefruit
juice and stir.*

⬜ SCREWDRIVER

1½ oz. vodka
5 oz. fresh orange juice

*Pour into ice-filled highball
glass. Stir well.*

⬜ SEA BREEZE

1½ oz. vodka
4 oz. cranberry juice
1 oz. fresh grapefruit juice
Garnish: Lime wedge

*Pour into ice-filled highball
glass. Garnish with lime.*

⬜ SHALOM

1½ oz. 100-proof vodka
1 oz. madeira
½ oz. fresh orange juice
Garnish: Orange wheel

*Shake with ice and strain
into ice-filled old-fashioned
glass. Add orange wheel.*

⬜ SONIC BLASTER

½ oz. vodka
½ oz. light rum
½ oz. crème de banana
1 oz. pineapple juice
1 oz. fresh orange juice
1 oz. cranberry juice
Garnish: Orange and lime wheels

*Shake and pour into ice-filled
Collins glass. Garnish with
orange and lime.*

▽ STUPID CUPID

2 oz. citrus-flavored vodka
½ oz. sloe gin
1 splash simple syrup
1 splash fresh lemon juice
Garnish: Maraschino cherry

*Shake with ice and strain
into chilled cocktail glass.
Garnish with cherry.*

⬜ SURF RIDER

2 oz. vodka
½ oz. sweet vermouth
2 oz. fresh orange juice
½ oz. fresh lemon juice
¼ oz. grenadine
Garnish: Orange half-wheel,
    maraschino cherry

*Shake with ice and strain
into ice-filled highball glass.
Garnish with orange and
cherry.*

▽ TABBY CAT

2 oz. Dubonnet Rouge
1 oz. orange-flavored vodka
2 dashes orange bitters
Garnish: Lemon twist

Stir with ice and strain into chilled cocktail glass. Add lemon twist.

☐ THYME COLLINS

Created by JOSHUA PEKAR, Fairfield, CT

2 oz. citrus-flavored vodka
1 oz. mint syrup
1 oz. fresh lemon juice
1 thyme sprig
3 oz. bitter lemon soda
Garnish: 2 long thyme sprigs

Put first four ingredients in mixing glass, add ice, and shake well. Strain into ice-filled Collins glass. Top with bitter lemon soda and stir briefly. Garnish with long thyme sprigs.

▽ TIGER TANAKA

3 fresh cilantro leaves
1 (¼-inch-thick) slice peeled fresh ginger
2 oz. citrus-flavored vodka
½ oz. limoncello
¾ oz. pineapple juice

Muddle cilantro and ginger in mixing glass. Add remaining ingredients and shake. Double-strain into chilled cocktail glass.

▽ THE TITIAN

1 oz. orange-flavored vodka
½ oz. Grand Marnier
1 oz. passion fruit juice
½ oz. fresh lime juice
½ oz. pomegranate syrup
Garnish: Fresh raspberry

Shake with ice and strain into chilled cocktail glass. Garnish with raspberry.

℣ TOASTED DROP

For glass: Lemon wedge,
    Cinnamon Sugar (page 113)
1½ oz. citrus-flavored vodka
¾ oz. limoncello
¼ oz. amaretto
¾ oz. fresh lemon juice
1 egg white
Garnish: Lemon twist

*Rim chilled cocktail glass
with lemon and cinnamon
sugar. Shake ingredients
without ice. Add ice and
shake again. Strain into
glass. Add lemon twist.*

☐ TOP BANANA

1 oz. vodka
1 oz. crème de banana
2 oz. fresh orange juice

*Shake with ice and strain into
ice-filled old-fashioned glass.*

☐ TWISTER

2 oz. vodka
½ oz. fresh lime juice
Lime wedge
Lemon-lime soda

*Pour vodka and lime juice
into Collins glass. Add several ice cubes. Squeeze lime
into glass and add. Fill with
lemon-lime soda and stir.*

☐ UNDERNEATH THE MANGO TREE

**Created by JONATHAN POGASH,
New York, NY**

For glass: Lime wedge, Sweet
    Chili Powder (recipe follows)
1 oz. mango-flavored vodka
½ oz. peach liqueur
¾ oz. fresh lime juice
½ oz simple syrup
2 oz. ginger ale

*Rim Collins glass with lime
and sweet chili powder. Fill
glass with ice. Shake next four
ingredients with ice. Strain
into glass. Top with ginger ale.*

SWEET CHILI POWDER

*Combine 2 Tbs. chili powder
with 2 Tbs. superfine sugar.*

☐ VELVET PEACH HAMMER

1¾ oz. vodka
¾ oz. peach schnapps
¼ oz. simple syrup
½ oz. fresh lemon juice
Garnish: Peach slice

*Pour vodka and schnapps
into ice-filled old-fashioned
glass. Stir and top with syrup
and lemon juice. Garnish
with peach.*

☐ VICTORY COLLINS

1½ oz. vodka
2 oz. unsweetened grape juice
1 oz. fresh lemon juice
½ oz. simple syrup
Garnish: Orange half-wheel

Shake with ice and strain into ice-filled Collins glass. Garnish with orange.

☐ VODKA AND TONIC

2 oz. vodka
Tonic water
Garnish: Lemon or lime wedge

Pour vodka into highball glass over ice. Add tonic and stir. Garnish with lemon or lime wedge.

☐ VODKA COLLINS

2 oz. vodka
¾ oz. fresh lemon juice
¾ oz. simple syrup
Soda water
Garnish: Lemon and orange
    wheels, maraschino cherry

Shake vodka, lemon juice, and syrup and strain into ice-filled Collins glass. Fill with soda water and stir. Garnish with citrus and cherry. Serve with a straw.

☐ VODKA GIMLET

If you are used to Gimlets made with bottled lime juice, you owe it to yourself to try one with fresh lime juice and simple syrup.

1½ oz. vodka
1 oz. fresh lime juice
½ oz. simple syrup

Shake with ice and strain into chilled cocktail glass.

Note: If desired, substitute 1 oz. Rose's Sweetened Lime Juice for the fresh lime juice and simple syrup.

☐ VODKA GRASSHOPPER

¾ oz. vodka
¾ oz. green crème de menthe
¾ oz. white crème de cacao
¾ oz. half-and-half

Shake with ice and strain into chilled cocktail glass.

☐ VODKA STINGER

1 oz. vodka
1 oz. white crème de menthe

Shake with ice and strain into chilled cocktail glass.

☗ WARSAW COCKTAIL

1½ oz. vodka
½ oz. blackberry-flavored
    brandy
½ oz. dry vermouth
1 tsp. fresh lemon juice

*Shake with ice and strain
into chilled cocktail glass.*

☗ WEST SIDE

1½ oz. lemon-flavored vodka
¾ oz. fresh lemon juice
½ oz. simple syrup
6 fresh mint leaves
Soda water

*Shake first four ingredients
with ice and double-strain
into chilled cocktail glass. Top
with a splash of soda water.*

☗ WHITE RUSSIAN

2 oz. vodka
1 oz. coffee liqueur
Milk or half-and-half

*Pour vodka and coffee
liqueur into ice-filled old-
fashioned glass. Fill with milk
or half-and-half.*

WHISKIES

WHISKEY IS AN UMBRELLA term for four distinct spirits—Irish, Scotch, bourbon, and rye—distilled from a fermented mash of grain and aged in oak barrels. In Ireland and the United States, it's spelled with an "e"; in Scotland and Canada it's spelled without one.

Irish whiskey comprises corn-based grain whiskey, barley, and barley malt. In Scotch whisky production, a peat-fueled fire is used to flavor the final product. The whiskeys of Islay and Skye are especially smoky. American whiskey falls into two categories: straight whiskey, which is made from at least 51 percent of a grain, and blended whiskey, a combination of at least two 100-proof straight whiskies blended with neutral spirits, grain spirits, or light whiskies. Straight whiskey is made in three styles: bourbon, Tennessee, and rye. Bourbon can be made with one of two types of mash: sweet, which employs fresh yeast to start fermentation, or sour, which combines a new batch of sweet mash with residual mash from the previous fermentation.

Tennessee whiskey is similar to bourbon, except that before the whiskey goes into charred barrels to mature, it is painstakingly filtered through ten feet of sugar maple charcoal.

Rye (aka straight rye), once the leading brown spirit before Prohibition, is making a comeback. Though wheat and barley are commonly used to make rye whiskey, by U.S. law it must be made with a minimum of 51 percent rye, whereas in Canada anything goes.

The following recipes list a specific whiskey if it's traditional or integral to the drink. Where simply "whiskey" is listed, feel free to experiment.

☐ 1626

Created by BLAIR FRODELIUS,
Syracuse, NY

2½ oz. bourbon whiskey
¾ oz. gingerbread liqueur
½ tsp. cherry-flavored
    brandy
2 dashes Angostura bitters
Garnish: Italian preserved
    cherry

Shake well with ice and strain into chilled cocktail glass. Garnish with cherry.

☐ ACADEMIC REVIEW

Created by HAL WOLIN,
New York, NY

1½ oz. Irish whiskey
½ oz. applejack
½ oz. Amaro Nonino
½ oz. rye whiskey
¼ oz. Demerara Syrup
    (page 20)
2 dashes mole bitters
1 dash orange bitters
Garnish: Orange twist

Stir with ice and strain into ice-filled old-fashioned glass. Add orange twist.

ADDERLY COCKTAIL

2 oz. straight rye whiskey
¾ oz. maraschino liqueur
¾ oz. fresh lemon juice
2 dashes orange bitters
Garnish: Orange twist,
    flamed (see page 46)

*Shake with ice and strain
into cocktail glass. Flame
orange twist and add.*

AKOGARE

Created by MICHAEL
GRONFORS and JYRI
PYLKKANEN, Helsinki,
Finland

1½ oz. straight rye whiskey
¾ oz. Ginger Syrup (page 21)
¾ oz. cold brewed black tea,
    preferably Japanese
¾ oz. fresh lemon juice
Garnish: Orange twist

*Shake with ice and strain
into chilled cocktail glass.
Add orange twist.*

ALGONQUIN

1½ oz. straight rye whiskey
1 oz. dry vermouth
1 oz. pineapple juice

*Shake with ice and strain
into chilled cocktail glass.*

ALLEGHENY

1 oz. bourbon whiskey
1 oz. dry vermouth
½ oz. blackberry-flavored brandy
½ oz. fresh lemon juice
Garnish: Lemon twist

*Shake with ice and strain
into chilled cocktail glass.
Add lemon twist.*

AMERICANA

1 oz. Tennessee whiskey
½ oz. simple syrup
2 dashes Angostura bitters
Chilled American sparkling
    wine
Garnish: Peach slice

*Stir first three ingredients in
ice-filled Collins glass. Fill
with sparkling wine. Garnish
with peach.*

AMERICAN TRILOGY

1 brown sugar cube, such as
    Demerara
1 oz. straight rye whiskey
1 oz. applejack
Garnish: Orange twist

*Muddle sugar cube in mixer
glass. Add whiskey, applejack, and ice. Stir and strain
into chilled old-fashioned
glass. Add orange twist.*

▢ AUTUMN LEAVES

¾ oz. straight rye whiskey
¾ oz. apple brandy
¾ oz. sweet vermouth
¼ oz. Strega
2 dashes Angostura bitters
Garnish: Orange twist

*Stir with ice and strain into
ice-filled old-fashioned glass.
Add orange twist.*

▢ BACK PORCH SWIZZLE

1½ oz. bourbon whiskey
½ oz. dry vermouth
1 oz. pineapple juice
1 oz. ginger beer
Green Chartreuse
Garnish: Fresh mint sprig

*Pour first four ingredients
in crushed ice–filled highball glass. With barspoon
between your palms, move
hands back and forth and
up and down to quickly
rotate and lift spoon, until
glass is frosted. Float
Chartreuse (see page 12)
on top, and garnish with
mint.*

▢ THE BEAUTIFUL DAY

**Created by TED HENWOOD,
New York, NY**

More and more bartenders
are paying attention to the
sustainable agriculture
movement with seasonal
drinks. When spring comes
around and rhubarb is at its
peak, offer this cocktail.

1¼ oz. Irish whiskey
¾ oz. Rhubarb Syrup (page 21)
2 oz. cold brewed green tea
Garnish: Edible flowers

*Shake with ice and strain
into ice-filled old-fashioned
glass. Garnish with edible
flowers.*

▽ BENSONHURST

**Created by CHAD SOLOMON,
New York, NY**

1 splash Cynar
2 oz. straight rye whiskey
1 oz. dry vermouth
¼ oz. maraschino liqueur

*Swirl Cynar in chilled
cocktail glass to coat inside;
discard excess Cynar. Stir
remaining ingredients with
ice and strain into glass.*

☐ THE BLINKER

The original recipe, published in 1934, used grenadine, but the raspberry syrup complements the grapefruit better. In this recipe, a thick ice-cream topping syrup is preferable to the thin beverage flavoring syrup.

2 oz. straight rye whisky
1½ oz. fresh grapefruit juice
1 tsp. raspberry syrup
Garnish: Grapefruit twist
    or skewered raspberry

Shake and strain into cocktail glass. Garnish with grapefruit twist or raspberry.

☐ BLOOD AND SAND

Blood and Sand, the iconic bullfighter movie, was made first in 1922 with Rudolph Valentino. The cocktail's color will give you a hint as to how the drink got its name.

½ oz. blended Scotch whisky
½ oz. cherry-flavored brandy
½ oz. sweet vermouth
½ oz. fresh orange juice

Shake with ice and strain into chilled cocktail glass.

☐ BLOODY SCOTSMAN

Created by JONATHAN POGASH, New York, NY

A busy barkeeper (or organized home bartender serving a big brunch) will make up large batches of morning cocktails to get a head start on serving. This great variation on the Bloody Mary theme uses Scotch to give it a smoky note.

Makes 14 to 16 servings

24 oz. smoky Scotch whisky, such as Laphroaig
24 oz. tomato juice
24 oz. V8 cocktail juice
1 c. ketchup
3 oz. fresh lime juice
3 oz. simple syrup
¾ oz. Worcestershire sauce
1 tsp. freshly ground white pepper
1 tsp. freshly ground black pepper
⅛ tsp. cayenne pepper
Fine sea salt

Mix ingredients together, stirring often, in a large container, adding salt to taste. Chill for at least 24 hours before serving. Serve in ice-filled old-fashioned glasses.

♈ BOBBY BURNS COCKTAIL

Mr. Burns, a cigar salesman, was such a good customer at the old Waldorf bar in the late nineteenth century that the establishment named this drink after him . . . probably.

1½ oz. blended Scotch whisky
1½ oz. sweet vermouth
1 tsp. Bénédictine
Garnish: Lemon twist

Stir with ice and strain into chilled cocktail glass. Add lemon twist.

☐ BOURBON COOLER

2½ oz. bourbon whiskey
½ oz. fresh lemon juice
½ oz. grapefruit juice
½ oz. orgeat syrup
Garnish: Peach slice

Shake with ice in mixing glass. Pour with ice into old-fashioned glass. Garnish with peach.

☐ BOURBON AND ELDER

2 oz. bourbon whiskey
¾ oz. elderflower liqueur
1 dash Angostura bitters
Garnish: Lemon twist

Stir with ice and strain into chilled old-fashioned glass. Add lemon twist.

☐ BOURBON HIGHBALL

2 oz. bourbon whiskey
Ginger ale or soda water
Garnish: Lemon twist

Pour whiskey into ice-filled highball glass. Fill with ginger ale or soda water and stir. Add lemon twist.

☐ BRIGHTON PUNCH

¾ oz. bourbon whiskey
¾ oz. brandy
¾ oz. Bénédictine
2 oz. fresh orange juice
1 oz. fresh lemon juice
Soda water
Garnish: Orange and lemon wheels

Shake first five ingredients with ice and pour with ice into Collins glass. Fill with soda water and stir gently. Garnish with orange and lemon and serve with a straw.

⏤ BROOKLYN

1½ oz. rye or bourbon
  whiskey
½ oz. sweet vermouth
1 dash Amer Picon or Torani
  Amer
1 dash maraschino liqueur

Stir with ice and strain into chilled cocktail glass.

⏤ BULL AND BEAR

1½ oz. bourbon whiskey
¾ oz. orange curaçao
1 oz. fresh lemon juice
¼ oz. grenadine
Garnish: Maraschino cherry,
  orange half-wheel

Shake with ice and strain into chilled cocktail glass. Garnish with cherry and orange.

⏤ CALIFORNIA LEMONADE

2 oz. bourbon whiskey
1 oz. fresh lemon juice
1 oz. fresh lime juice
1 oz. simple syrup
¼ oz. grenadine
Soda water
Garnish: Orange and lemon
  wheels, maraschino cherry

Shake first five ingredients with ice. Strain into shaved ice–filled Collins glass. Fill with soda water and garnish with orange, lemon, and cherry. Serve with straws.

⏤ CAMERON'S KICK COCKTAIL

¾ oz. blended Scotch whisky
¾ oz. Irish whiskey
½ oz. fresh lemon juice
2 dashes orange bitters

Shake with ice and strain into chilled cocktail glass.

☐ CANADIAN BREEZE

1½ oz. Canadian whisky
¾ oz. pineapple juice
½ oz. fresh lemon juice
¼ oz. maraschino liqueur
Garnish: Pineapple wedge,
    maraschino cherry

*Shake with ice. Strain into
ice-filled old-fashioned glass.
Garnish with pineapple and
cherry.*

☐ CANADIAN CHERRY

For glass: Maraschino liqueur
1½ oz. Canadian whisky
½ oz. maraschino liqueur
½ oz. fresh lemon juice
½ oz. fresh orange juice

*Moisten rim of old-fashioned
glass with maraschino
liqueur. Fill with ice. Shake
ingredients with ice and
strain into glass.*

☐ CANADIAN COCKTAIL

1½ oz. Canadian whisky
½ oz. triple sec
½ oz. simple syrup
1 dash Angostura bitters

*Shake with ice and strain
into chilled cocktail glass.*

☐ CANAL STREET DAISY

1 oz. blended Scotch whisky
1 oz. fresh orange juice
¾ oz. fresh lemon juice
Soda water
Garnish: Orange wheel

*Add Scotch and juices to ice-
filled Collins glass and stir.
Fill with soda water and stir
again. Garnish with orange.*

☐ CHARACTER DEVELOPMENT

Created by HAL WOLIN,
New York, NY

2 oz. Scotch whiskey
½ oz. coconut liqueur
½ oz. dry sherry
2 dashes grapefruit bitters
Garnish: Grapefruit twist

*Stir with ice and strain into
chilled cocktail glass. Add
grapefruit twist.*

☐ CHEF'S PAIN

2 oz. bourbon whiskey
¾ oz. fresh lime juice
½ oz. blackberry liqueur
½ oz. B & B

*Shake with ice and strain
into chilled cocktail glass.*

▢ COFFEE OLD-FASHIONED

2 oz. bourbon whiskey
¾ oz. simple syrup
2 dashes Angostura bitters
½ c. cold brewed coffee
2 oz. soda water
Garnish: Orange wheel, maraschino cherry

Pour bourbon, syrup, bitters, and coffee into ice-filled old-fashioned glass and stir. Add soda water and stir again. Garnish with orange and cherry.

▢ COMMODORE COCKTAIL

The whiskey used in this recipe has a higher-than-average proportion of rye than usual bourbons, but any rye or bourbon will do.

2 oz. 1792 Ridgemont Reserve Bourbon Whiskey
¾ oz. white crème de cacao
½ oz. fresh lemon juice
1 dash grenadine

Shake with ice and strain into chilled champagne flute.

▢ COTTON CLUB FLIP

Created by DUANE FERNANDEZ, Jr., New York, NY

Buy some packaged cotton candy for this cocktail's garnish, or skip the candy and garnish with an edible flower.

2 oz. Vanilla-Infused Bourbon (recipe follows)
½ oz. Honey-Currant Syrup (recipe follows)
¾ oz. fresh lime juice
1 egg white
2 dashes rhubarb bitters
Garnish: Stick of cotton candy

Shake first four ingredients without ice. Add ice and shake again. Strain into ice-filled old-fashioned glass. Top with bitters. Garnish with cotton candy.

VANILLA-INFUSED BOURBON

Split 3 Tahitian vanilla beans lengthwise. Insert into 750-ml bottle of bourbon. Close bottle and let stand at room temperature for 3 to 5 days. Remove vanilla beans. Store bourbon at room temperature for up to 1 month.

HONEY-CURRANT SYRUP

Bring 1 c. honey, ½ c. dried currants, and ¼ c. water to a simmer over medium heat in small saucepan, stirring to dissolve honey. Simmer over low heat for 10 minutes. Remove from heat and let cool. Strain into jar, cover, and refrigerate for up to 3 weeks.

☐ THE DEBONAIR

2½ oz. single-malt Scotch whisky
1 oz. ginger liqueur
Garnish: Lemon twist

Stir and strain into chilled cocktail glass. Add lemon twist.

☐ DE LA LOUISIANE

¾ oz. straight rye whiskey
¾ oz. sweet vermouth
¾ oz. Bénédictine
3 dashes absinthe or pastis
3 dashes Peychaud's bitters
Garnish: Maraschino cherry

Stir with ice and strain into chilled cocktail glass. Garnish with cherry.

☐ DERBY

2 oz. bourbon whiskey
¼ oz. Bénédictine
1 dash Angostura bitters
Garnish: Lemon twist

Stir with ice and strain into chilled cocktail glass. Add lemon twist.

☐ DESHLER

1½ oz. straight rye whiskey
½ oz. Dubonnet Rouge
¼ oz. triple sec
2 dashes Angostura bitters
Garnish: Lemon twist

Stir with ice and strain into chilled champagne flute. Add lemon twist.

☐ DEVIL'S SOUL

Created by TED KILGORE, St. Louis, MO

1½ oz. straight rye whiskey
½ oz. mezcal
½ oz. amaro, such as Ramazzotti or Averna
¼ oz. Aperol
¼ oz. elderflower liqueur
Garnish: Orange twist, flamed

Stir with ice and strain into cocktail glass. Flame orange twist and add to glass.

Y DIRTY HARRY

1 splash absinthe
2 oz. straight rye whiskey
½ oz. sweet vermouth
¼ oz. maraschino liqueur
Garnish: Maraschino cherry

Swirl absinthe in chilled cocktail glass to coat inside; discard excess absinthe. Stir remaining ingredients with ice and strain into glass. Garnish with cherry.

Y DIXIE WHISKEY COCKTAIL

2 oz. bourbon whiskey
½ oz. white crème de menthe
¼ oz. triple sec
¼ oz. simple syrup
1 dash Angostura bitters

Shake with ice and strain into chilled cocktail glass.

Y DOUBLE STANDARD SOUR

¾ oz. rye or bourbon whiskey
¾ oz. gin
1 oz. fresh lemon juice
½ tsp. white crème de menthe
½ oz. grenadine
¼ oz. simple syrup
Garnish: Lemon half-wheel, maraschino cherry

Shake with ice and strain into chilled cocktail glass. Garnish with lemon and cherry.

Y THE DUBOUDREAU COCKTAIL

Created by JIM MEEHAN, New York, NY, in honor of bartender Jamie Boudreau, Seattle, WA

2 oz. straight rye whiskey
¾ oz. Dubonnet Rouge
¼ oz. Fernet-Branca
¼ oz. elderflower liqueur
Garnish: Lemon twist

Stir with ice and strain into chilled cocktail glass. Add lemon twist.

♉ DUFFTOWN FLIP

2 oz. blended Scotch whisky
½ oz. port
½ oz. Demerara Syrup
(page 20)
½ oz. almond milk
1 whole egg
Garnish: Freshly grated nutmeg

*Shake without ice. Then
shake with ice and strain into
snifter. Top with nutmeg.*

▯ EASTERN SOUR

2 oz. bourbon whiskey
1½ oz. fresh orange juice
1 oz. fresh lime juice
¼ oz. orgeat or almond syrup
¼ oz. simple syrup
Garnish: Orange and lime
wheels

*Shake with ice and strain
into ice-filled highball glass.
Garnish with orange and
lime.*

▽ EASTERNER

2 oz. straight rye whiskey
1 oz. fresh grapefruit juice
½ oz. maple syrup
Garnish: Grapefruit twist

*Shake with ice and strain
into chilled cocktail glass.
Add grapefruit twist.*

▯ EMPEROR NORTON'S MISTRESS

Emperor Norton was a famous
eccentric of San Francisco's
post–Gold Rush period.

3 fresh strawberries, cut in
halves
1½ oz. bourbon whiskey
½ oz. vanilla liqueur
¼ oz. triple sec
Garnish: Strawberry slice

*Muddle halved strawberries
in mixing glass. Add remaining ingredients. Shake with
ice and double-strain into
ice-filled old-fashioned glass.
Garnish with strawberry
slice.*

▽ FANCY-FREE COCKTAIL

2 oz. bourbon whiskey
½ oz. maraschino liqueur
1 dash Angostura bitters
1 dash orange bitters

*Stir with ice and strain into
chilled cocktail glass.*

⅂ FANCY WHISKEY

2 oz. bourbon or rye whiskey
1 dash Angostura bitters
¼ oz. triple sec
¼ oz. simple syrup
Garnish: Lemon twist

*Shake with ice and strain
into chilled cocktail glass.
Add lemon twist.*

⅂ FOX RIVER COCKTAIL

2 oz. bourbon or rye whiskey
½ oz. dark crème de cacao
4 dashes Angostura bitters

*Stir with ice and strain into
chilled cocktail glass.*

⅂ FRISCO SOUR

2 oz. bourbon or rye whiskey
¾ oz. fresh lemon juice
½ oz. fresh lime juice
½ oz. Bénédictine
Garnish: Lemon and lime
    wheels

*Shake with ice and strain
into chilled sour glass.
Garnish with lemon and
lime.*

⅂ GILCHRIST

1¼ oz. blended Scotch whisky
¾ oz. pear brandy
¾ oz. fresh grapefruit juice
½ oz. amaro, such as Averna
2 dashes grapefruit bitters
Garnish: Lemon twist

*Shake with ice and strain
into chilled cocktail glass.
Add lemon twist.*

⌷ GODFATHER

1½ oz. blended Scotch whisky
¾ oz. amaretto

*Pour into ice-filled
old-fashioned glass and stir.*

⌷ GOLDRUSH

2 oz. bourbon whiskey
¾ oz. fresh lemon juice
1 oz. Honey Syrup (page 21)

*Shake and strain into ice-
filled old-fashioned glass.*

⅂ GRANDFATHER

1 oz. bourbon whiskey
1 oz. applejack
1 oz. sweet vermouth
1 dash Angostura bitters
1 dash Peychaud's bitters
Garnish: Maraschino cherry

*Stir with ice and strain into
chilled cocktail glass. Garnish
with cherry.*

⅋ GREENPOINT

Created by MICHAEL McILROY,
New York, NY

2 oz. straight rye whiskey
½ oz. yellow Chartreuse
½ oz. sweet vermouth
1 dash Angostura bitters
1 dash orange bitters
Garnish: Lemon twist

*Stir with ice and strain into
chilled cocktail glass. Add
lemon twist.*

⅋ HARVEST MOON

1½ oz. straight rye whiskey
1 oz. Lillet Blanc
½ oz. apple brandy
¼ oz. green Chartreuse
2 dashes Angostura bitters
Garnish: Orange twist

*Stir with ice and strain into
chilled cocktail glass. Add
orange twist.*

⅋ HEATHER BLUSH

1 oz. blended Scotch whisky
1 oz. strawberry liqueur
3 oz. chilled sparkling wine
Garnish: Whole strawberry

*Pour Scotch and liqueur into
chilled champagne flute. Top
with sparkling wine. Garnish
with strawberry.*

⅋ HEATHER'S KISS

Created by BLAIR FRODELIUS,
Syracuse, NY

2¼ oz. blended Scotch whisky
½ oz. fresh lemon juice
¼ oz. agave nectar
1 tsp. absinthe
Garnish: Apple slice

*Shake with ice strain into
chilled cocktail glass. Garnish
with apple slice.*

☐ HEBRIDES

1½ oz. single-malt Scotch
   whisky
½ oz. maraschino liqueur
½ oz. triple sec
2 oz. apple juice
½ oz. fresh lemon juice
1 dash Angostura bitters

*Pour into ice-filled Collins
glass and stir.*

⅋ HIGH COTTON

2 oz. straight rye whiskey
½ oz. Pimm's No. 1 Cup
½ oz. Dubonnet Rouge
2 dashes peach bitters
Garnish: Lemon twist, fresh
   mint sprig

*Stir with ice and strain into
chilled cocktail glass. Garnish
with lemon and mint.*

🍸 HILL DOG

Created by CARLOS CUERTA, Chicago, IL

White whiskey is none other than moonshine or white lightning, which isn't colored because it hasn't been aged in wood.

1½ oz. white whiskey
½ oz. Grand Marnier
½ oz. dry sherry
½ oz. Lavender Syrup (page 21)
Garnish: Orange twist

Stir with ice and strain into chilled cocktail glass. Add orange twist.

🍸 HOLE-IN-ONE

1¾ oz. blended Scotch whisky
¾ oz. dry vermouth
¼ oz fresh lemon juice
1 dash orange bitters

Shake with ice and strain into chilled cocktail glass.

🥃 HORSE'S NECK (WITH A KICK)

The Horse's Neck was originally a soft drink with iced ginger ale garnished with lots of lemon peel but an enterprising bartender added spirits to give it a "kick."

1 long, wide spiral of lemon zest (use a vegetable peeler)
2 oz. bourbon whiskey
Ginger ale

Insert the lemon spiral in Collins glass with one end hanging over the rim. Fill glass with ice cubes. Add whiskey. Fill with ginger ale and stir well.

🥃 HOTEL D'ALSACE

1 fresh rosemary sprig
2 oz. Irish whiskey
½ oz. Bénédictine
½ oz. triple sec

Muddle leaves from half-sprig of rosemary in mixing glass and reserve the other half. Add remaining ingredients. Stir with ice and strain into ice-filled old-fashioned glass. Garnish with remaining half-sprig of rosemary.

☐ I.A.P.

2 oz. Tennessee whiskey
¼ oz. Fernet-Branca
3 oz. cola

*Build in ice-filled Collins
glass.*

☐ IMPERIAL FIZZ

1½ oz. bourbon or rye whiskey
½ oz. light rum
1 oz. fresh lemon juice
½ oz. simple syrup
Soda water

*Shake first four ingredients
with ice and strain into ice-
filled highball glass. Fill with
soda water and stir.*

☐ INCIDER COCKTAIL

1½ oz. rye or bourbon whiskey
4 oz. apple cider
Garnish: Apple slice

*Stir whiskey and apple cider
in ice-filled old-fashioned
glass. Garnish with apple.*

🍸 IRISH SHILLELAGH

1½ oz. Irish whiskey
1 oz. light rum
½ oz. sloe gin
1 oz. fresh lemon juice
½ oz. simple syrup
Garnish: Fresh raspberries
    and strawberries, 2 peach
    slices, maraschino cherry

*Shake with ice and strain
into ice-filled Irish coffee
glass. Garnish with berries,
peach slices, and cherry.*

🍸 JITTERBUG SOUR

2 oz. straight rye whiskey
½ oz. Bénédictine
¾ oz. fresh lemon juice
½ oz. Honey Syrup (page 21)
1 egg white
1 dash Angostura bitters
Garnish: Lemon twist

*Shake first five ingredients
with ice and strain into
chilled cocktail glass. Add
bitters and lemon twist.*

☐ JOCOSE JULEP

2½ oz. bourbon whiskey
½ oz. green crème de menthe
1 oz. fresh lime juice
½ oz. simple syrup
5 fresh mint leaves
Soda water
Garnish: Fresh mint sprig

Combine first five ingredients in blender without ice until smooth. Pour into ice-filled Collins glass. Fill with soda water and stir. Garnish with mint sprig.

☐ THE JOE LEWIS

Created by CHRIS PATINO, New York, NY

1½ oz. Scotch whisky
1 oz. fresh carrot juice
¾ oz. tawny port
½ oz. fresh lemon juice
1 tsp. agave nectar

Shake with ice and strain into chilled cocktail glass.

☐ JOHN COLLINS

2 oz. bourbon whiskey
1 oz. fresh lemon juice
½ oz. simple syrup
Soda water
Garnish: Orange and lemon
　　wheels, maraschino cherry

Shake first three ingredients with ice and strain into Collins glass. Add ice, fill with soda water, and stir. Garnish with orange, lemon, and cherry. Serve with straws.

☐ KENTUCKY BLIZZARD

1½ oz. bourbon whiskey
1½ oz. cranberry juice
½ oz. fresh lime juice
½ oz. grenadine
½ oz simple syrup
Garnish: Orange half-wheel

Shake ingredients with ice. Strain into chilled cocktail (or ice-filled old-fashioned) glass. Garnish with orange.

☐ KENTUCKY COCKTAIL

1½ oz. 1792 Ridgemont
　　Reserve Bourbon Whiskey
¾ oz. pineapple juice

Shake with ice and strain into chilled cocktail glass.

⍩ KENTUCKY COLONEL COCKTAIL

2 oz. bourbon whiskey
1 oz. Bénédictine
Garnish: Lemon twist

Stir with ice and strain into chilled cocktail glass. Add lemon twist.

⍩ THE KENTUCKY LONGSHOT

2 oz. bourbon whiskey
½ oz. ginger liqueur
½ oz. peach-flavored brandy
1 dash Angostura bitters
1 dash Peychaud's bitters
Garnish: Candied ginger slice

Stir with ice and strain into chilled cocktail glass. Garnish with candied ginger perched on the rim of the glass.

▢ KING COLE COCKTAIL

1 orange wheel
1 pineapple wedge, peeled
¼ oz. simple syrup
2 oz. rye or bourbon whiskey

Muddle first three ingredients well in old-fashioned glass. Add whiskey and ice. Stir.

▢ KISS ON THE LIPS

2 oz. bourbon whiskey
6 oz. apricot nectar

Pour into ice-filled Collins glass and stir. Serve with straw.

KLONDIKE COOLER

2 oz. bourbon whiskey
¼ oz simple syrup
Soda water or ginger ale
Garnish: Orange and/or lemon zest spiral(s)

Stir bourbon and syrup in Collins glass. Add ice. Fill with soda and stir again. Insert citrus spiral(s) and dangle end(s) over rim of glass.

⍩ LA TAVOLA ROTONDA

1½ oz. bourbon whiskey
¾ oz. pineapple juice
½ oz. Campari
½ oz. amaro, such as Ramazzotti or Averna
½ oz. maraschino liqueur
2 dashes Peychaud's bitters
Garnish: Maraschino cherry

Shake with ice and strain into chilled cocktail glass. Garnish with cherry.

🍸 LIBERAL

1½ oz. straight rye whiskey
½ oz. sweet vermouth
¼ oz. Amer Picon or Torani
    Amer
1 dash orange bitters
Garnish: Orange twist

*Stir with ice and strain into
chilled cocktail glass. Add
orange twist.*

🍸 LINSTEAD COCKTAIL

1½ oz. bourbon whiskey
¾ oz. pineapple juice
½ oz. simple syrup
1 tsp. anisette
½ tsp. fresh lemon juice

*Shake with ice and strain
into chilled cocktail glass.*

🍸 LOCH LOMOND

1 oz. blended Scotch whisky
1 oz. blue curaçao
½ oz. peach schnapps
3 oz. fresh grapefruit juice
½ oz. fresh lemon juice
Garnish: Star fruit slice

*Shake ingredients with ice
and strain into ice-filled
hurricane or parfait glass.
Garnish with star fruit.*

🍸 LOUISVILLE COOLER

1½ oz. 1792 Ridgemont
    Reserve Bourbon Whiskey
1 oz. fresh orange juice
½ oz. fresh lime juice
½ oz. simple syrup
Garnish: Orange half-wheel

*Shake ingredients with ice.
Strain into old-fashioned
glass over fresh ice. Garnish
with orange.*

🍸 MAGNOLIA MAIDEN

1¼ oz. bourbon whiskey
1¼ oz. Mandarine Napoléon
1 splash simple syrup
1 splash soda water

*Shake bourbon, Mandarine
Napoléon, and syrup with
ice. Strain into ice-filled
old-fashioned glass. Top with
soda water.*

🍸 MAMIE GILROY

2 oz. blended Scotch whisky
½ oz. fresh lime juice
Ginger ale

*Stir Scotch and lime juice in
ice-filled Collins glass. Top
with ginger ale and stir.*

☿ MANHASSET

1½ oz. bourbon whiskey
¾ oz. dry vermouth
¾ oz. sweet vermouth
½ oz. fresh lemon juice

*Shake with ice and strain
into chilled cocktail glass.*

☿ MANHATTAN

For more on the Manhattan,
see page 28.

2 oz. rye or bourbon whiskey
½ oz. sweet vermouth
1 dash Angostura bitters
Garnish: Maraschino cherry

*Stir with ice and strain into
chilled cocktail glass. Garnish
with cherry.*

☿ MANHATTAN (DRY)

For a perfect Manhattan, use
¼ oz. each dry and sweet
vermouth.

2 oz. rye or bourbon whiskey
½ oz. dry vermouth
1 dash Angostura bitters
Garnish: Maraschino cherry

*Stir with ice and strain into
chilled cocktail glass. Garnish
with cherry.*

☿ THE MANUSCRIPT

Created by CHAD MICHAEL
GEORGE, Clayton, MO

1½ oz. straight rye whiskey
¾ oz. cherry brandy
½ oz. fresh lemon juice
½ oz. simple syrup
1 oz. chilled Champagne
Garnish: Orange twist, flamed

*Shake first four ingredients
with ice. Strain into chilled
cocktail glass. Top with
Champagne. Flame orange
twist and add.*

☿ MIAMI BEACH COCKTAIL

¾ oz. blended Scotch whisky
¾ oz. dry vermouth
¾ oz. fresh grapefruit juice

*Shake with ice and strain
into chilled cocktail glass.*

▯ MINT JULEP

Follow this advice from
Frances Parkinson Keyes:
"Never insult a decent woman,
never bring a horse into the
house, and never crush
the mint in a julep."

½ oz. simple syrup
2½ oz. bourbon whiskey
Garnish: 5 fresh mint sprigs

*Pour syrup into silver julep
cup, silver mug, or Collins
glass. Fill with shaved or
crushed ice and add bourbon.
Stir until glass is heavily
frosted, adding more ice if necessary. (Do not hold glass with
hand while stirring.) Garnish
with mint so that the tops are
about 2 inches above rim of
glass. Use short straws so that
it will be necessary to bury
nose in mint, which is intended
for scent rather than taste.*

▽ MODERN COCKTAIL

1½ oz. blended Scotch whisky
½ tsp. Jamaican rum
¼ oz. anisette
½ tsp. fresh lemon juice
1 dash orange bitters
Garnish: Maraschino cherry

*Shake with ice and strain
into chilled cocktail glass.
Garnish with cherry.*

▽ MOTO GUZZI

1½ oz. bourbon whiskey
1½ oz. Punt e Mes

*Stir with ice and strain into
chilled cocktail glass.*

▯ NARRAGANSETT

1 splash anisette
1½ oz. bourbon whiskey
1 oz. sweet vermouth
Garnish: Lemon twist

*Swirl anisette in old-fashioned
glass to coat inside. Add ice,
then whiskey and vermouth
and stir. Add lemon twist.*

▼ NEW YORK COCKTAIL

Sometimes called the
New Yorker, this is a reminder
that rye was once the whiskey
of choice in the Big Apple.

1½ oz. straight rye whiskey
¾ oz. fresh lemon juice
¼ oz. simple syrup
¼ oz. grenadine
Garnish: Lemon twist

*Shake with ice and strain
into chilled cocktail glass.
Add lemon twist.*

☐ NEW YORK SOUR

2 oz. rye or bourbon whiskey
¾ oz. fresh lemon juice
¾ oz. simple syrup
1 oz. red wine
Garnish: Lemon half-wheel,
    maraschino cherry

*Shake first three ingredients
with ice. Strain into ice-filled
old-fashioned glass. Float
red wine (see page 12) on
top. Garnish with lemon and
cherry.*

☐ NUTCRACKER

2 oz. bourbon whiskey
½ oz. hazelnut liqueur
½ oz. amaretto
½ oz. orgeat or almond
    syrup
¾ oz. fresh lemon juice
1 egg white
Garnish: Freshly grated nutmeg

*Shake without ice. Shake
with ice and strain into ice-
filled old-fashioned glass. Top
with nutmeg.*

☐ OLD BAY RIDGE

1 oz. straight rye whiskey
1 oz. aquavit
½ oz. Demerara Syrup
    (page 20)
2 dashes Angostura bitters
Garnish: Lemon twist

*Stir with ice and strain into
chilled old-fashioned glass.
Add lemon twist.*

OLD-FASHIONED COCKTAIL

For more information on the Old-Fashioned Cocktail, see page 24.

2 oz. rye or bourbon whiskey
¼ oz. simple syrup
2 dashes orange or Angostura bitters
Garnish: Orange wheel, Italian preserved cherry

Pour whiskey, syrup, and bitters into cracked ice–filled old-fashioned glass and stir. Garnish with orange and cherry.

PADDY COCKTAIL

1½ oz. Irish whiskey
1½ oz. sweet vermouth
1 dash Angostura bitters

Stir with ice and strain into chilled cocktail glass.

PENICILLIN

Created by SAM ROSS, New York, NY

1¾ oz. Scotch whisky
¾ oz. fresh lemon juice
½ oz. Honey Syrup (page 21)
½ oz ginger liqueur
¼ oz. smoky Scotch whisky, such as Islay
Garnish: Lemon wheel

Shake first four ingredients with ice and strain into ice-filled old-fashioned glass. Float smoky Scotch on top and garnish with lemon.

THE PITBULL

Created by CHRIS CARLSSON, Rochester, NY

1 oz. white whiskey, preferably Buffalo Trace White Dog
¾ oz. fresh lemon juice
1 oz. simple syrup
1 egg white
Garnish: 3 drops Angostura bitters

Shake without ice. Then shake with ice and strain into chilled cocktail glass. Top with bitters.

PLUMMED AWAY

¾ oz. Irish whiskey
¾ oz. plum wine
1½ oz. apple juice
½ oz. fresh lemon juice
½ oz. simple syrup
Garnish: Lemon twist

Pour into ice-filled highball glass. Stir, then add lemon twist.

QUEBEC

For glass: Lemon wedge, superfine sugar
1½ oz. Canadian whisky
½ oz. dry vermouth
1 tsp. Amer Picon or Torani Amer
1 tsp. maraschino liqueur

Rim chilled cocktail glass with lemon and sugar. Shake remaining ingredients with ice and strain into glass.

THE RECONCILIATION

Created by RICHARD BOCCATO, New York, NY

¼ tsp. sambuca
1½ oz. straight rye whiskey
½ oz. amaro, such as Ramazzotti or Averna
1 tsp. orgeat syrup
Garnish: Orange twist

Swirl sambuca in old-fashioned glass to coat inside; discard excess sambuca. Add ice to glass. Shake remaining ingredients with ice and strain into prepared glass. Add orange twist.

RED HOOK

Created by ENZO ENRICO, New York, NY

2 oz. straight rye whiskey
¼ oz. maraschino liqueur
¼ oz. Punt e Mes
Garnish: Maraschino cherry

Stir with ice and strain into chilled cocktail glass. Garnish with cherry.

🍸 RED-HOT PASSION

½ oz. bourbon whiskey
½ oz. amaretto
½ oz. Tennessee sour mash
    whiskey
¼ oz. sloe gin
1 splash triple sec
1 splash fresh orange juice
1 splash pineapple juice
Garnish: Orange half-wheel

Pour ingredients into ice-filled hurricane or parfait glass and stir gently. Garnish with orange.

🍸 RED RAIDER

1 oz. bourbon whiskey
½ oz. triple sec
1 oz. fresh lemon juice
1 tsp. grenadine

Shake with ice and strain into chilled cocktail glass.

🍸 REMEMBER THE MAINE

2 oz. straight rye whiskey
¾ oz. sweet vermouth
½ oz. Cherry Heering
1 tsp. absinthe or pastis
Garnish: Lemon twist

Stir with ice and strain into chilled cocktail glass. Add lemon twist.

🍸 REVOLVER

Created by JON SANTER,
San Francisco, CA

2 oz. bourbon
½ oz. Tia Maria
2 dashes orange bitters
Garnish: Orange twist,
    flamed

Stir with ice and strain into chilled cocktail glass. Flame orange twist and add.

🍸 ROBERT BURNS

1½ oz. blended Scotch
    whisky
½ oz. sweet vermouth
1 dash orange bitters
1 dash absinthe or pastis

Stir with ice and strain into chilled cocktail glass.

🍸 ROB ROY

1½ oz. blended Scotch whisky
¾ oz. sweet vermouth

Stir with ice and strain into chilled cocktail glass.

🍸 RORY O'MORE

Here is an Irish version of the
Rob Roy, with orange bitters

1½ oz. Irish whiskey
¾ oz. sweet vermouth
1 dash orange bitters

*Stir with ice and strain into
chilled cocktail glass.*

☐ RUSTY NAIL

1½ oz. blended Scotch whisky
½ oz. Drambuie

*Pour Scotch into ice-filled
old-fashioned glass. Float
Drambuie (see page 12) on
top.*

☐ SAZERAC (RYE)

The official cocktail of New
Orleans, nowadays made with
rye. The original used cognac,
which also makes a fine
Sazerac.

1 sugar cube
3 dashes Peychaud's bitters
2 oz. rye whiskey, preferably
    Buffalo Trace or Sazerac
¼ oz. absinthe, Herbsaint, or
    Pernod
Lemon twist

*Fill old-fashioned glass with
ice. Muddle sugar and bitters in second old-fashioned
glass. Add whiskey and stir.
Discard ice from first glass.
Add absinthe to chilled glass,
swirl to coat inside, and
discard excess absinthe. Pour
whiskey mixture from second
glass into chilled glass. Twist
lemon over drink, but do not
add to glass.*

♈ SCOFFLAW

1 oz. Canadian whisky
1 oz. dry vermouth
¼ oz. fresh lemon juice
1 dash grenadine
1 dash orange bitters
Garnish: Lemon wedge

Stir with ice and strain into chilled cocktail glass. Garnish with lemon.

♈ SCOTCH BISHOP COCKTAIL

1 oz. blended Scotch whisky
½ oz. fresh orange juice
½ oz. dry vermouth
½ tsp. triple sec
¼ oz simple syrup
Garnish: Lemon twist

Shake with ice and strain into chilled cocktail glass. Add lemon twist.

♈ SCOTCH BONNET

1¼ oz. single-malt Scotch whisky
¼ oz. dry vermouth
¼ oz. Aperol
2 dashes hot red pepper sauce
Garnish: Orange twist, flamed (see page 46)

Stir with ice and strain into chilled cocktail glass. Flame orange twist and add.

▯ SCOTCH HIGHBALL

2 oz. blended Scotch whisky
Ginger ale or soda water
Garnish: Lemon twist

Pour Scotch into ice-filled highball glass and fill with ginger ale or soda water. Add lemon twist and stir.

▯ SCOTCH HOLIDAY SOUR

1½ oz. blended Scotch whisky
1 oz. cherry-flavored brandy
½ oz. sweet vermouth
1 oz. fresh lemon juice
Garnish: Lemon half-wheel

Shake with ice and strain into ice-filled old-fashioned glass. Garnish with lemon.

▮ SCOTCH ROYALE

1 sugar cube
1 dash Angostura bitters
1½ oz. blended Scotch whisky
Chilled Champagne

Place sugar cube and bitters in chilled champagne flute. Stir Scotch with ice in mixing glass and strain into flute. Fill with Champagne.

∀ SCOTCH STINGER

1½ oz. blended Scotch
  whisky
½ oz. white crème
  de menthe

*Shake with ice and strain
into chilled cocktail glass.*

∀ SCOTTISH GUARD

1½ oz. bourbon whiskey
½ oz. fresh lemon juice
½ oz. fresh orange juice
1 tsp. grenadine

*Shake with ice and strain
into chilled cocktail glass.*

∀ THE SCOTTISH
BANDIT

Created by HAL WOLIN,
New York, NY

1¾ oz. blended Scotch
  whisky
1 tsp. green Chartreuse
¾ oz. fig juice
½ oz. Cinnamon Syrup
  (page 20)
2 dashes whiskey barrel
  bitters
Garnish: Orange twist

*Shake with ice and strain
into cocktail glass. Add
orange twist.*

∀ THE SEELBACH
COCKTAIL

A namesake of the famous
hotel in Louisville, KY, this
cocktail is loaded with bitters,
so decrease the amount if
you wish.

¾ oz. bourbon whiskey
½ oz. triple sec
7 dashes Angostura bitters
7 dashes Peychaud's bitters
4 oz. chilled Champagne
Garnish: Orange twist

*Add, in order given, to chilled
champagne flute. Add orange
twist.*

▢ SHRUFF'S END

1 oz. Islay or other peaty
  single-malt Scotch whisky
1 oz. apple brandy
½ oz. Bénédictine
2 dashes Peychaud's bitters

*Stir with ice and strain into
chilled old-fashioned glass.*

☐ SILVER LINING

1½ oz. straight rye whiskey
¾ oz. fresh lemon juice
¾ oz. vanilla liqueur
1 egg white
Soda water

*Shake first four ingredients
without ice. Then shake with
ice and strain into ice-filled
Collins glass. Top with soda
water.*

☐ SLEEPING MONK

Created by KENTA GOTA,
New York, NY

2 oz. Chamomile Tea–infused
   Scotch (recipe follows)
¼ oz. yellow Chartreuse
¼ oz. Bénédictine
¾ oz. fresh lemon juice
¾ oz. Honey Syrup (page 21)
1 dash orange bitters
Garnish: Apple slice

*Shake with ice and strain
into chilled cocktail glass.
Garnish with apple slice.*

**CHAMOMILE TEA–INFUSED
SCOTCH**

*Combine 2 chamomile tea
bags with 8 oz. Scotch in
a bowl and let stand for 30
minutes. Strain into a jar or
bottle, pressing hard on the tea
bags. Cover, and store in the
refrigerator for up to 2 weeks.*

☐ THE SLOPE

2 oz. straight rye whiskey
¾ oz. Punt e Mes
½ oz. apricot liqueur
2 dashes Angostura bitters
Garnish: Maraschino cherry

*Stir with ice and strain into
chilled cocktail glass. Garnish
with cherry.*

☐ SOUTHERN BELLE

1½ oz. Tennessee bourbon
    whiskey
½ oz. triple sec
6 oz. pineapple juice
2 oz. fresh orange juice
1 splash grenadine

*Combine whiskey, triple sec,
and juices in ice-filled Collins
glass. Top with grenadine and
stir once.*

☐ SOUTHERN PEACH

¼ oz. grenadine
1½ oz. bourbon whiskey
2 oz. fresh orange juice
1 oz. simple syrup
1 oz. fresh lemon juice
1 oz. peach schnapps
Garnish: Peach slice

*Fill hurricane or parfait glass
with ice. Pour grenadine
over ice; add bourbon. Shake
remaining ingredients with
ice and pour slowly into glass.
Garnish with peach.*

☐ STILETTO

1½ oz. bourbon whiskey
1 oz. fresh lemon juice
½ oz. amaretto

*Pour into ice-filled
old-fashioned glass and stir.*

☐ STONE FENCE

2 oz. blended Scotch whisky
2 dashes Angostura bitters
Apple cider

*Pour Scotch and bitters into
ice-filled highball glass. Fill
with cider. Stir.*

☐ STRAIGHT RYE WITCH

2 oz. straight rye whiskey
¼ oz. Strega
¼ oz. palo cortado sherry
¼ oz. simple syrup
2 dashes orange bitters
Garnish: Orange twist

*Stir with ice and strain into
chilled cocktail glass. Add
orange twist.*

☐ T-BIRD

1½ oz Canadian whisky
¾ oz. amaretto
2 oz. pineapple juice
1 oz. fresh orange juice
2 dashes grenadine
Garnish: Orange half-wheel,
    maraschino cherry

*Shake with ice and strain
into ice-filled highball glass.
Garnish with orange and
cherry. Serve with straw.*

🍶 THOROUGHBRED COOLER

1 oz. bourbon whiskey
1 oz. fresh orange juice
½ oz. fresh lemon juice
½ oz. simple syrup
Lemon-lime soda
1 dash grenadine
Garnish: Orange wedge

Pour first four ingredients over ice in highball glass. Fill with lemon-lime soda and stir. Add grenadine. Garnish with orange.

🍸 TIPPERARY COCKTAIL

¾ oz. Irish whiskey
¾ oz. green Chartreuse
¾ oz. sweet vermouth

Stir with ice and strain into chilled cocktail glass.

🍸 TWIN HILLS

1½ oz. bourbon whiskey
¼ oz. Bénédictine
½ oz. fresh lemon juice
½ oz. fresh lime juice
¾ oz. simple syrup
Garnish: Lemon wheel, lime wheel

Shake with ice and strain into chilled cocktail glass. Garnish with lemon and lime.

🍸 VERRAZANO

1 splash Campari
2 oz. bourbon whiskey
1 oz. sweet vermouth
¼ oz. apricot liqueur
Garnish: Orange twist

Swirl Campari in chilled cocktail glass to coat inside; discard excess Campari. Stir remaining ingredients with ice and strain into glass. Add orange twist.

🍸 VIEUX CARRÉ

Another contender in the Most Beloved New Orleans Cocktail roundup, this has been around since 1938, when it was introduced by Walter Bergeron, head bartender at the Hotel Monteleone.

¾ oz. straight rye whiskey
¾ oz. brandy
¾ oz. sweet vermouth
¼ oz. Bénédictine
1 dash Peychaud's bitters
1 dash Angostura bitters

Pour into ice-filled old-fashioned glass and stir.

⟁ WALTERS

1½ oz. blended Scotch whisky
½ oz. fresh orange juice
½ oz. fresh lemon juice

Shake with ice and strain into chilled cocktail glass.

⟁ WARD EIGHT

Of the many stories telling how this drink got its name, the one that sticks is its invention at Locke-Ober restaurant to honor a local politician from Boston's Eighth Ward. The clincher? The honoree became a teetotaler.

2 oz. rye whiskey
¾ oz. fresh lemon juice
½ oz. simple syrup
¼ oz. grenadine
Garnish: Orange and lemon
    half-wheels, maraschino
    cherry

Shake with ice and strain into red-wine glass filled with ice. Garnish with orange, lemon, and cherry. Serve with straws.

⬚ WASHINGTON APPLE

2 oz. Canadian whisky
2 oz. sour apple schnapps
2 oz. cranberry juice

Pour into ice-filled highball glass and stir.

⟁ THE WELSHMAN

Created by JONATHAN POGASH, New York, NY

2 oz. Penderyn single-malt
    Welsh whisky
¾ oz. sweet vermouth
1 dash Angostura bitters
1 dash orange bitters
Garnish: Orange twist

Stir with ice and strain into chilled cocktail glass. Add orange twist.

⟁ THE WHIMSY

Created by TED HENWOOD, New York, NY

For glass: Lemon wedge,
    orange volcanic sea salt
2 oz. bourbon whiskey
1 oz. fresh lemon juice
½ oz. agave nectar
1 tsp. Fernet-Branca

Rim a chilled cocktail glass with lemon and salt. Shake remaining ingredients with ice and strain into glass.

▯ WHISKEY ORANGE

1½ oz. rye or bourbon whiskey
2 oz. fresh orange juice
½ oz. simple syrup
½ tsp. anisette
Garnish: Orange half-wheel,
    lemon half-wheel

*Shake with ice and strain
into ice-filled highball glass.
Garnish with orange and
lemon.*

▯ WHISKEY SQUIRT

1½ oz. rye or bourbon whiskey
¼ oz. simple syrup
¼ oz. grenadine
Soda water
Garnish: Pineapple cubes,
    whole strawberries

*Shake first three ingredients
with ice and strain into
chilled highball glass. Add
ice and fill with soda water.
Garnish with pineapple and
strawberries.*

▯ WHISPERS-OF-THE-FROST COCKTAIL

¾ oz. bourbon whiskey
¾ oz. cream sherry
¾ oz. tawny port
¼ oz. simple syrup
Garnish: Orange and lemon
    half-wheels

*Stir with ice and strain into
chilled cocktail glass. Garnish
with orange and lemon.*

▯ WHOA, NELLIE!

1½ oz. straight rye whiskey
¾ oz. dark rum
½ oz. fresh lemon juice
½ oz. fresh grapefruit juice
½ oz. simple syrup
Garnish: Grapefruit twist

*Shake with ice and strain
into chilled cocktail glass.
Add grapefruit twist.*

☐ WOODWARD COCKTAIL

1½ oz. blended Scotch whisky
½ oz. dry vermouth
½ oz. fresh grapefruit juice

Shake with ice and strain into chilled cocktail glass.

☐ WOOLWORTH

2 oz. blended Scotch whisky
1 oz. palo cortado or fino sherry
½ oz. Bénédictine
2 dashes orange bitters

Stir with ice and strain into chilled cocktail glass.

CORDIALS AND LIQUEURS

ORDIALS AND LIQUEURS have been around since the Middle Ages, when they were concocted in European monasteries primarily for medicinal purposes. The historical distinction between cordials (fruit based) and liqueurs (herb based) doesn't really exist anymore, and the word "liqueur" is typically used for both. Crèmes, another common designation, are liqueurs with an especially high sugar content, which gives them a creamy texture. In Europe, liqueurs have long been savored as after-dinner drinks, while Americans have tended to enjoy them mixed with other ingredients.

Liqueurs by today's definition are flavored spirits with between 2.5 percent and 40 percent sweetener, which can come from just about anything, including fruits, herbs, roots, spices, and nuts. The alcohol base used to make liqueurs is produced from grain, grapes, other fruits, or vegetables, and must be flavored in one of four ways: distillation, infusion, maceration, or percolation.

Do not confuse liqueur with fruit brandy, which is distilled from a mash of the fruit itself. Some producers mislabel their liqueurs as brandies, such as "blackberry brandy," when they are technically cordials (or liqueurs). Artificial colors and flavors are permitted in liqueurs. Colorless double-distilled fruit brandy is called eau-de-vie.

The best liqueurs come from all over the globe, and many have closely guarded secret recipes and processes, as well as their own proprietary brand names. Some of the most popular include crème de cacao (cacao and vanilla beans); curaçao (made from dried citrus peel); sambuca (licorice-flavored, made from the elderberry bush's white flowers); sloe gin (sloe berries, from the blackthorn bush); and triple sec (orange-flavored, and similar to curaçao).

♈ ABSINTHE SPECIAL COCKTAIL

1½ oz. absinthe
¼ oz. simple syrup
1 dash orange bitters

Shake with ice and strain into chilled cocktail glass.

♈ AMARETTO AND CREAM

1½ oz. amaretto
1½ oz. half-and-half

Shake with ice and strain into chilled cocktail glass.

▢ AMARETTO ROSE

1½ oz. amaretto
½ oz. fresh lemon juice
½ oz. simple syrup
Soda water

Pour first three ingredients into ice-filled Collins glass and fill with soda water. Stir.

♀ AMARETTO SOUR

1½ oz. amaretto
¾ oz. fresh lemon juice
½ oz. simple syrup
Garnish: Orange half-wheel

Shake with ice and strain into chilled sour glass. Garnish with orange.

⏺ AMARETTO STINGER

1½ oz. amaretto
¾ oz. white crème de menthe

*Shake with ice and strain
into chilled cocktail glass.*

⏺ APPLE PIE

3 oz. apple schnapps
1 splash cinnamon schnapps
Garnish: Apple slice, ground
  cinnamon

*Pour into ice-filled old-
fashioned glass. Garnish with
apple and top with cinnamon.*

⏺ ARISE MY LOVE

1 tsp. green crème de menthe
Chilled Champagne

*Pour crème de menthe into
champagne flute. Fill with
Champagne.*

⏺ BANSHEE

1 oz. crème de banana
½ oz. white crème de cacao
½ oz. half-and-half

*Shake with ice and strain
into chilled cocktail glass.*

⏺ BITTER MAI TAI

Created by JEREMY OERTEL,
New York, NY

1½ oz. Campari
¾ oz. dark rum
½ oz. orange curaçao
1 oz. fresh lime juice
¾ oz. orgeat syrup
Garnish: Fresh mint sprig

*Shake with ice and strain
into crushed ice–filled old-
fashioned glass. Garnish
with mint.*

⏺ BLACKJACK

1 oz. cherry-flavored
  brandy
½ oz. brandy
1 oz. cold brewed coffee

*Shake with ice and strain
into ice-filled old-fashioned
glass.*

⏺ BLACKTHORN

1½ oz. sloe gin
1 oz. sweet vermouth
Garnish: Lemon twist

*Stir with ice and strain into
chilled cocktail glass. Add
lemon twist.*

BOCCE BALL

1½ oz. amaretto
1½ oz. fresh orange juice
2 oz. soda water

Pour into ice-filled highball glass and stir gently.

BOSTON ICED COFFEE

6 oz. cold brewed coffee
1 oz. white crème de menthe
1 oz. white crème de cacao
1 oz. brandy
Garnish: Lemon twist

Pour into ice-filled highball glass and stir. Add lemon twist.

BURNING SUN

1½ oz. strawberry schnapps
4 oz. pineapple juice
Garnish: Whole strawberry

Pour into ice-filled highball glass and stir. Garnish with strawberry.

BUSHWHACKER

½ oz. coffee liqueur
½ oz. amaretto
½ oz. light rum
½ oz. Irish cream liqueur
2 oz. half-and-half

Shake with ice. Pour into ice-filled old-fashioned glass.

CAFÉ CABANA

1 oz. coffee liqueur
Soda water
Garnish: Lime wedge

Pour liqueur into ice-filled Collins glass. Fill with soda water and stir. Garnish with lime.

CHARTREUSE SWIZZLE

Created by MARCOVALDO DIONYSOS, San Francisco, CA

1½ oz. green Chartreuse
1 oz. pineapple juice
¾ oz. fresh lime juice
½ oz. Taylor's Velvet Falernum
Garnish: Freshly grated nutmeg, fresh mint sprig

Pour ingredients into Collins glass and add crushed ice. Swizzle with bar spoon until glass is frosted. Top with nutmeg and garnish with mint.

CHOCOLATE-COVERED STRAWBERRY

1 oz. strawberry schnapps
¼ oz. white crème de cacao
½ oz. heavy cream or half-and-half
Garnish: Whole strawberry

Stir with ice and strain into ice-filled red-wine glass. Garnish with strawberry.

COFFEE NUDGE

½ oz. brandy
½ oz. coffee liqueur
½ oz. dark crème de cacao
4½ oz. hot brewed coffee
Garnish: Whipped cream, chocolate shavings

Pour first three ingredients into preheated Irish coffee glass. Fill with coffee and stir. Top with whipped cream and chocolate.

CRÈME DE MENTHE FRAPPÉ

2 oz. green crème de menthe

Fill cocktail glass up to brim with shaved ice. Add crème de menthe. Serve with two short straws.

DEPTH CHARGE

Add a shot of any flavor of schnapps to a mug of cold beer.

DIANA COCKTAIL

1½ oz. white crème de menthe
1½ oz. brandy

Fill cocktail glass with ice. Add crème de menthe, then float (see page 12) brandy on top.

FRENCH CONNECTION

1½ oz. cognac
¾ oz. amaretto

Pour into ice-filled old-fashioned glass, but do not stir.

☐ FRENCH FANTASY

1 oz. black raspberry liqueur
1 oz. Mandarine Napoléon
2 oz. cranberry juice
2 oz. fresh orange juice
Garnish: Orange half-wheel,
    maraschino cherry

*Pour into ice-filled highball
glass and stir. Garnish with
orange and cherry.*

☐ FUZZY NAVEL

2 oz. 48-proof peach
    schnapps
3 oz. fresh orange juice
Garnish: Orange half-wheel

*Pour schnapps and
orange juice into ice-filled
highball glass. Garnish
with orange.*

☐ GOLDEN DREAM

1 oz. Galliano
½ oz. triple sec
½ oz. fresh orange juice
½ oz. half-and-half

*Shake with ice and strain
into chilled cocktail glass.*

☐ GOOBER

1 oz. vodka
1 oz. black raspberry
    liqueur
1 oz. melon liqueur
¾ oz. triple sec
½ oz. grenadine
2 oz. fresh orange juice
2 oz. pineapple juice
Garnish: Orange wheel,
    maraschino cherry

*Shake with ice and strain
into ice-filled Collins
glass. Garnish with orange
and cherry. Serve with a
straw.*

☐ GRAPE SOUR

Created by CHARLES VEXENAT,
London, UK

10 white seedless grapes
1 oz. absinthe
1 oz. fresh lemon juice
2 dashes orange bitters
1 egg white
Garnish: Fennel seeds

*Muddle grapes in mixing glass.
Add remaining ingredients and
shake without ice. Add ice and
shake again. Double-strain into
chilled cocktail glass. Top with
fennel seeds.*

🍸 GRASSHOPPER

¾ oz. green crème de menthe
¾ oz. white crème de cacao
¾ oz. half-and-half

Shake with ice and strain into chilled cocktail glass.

🍹 HEAT WAVE

1¼ oz. coconut-flavored rum
½ oz. peach schnapps
3 oz. pineapple juice
3 oz. fresh orange juice
½ oz. grenadine
Garnish: Peach slice

Shake first four ingredients with ice and strain into ice-filled hurricane glass. Top with grenadine. Garnish with peach.

🍸 ITALIAN SOMBRERO

1½ oz. amaretto
3 oz. half-and-half

Shake well with ice. Strain, with or without ice, into chilled champagne flute.

🥃 ITALIAN SURFER

1 oz. amaretto
1 oz. brandy
3 oz. pineapple juice
Garnish: Pineapple spear, maraschino cherry

Pour amaretto and brandy into ice-filled Collins glass. Add pineapple juice and stir. Garnish with pineapple and cherry.

🥃 LIMONCELLO SUNRISE

1 oz. limoncello
3 oz. fresh orange juice
1 dash grenadine

Shake limoncello and orange juice with ice and strain into chilled old-fashioned glass. Top with grenadine.

♈ KARMA SUTRA

Created by JONATHAN POGASH,
New York, NY

1 oz. Darjeeling Tea–Infused
    Amaro (recipe follows)
1 oz. Plymouth gin
1 tsp. orange marmalade
¼ oz. fresh orange juice
Garnish: Freshly grated nutmeg

*Shake with ice and strain
through wire sieve into chilled
cocktail glass.*

DARJEELING TEA–INFUSED
AMARO

*Combine 8 oz. amaro (such
as Ramazzotti or Averna)
and 1 Darjeeling tea bag in
bowl and let stand at room
temperature for 45 minutes.
Strain into covered jar, pressing hard on tea bag. Store
in refrigerator for up to
2 months.*

♉ LOVER'S KISS

½ oz. amaretto
½ oz. cherry-flavored brandy
½ oz. dark crème de cacao
1 oz. half-and-half
Garnish: Whipped cream,
    chocolate shavings,
    maraschino cherry

*Shake with ice and pour with
ice into parfait glass. Top
with whipped cream, sprinkle
with chocolate shavings, and
garnish with cherry.*

♊ MARMALADE

1½ oz. triple sec
Tonic water
Garnish: Orange half-wheel

*Pour triple sec into ice-filled
highball glass. Fill with tonic
water. Garnish with orange.*

♈ MELON COOLER

¾ oz. melon liqueur
½ oz. peach schnapps
½ oz. raspberry schnapps
1 oz. pineapple juice
Garnish: Lime wheel,
    maraschino cherry

*Shake with ice and pour into
chilled cocktail glass. Garnish
with lime and cherry.*

� MOULIN ROUGE

1½ oz. sloe gin
¾ oz. sweet vermouth
1 dash Angostura bitters

Stir with ice and strain into chilled cocktail glass.

� THE OSCAR WILDE

Created by JONATHAN POGASH, New York, NY

1¼ oz. absinthe
¾ oz. fresh lemon juice
¾ oz. simple syrup
1 egg white
1 oz. chilled Champagne
Garnish: Freshly grated
   nutmeg, orange twist

Shake first four ingredients without ice. Add ice and shake again. Strain into white-wine glass. Top with Champagne. Sprinkle with nutmeg and add orange twist.

▢ PEACH MELBA

1 oz. peach schnapps
½ oz. black raspberry liqueur
3 oz. half-and-half
Garnish: Peach slice

Shake with ice. Strain into ice-filled old-fashioned glass. Garnish with peach. Serve with short straw.

� PEPPERMINT STICK

1 oz. peppermint schnapps
1½ oz. white crème de cacao
1 oz. half-and-half

Shake with ice and strain into chilled cocktail glass.

▢ PIMM'S CUP

James Pimm, a London restaurateur of the early nineteenth century, originally had six different flavors of his Pimm's Cup liqueurs, but only No. 1, based on gin, is still easily found.

2 oz. Pimm's No. 1
3 oz. ginger ale or lemon-lime
   soda
Garnish: Cucumber slices
   and/or lemon wheel

Pour Pimm's into ice-filled Collins glass. Top with chilled ginger ale. Garnish with cucumbers and/or lemon.

� PINK SQUIRREL

1 oz. crème de noyaux
½ oz. white crème de cacao
½ oz. half-and-half

Shake with ice and strain into chilled cocktail glass.

🍸 POUSSE-CAFÉ

See the detailed instructions on page 12 on how to float the liqueur layers on each other for a striped effect.

½ oz. grenadine
½ oz. yellow Chartreuse
½ oz. crème de cassis
½ oz. white crème de menthe
½ oz. green Chartreuse
½ oz. brandy

In order given, carefully float liquors over back of barspoon into pousse-café glass, so that each ingredient layers on preceding one.

🥃 PRIZEFIGHTER

Created by NICHOLAS JARRETT, New York, NY

8–10 fresh mint leaves
2–3 lemon wedges
¾ oz. simple syrup
1 oz. Fernet-Branca
1 oz. sweet vermouth
¼ oz. fresh lemon juice
Garnish: 2 fresh mint sprigs

Muddle mint leaves, lemon, and syrup in mixing glass. Add remaining ingredients with ice and shake. Double-strain into crushed ice-filled old-fashioned glass. Garnish with mint.

🥃 QUAALUDE

1 oz. vodka
1 oz. hazelnut liqueur
1 oz. coffee liqueur
1 splash milk

Shake with ice and pour into ice-filled old-fashioned glass.

🍸 RITZ FIZZ

1 dash fresh lemon juice
1 dash blue curaçao
1 dash amaretto
Chilled Champagne
Garnish: Lemon twist

Add first three ingredients to chilled champagne flute. Fill with Champagne and stir briefly. Add lemon twist.

🥃 ROCKY MOUNTAIN COOLER

1½ oz. peach schnapps
4 oz. pineapple juice
2 oz. lemon-lime soda

Pour into ice-filled Collins glass and stir.

🍸 ST. PATRICK'S DAY

¼ oz. green crème de menthe
¾ oz. green Chartreuse
¾ oz. Irish whiskey
1 dash Angostura bitters

Stir with ice and strain into chilled cocktail glass.

♗ SAMBUCA CON MOSCA

2 oz. sambuca
3 coffee beans

Pour sambuca into snifter and float coffee beans on top.

♓ SAN FRANCISCO COCKTAIL

¾ oz. sloe gin
¾ oz. sweet vermouth
¾ oz. dry vermouth
1 dash Angostura bitters
1 dash orange bitters
Garnish: Maraschino cherry

Shake with ice and strain into chilled cocktail glass. Garnish with cherry.

♗ SANTINI'S POUSSE-CAFÉ

½ oz. brandy
½ oz. maraschino liqueur
½ oz. triple sec
½ oz. gold rum

Pour ingredients, in order given, into pousse-café glass. Ingredients should blend, and not layer.

♓ SHANGRI-LITA

Created by BLAIR FRODELIUS, Rochester, NY

1½ oz. pomegranate liqueur
1 oz. fresh orange juice
¾ oz. fresh lime juice
1 tsp. simple syrup
2 dashes hot red pepper sauce
½ oz. soda water

Shake first five ingredients with ice. Strain into chilled cocktail glass. Top with soda water and stir briefly.

♓ SHEER ELEGANCE

1½ oz. amaretto
1½ oz. black raspberry liqueur
½ oz. vodka

Shake with ice and strain into chilled cocktail glass.

♒ SLOE DRIVER

1½ oz. sloe gin
5 oz. fresh orange juice

Pour ingredients into ice-filled highball glass and stir.

♓ SLOE GIN COCKTAIL

2 oz. sloe gin
¼ oz. dry vermouth
1 dash orange bitters

Stir with ice and strain into chilled cocktail glass.

☐ SLOE GIN COLLINS

2 oz. sloe gin
1 oz. fresh lemon juice
Soda water
Garnish: Lemon and orange
   half-wheels, maraschino
   cherry

*Shake sloe gin and lemon
juice with ice and strain into
ice-filled Collins glass. Fill
with soda water and stir.
Garnish with lemon, orange,
and cherry. Serve with
straws.*

☐ SLOE GIN FIZZ

2 oz. sloe gin
1 oz. fresh lemon juice
½ oz. simple syrup
Soda water
Garnish: Lemon wheel

*Pour sloe gin, lemon juice,
and syrup into highball glass.
Add ice, fill with soda water,
and stir. Garnish with lemon.*

☐ SLOE GIN RICKEY

1 lime
2 oz. sloe gin
Soda water

*Squeeze ½ oz. lime juice
from lime; reserve 1 spent
rind. Pour lime juice and sloe
gin into ice-filled highball
glass. Fill with soda water,
add lime rind, and stir.*

☐ THE SLOE STARTER

Created by RYAN ALVA
LAYMAN, Denver, CO

2 oz. sloe gin
¾ oz. green Chartreuse
¾ oz. fresh lemon juice
3 dashes Peychaud's bitters
1 splash soda water
Garnish: Lemon wheel

*Shake first four ingredients
with ice. Strain into ice-filled
old fashioned glass. Top with
soda water. Garnish with
lemon.*

◻ SOMETHING DIFFERENT

1 oz. peach schnapps
1 oz. amaretto
2 oz. pineapple juice
2 oz. cranberry juice

Shake with ice and pour into ice-filled highball glass.

◻ STRAWBERRY FIELDS FOREVER

2 oz. strawberry schnapps
½ oz. brandy
Soda water
Garnish: Whole strawberry

Pour schnapps and brandy into ice-filled highball glass. Fill with soda water. Garnish with strawberry.

◻ STRAWBERRY SUNRISE

2 oz. strawberry schnapps
½ oz. grenadine
3 oz. fresh orange juice
Garnish: Whole strawberry

Pour schnapps and grenadine into ice-filled highball glass. Fill with orange juice. Garnish with strawberry.

◻ SUN KISS

2 oz. amaretto
4 oz. fresh orange juice
Garnish: Lime wedge

Pour amaretto into ice-filled Collins glass. Add orange juice. Garnish with lime.

◻ TOASTED ALMOND

1½ oz. coffee liqueur
1 oz. amaretto
1½ oz. half-and-half or milk

Shake with ice and strain into ice-filled old-fashioned glass.

▽ TROPICAL COCKTAIL

¾ oz. white crème de cacao
¾ oz. maraschino liqueur
¾ oz. dry vermouth
1 dash Angostura bitters

Stir with ice and strain into chilled cocktail glass.

◻ TWIN PEACH

2 oz. peach schnapps
4 oz. cranberry juice
Garnish: Peach slice or orange half-wheel

Pour schnapps into ice-filled highball glass, fill with cranberry juice, and stir. Garnish with peach or orange.

▯ WATERMELON

1 oz. strawberry liqueur
1 oz. vodka
½ oz. simple syrup
½ oz. fresh lemon juice
1 oz. fresh orange juice
Garnish: Orange half-wheel

Pour into ice-filled Collins glass and stir. Garnish with orange. Serve with a straw.

♟ ZWACKBERRY FLIP

Created by ROBERT E. GONZALES, San Francisco, CA

1½ oz. Zwack Unicum (Hungarian herbal liqueur)
¾ oz. blackberry puree
½ oz. espresso liqueur, such as Stirrings
1 tsp. allspice liqueur (pimento dram)
2 dashes vanilla extract
1 egg
Garnish: Chocolate shavings

Shake without ice. Add ice and shake again. Double-strain into chilled cocktail glass. Top with chocolate.

SHOOTERS

WHEN THIS BOOK debuted 75 years ago, a "shot" was 2 ounces of straight whiskey knocked back in a single gulp—just like the scenes in those dusty old Westerns. Today, shots are called shooters, slammers, even tooters, usually preceded by fanciful names—B-52, Sex on the Beach, Kamikaze—and concocted with virtually any spirit and mixer handy in a well-stocked bar.

The universal appeal of shooters is partly attributable to the fact that many are fairly low in alcohol content. Frequently made with several juices as well as lower-proof liqueurs, the small size of the shooter limits the amount of spirit contained in a single drink. Some, like the Rattlesnake, are skillfully layered works of art, similar to a Pousse-Café. Others, like the Bloody Caesar, incorporate surprising ingredients such as clams or oysters.

The granddaddy of all shooters—a lick of salt, washed down with a shot of straight tequila, followed by a suck on a wedge of lime and the obligatory shudder—is not only still alive and kicking, it has inspired similar drinks like the Lemon Drop Shot and the Cordless Screwdriver.

The common denominator for the drinks on the following pages is that they were created with a sense of humor and wit, which is how they should be enjoyed. Once you get the hang of making them, you can experiment with bumping up the recipes to make large batches for parties. You might also feel inspired to create your own, which is how every one of these recipes came to fruition. Imagination and creativity can create a great little drink.

AFFAIR

½ oz. strawberry schnapps
½ oz. cranberry juice
½ oz. fresh orange juice

Stir with ice and strain into chilled cordial glass.

ANGEL'S KISS

¼ oz. white crème de cacao
¼ oz. sloe gin
¼ oz. brandy
¼ oz. half-and-half

Float carefully (see page 12), in order given, over back of barspoon into chilled cordial glass, so that each ingredient layers on preceding one.

ANGEL'S TIP

¾ oz. white crème de cacao
¾ oz. half-and-half
Garnish: Maraschino cherry on long skewer

Pour crème de cacao into cordial glass. Carefully float cream (see page 12) over back of barspoon on top. Place skewered cherry over mouth of glass.

ANGEL'S WING

½ oz. white crème de cacao
½ oz. brandy
½ oz. half-and-half

Float carefully (see page 12), in order given, over back of barspoon into chilled cordial glass, so that each ingredient layers on preceding one.

B-52

½ oz. coffee liqueur
½ oz. Irish cream liqueur
½ oz. Mandarine Napoléon

Float carefully (see page 12), in order given, over back of barspoon into chilled shot glass, so that each ingredient layers on preceding one.

BANANA BOMBER

1 oz. banana-flavored
　schnapps, preferably
　99 Bananas
¾ oz. triple sec
1 splash grenadine

Shake with ice and strain into chilled shot glass.

BANANA SLIP

¾ oz. crème de banana
¾ oz. Irish cream liqueur

Pour crème de banana into cordial glass. Carefully float Irish cream liqueur (see page 12) over back of barspoon on top.

BETWEEN-THE-SHEETS

½ oz. fresh lemon juice
¼ oz. brandy
¼ oz. triple sec
¼ oz. light rum

Shake with ice and strain into chilled shot glass.

BLOODY CAESAR SHOOTER

1 littleneck clam, shucked
1 oz. vodka
1½ oz. tomato juice
2 drops hot red pepper sauce
2 drops Worcestershire sauce
1 dash prepared horseradish
Garnish: Celery salt, lime
　wedge

Put clam in the bottom of chilled shot glass. Shake vodka, tomato juice, sauces, and horseradish with ice, and strain into glass. Top with celery salt and garnish with lime.

BLUE MARLIN

¾ oz. light rum
¾ oz. blue curaçao
¼ oz. fresh lime juice

Stir with ice and strain into chilled shot glass.

▢ BONZAI PIPELINE

1 oz. tropical fruit schnapps
½ oz. vodka

Stir with ice and strain into chilled shot glass.

▢ BUZZARD'S BREATH

½ oz. amaretto
½ oz. peppermint schnapps
½ oz. coffee liqueur

Stir with ice and strain into chilled shot glass.

♀ CAPRI

¾ oz. white crème de cacao
¾ oz. crème de banana
¾ oz. half-and-half

Shake with ice and strain into chilled cordial glass.

▢ CARAMEL APPLE

1 oz. butterscotch schnapps
½ oz. apple-flavored schnapps, preferably 99 Apples

Shake with ice and strain into chilled shot glass.

♀ C.C. KAZI

¾ oz. blanco tequila
¾ oz. cranberry juice
¼ oz. fresh lime juice

Shake with ice and strain into chilled cordial glass.

▢ CORDLESS SCREWDRIVER

1¾ oz. vodka
Orange wedge
Sugar

Shake vodka with ice and strain into shot glass. Dip orange wedge in sugar. Shoot the vodka and immediately take a draw on the orange.

▢ COSMOS

1½ oz. vodka
½ oz. fresh lime juice

Shake with ice and strain into chilled shot glass.

♀ FIFTH AVENUE

½ oz. dark crème de cacao
½ oz. apricot-flavored brandy
½ oz. half-and-half

Float carefully (see page 12), in order given, over back of barspoon into chilled cordial glass, so that each ingredient layers on preceding one.

FLYING GRASSHOPPER

¾ oz. green crème de menthe
½ oz. white crème de cacao
½ oz. vodka

Stir with ice and strain into chilled cordial glass.

4TH OF JULY TOOTER

½ oz. grenadine
½ oz. vodka
½ oz. blue curaçao

Float carefully (see page 12), in order given, over back of barspoon into chilled cordial or shot glass, so that each ingredient layers on preceding one.

FOXY LADY

¾ oz. amaretto
¼ oz. dark crème de cacao
¾ oz. heavy cream

Shake with ice and strain into chilled cordial glass.

GREEN DEMON

½ oz. vodka
½ oz. light rum
½ oz. melon liqueur
½ oz. lemonade

Shake with ice and strain into chilled shot glass.

INTERNATIONAL INCIDENT

¼ oz. vodka
¼ oz. coffee liqueur
¼ oz. amaretto
¼ oz. hazelnut liqueur
½ oz. Irish cream liqueur

Shake with ice and strain into chilled shot glass.

IRISH CHARLIE

¾ oz. Irish cream liqueur
¾ oz. white crème de menthe

Shake with ice and strain into chilled cordial glass.

♀ IRISH FLAG

½ oz. green crème
   de menthe
½ oz. Irish cream liqueur
½ oz. Mandarine Napoléon

Float carefully (see page 12), in order given, over back of barspoon into chilled cordial glass, so that each ingredient layers on preceding one.

▢ JOHNNY ON THE BEACH

¾ oz. vodka
¼ oz. melon liqueur
¼ oz. black raspberry
   liqueur
¼ oz. pineapple juice
¼ oz. fresh orange juice
¼ oz. fresh grapefruit juice
¼ oz. cranberry juice

Shake with ice and strain into chilled shot glass.

▢ KAMIKAZE

½ oz. vodka
½ oz. triple sec
½ oz. fresh lime juice

Shake with ice and strain into chilled shot glass.

▢ LEMON DROP SHOT

1½ oz. vodka
Lemon wedge
Sugar

Stir vodka with ice. Strain into chilled shot glass. Dip lemon wedge in sugar. Shoot the vodka and immediately take a draw on the lemon.

♀ MELON BALL

½ oz. melon liqueur
½ oz. vodka
½ oz. pineapple juice

Shake with ice and strain into chilled cordial glass.

♀ MONKEY SHINE SHOOTER

½ oz. bourbon liqueur
½ oz. crème de banana
½ oz. Irish cream liqueur

Shake with ice and strain into chilled cordial glass.

▢ NUTTY PROFESSOR

½ oz. Mandarine Napoléon
½ oz. hazelnut liqueur
½ oz. Irish cream liqueur

Shake and strain into shot glass.

♀ PARISIAN BLONDE

½ oz. light rum
½ oz. triple sec
½ oz. Jamaican rum

Shake with ice and strain into chilled cordial glass.

♀ PEACH BUNNY

½ oz. peach-flavored brandy
½ oz. white crème de cacao
½ oz. half-and-half

Shake with ice and strain into chilled cordial glass.

▢ PEACH TART

1 oz. peach schnapps
½ oz. fresh lime juice

Stir with ice and strain into chilled shot glass.

♀ PEPPERMINT PATTIE

¾ oz. white crème de cacao
¾ oz. white crème de menthe

Shake with ice and strain into chilled cordial glass.

▢ PICKLEBACK

Created at the Bushwick Country Club, Brooklyn, NY

1½ oz. Irish whiskey
1½ oz. cold dill pickle brine

Shoot whiskey, followed by pickle brine.

▢ PIGSKIN SHOT

½ oz. vodka
½ oz. melon liqueur
¼ oz. simple syrup
¼ oz. fresh lemon juice

Shake with ice and strain into chilled shot glass.

▢ PINEAPPLE-UPSIDE-DOWN CAKE

½ oz. Irish cream liqueur
½ oz. vodka
½ oz. butterscotch schnapps
½ oz. pineapple Juice

Shake and strain into shot glass.

♀ PORT AND STARBOARD

½ oz. grenadine
½ oz. green crème de menthe

Pour grenadine into pousse-café glass. Carefully float crème de menthe (see page 12) over back of barspoon on top of grenadine.

□ PURPLE HOOTER

1 oz. citrus-flavored vodka
½ oz. triple sec
¼ oz. black raspberry liqueur

*Shake with ice and strain
into chilled shot glass.*

♀ RATTLESNAKE

½ oz. coffee liqueur
½ oz. white crème de cacao
½ oz. Irish cream liqueur

*Float carefully (see page 12),
in order given, over back of
barspoon into chilled cordial
or shot glass, so that each
ingredient layers on preceding one.*

□ ROCKY MOUNTAIN

¾ oz. Tennessee sour mash
　　whiskey
¾ oz. amaretto
¼ oz. fresh lime juice

*Shake with ice and strain
into chilled shot glass.*

□ SAMBUCA SLIDE

½ oz. sambuca
½ oz. vodka
½ oz. half-and-half

*Stir with ice and strain into
chilled shot glass.*

♀ SCOOTER

½ oz. amaretto
½ oz. brandy
½ oz. half-and-half

*Shake with ice and strain
into chilled cordial glass.*

♀ SEX ON THE BEACH

¼ oz. black raspberry liqueur
¼ oz. melon liqueur
¼ oz. vodka
¼ oz. pineapple juice
¼ oz. cranberry juice

*Shake first four ingredients
with ice and strain into
chilled cordial or shot glass.
Top with cranberry juice.*

□ SILVER SPIDER

½ oz. vodka
½ oz. light rum
½ oz. triple sec
½ oz. white crème de menthe

*Stir with ice and strain into
chilled shot glass.*

♀ SOUR APPLE

¼ oz. vodka
¼ oz. apple liqueur
½ oz. melon liqueur
½ oz. lemon-lime soda

*Shake first three ingredients
with ice. Add lemon-lime
soda and strain into cordial
glass.*

♀ STALACTITE

1¼ oz. sambuca
¼ oz. Irish cream liqueur
¼ oz. black raspberry liqueur

*Pour sambuca into cor-
dial glass. Using back of
barspoon, float Irish cream
(see page 12) on top.
Carefully pour raspberry
liqueur, drop by drop, as top
layer. The raspberry liqueur
will pull the Irish cream
through the sambuca and
settle on the bottom.*

♀ STARS AND STRIPES

½ oz. grenadine
½ oz. heavy cream
½ oz. blue curaçao

*Float carefully (see page 12),
in order given, over back of
barspoon into chilled cordial
or shot glass, so that each
ingredient layers on
preceding one.*

♀ TERMINATOR

½ oz. coffee liqueur
½ oz. Irish cream liqueur
½ oz. sambuca
½ oz. Mandarine Napoléon
½ oz. vodka

*Float carefully (see page 12),
in order given, over back of
barspoon into chilled cordial
glass, so that each ingredient
layers on preceding one.*

▢ **TO THE MOON**

½ oz. coffee liqueur
½ oz. amaretto
½ oz. Irish cream liqueur
½ oz. 151-proof rum

Stir with ice and strain into chilled shot glass.

♀ **TRAFFIC LIGHT**

½ oz. crème de noyaux
½ oz. Galliano
½ oz. melon liqueur

Float carefully (see page 12), in order given, over back of barspoon into chilled cordial or shot glass, so that each ingredient layers on preceding one.

▢ **WOO WOO**

½ oz. peach schnapps
½ oz. vodka
1 oz. cranberry juice

Shake with ice and strain into chilled shot glass.

FROZEN DRINKS

FROZEN DRINKS ARE certainly perfect for summertime sipping, but they're also enjoyed year-round—much like ice cream. In fact, some are creamy concoctions made with ice cream. Others are tropical in nature, combining spirits or liqueurs with fruit juices, blended with ice. Served in tall, generous glasses and garnished with an assortment of seasonal fruits, they're best sipped slowly—to prevent brain-freeze—through a straw.

Ice cream–based frozen drinks, often mixed with liqueurs such as crème de cacao, amaretto, or Irish cream and topped with whipped cream, also make delicious dessert substitutes. Just imagine sipping a strawberry shortcake or a raspberry cheesecake after a meal, and you sort of get the picture.

The most important ingredient to consider when planning to mix up frozen drinks is ice—and more than you think you could possibly need. Depending on the size and shape of the ice you use, it will melt differently when mixed with warm mixers and alcohol, and it will blend differently, too. And speaking of blending, having an electric blender to pulverize the ice will allow you to make professional-style smoothies at home. Otherwise, you'll need a hand-cranked crusher—or a Lewis bag and a mallet.

You'll find plenty of delicious recipes for every season in this section. Next time it's 90 degrees in the shade, you and your blender can quickly dispatch a Tidal Wave or a Maui Breeze to cool down. And when you have a hankering for a creamy treat any time of year, you'll find a recipe that will put you on cloud nine.

APPLE COLADA

2 oz. apple schnapps
1 oz. cream of coconut
1 oz. half-and-half
Garnish: Apple slice,
   maraschino cherry

*Process ingredients with
1 c. crushed ice in blender
until smooth. Pour into
highball glass and serve with
straw. Garnish with apple
and cherry.*

APPLE GRANNY CRISP

1 oz. apple schnapps
½ oz. brandy
½ oz. Irish cream liqueur
2 scoops vanilla ice cream
Garnish: Graham cracker
   crumbs, whipped cream,
   ground cinnamon

*Process ingredients in blender
until smooth. Pour into
hurricane glass. Top with
crumbs, whipped cream, and
cinnamon.*

BANANA FOSTER

1½ oz. spiced rum
½ oz. banana liqueur
2 scoops vanilla ice cream
1 medium banana, sliced
Garnish: Ground cinnamon

*Process ingredients in blender
until smooth. Pour into large
snifter. Top with cinnamon.*

🍸 BAY CITY BOMBER

½ oz. vodka
½ oz. light rum
½ oz. blanco tequila
½ oz. gin
½ oz. triple sec
1 oz. fresh orange juice
1 oz. pineapple juice
1 oz. cranberry juice
½ oz. simple syrup
½ oz. fresh lemon juice
¼ oz. 151-proof rum
Garnish: Orange half-wheel,
    maraschino cherry

*Process all ingredients
except 151-proof rum with
1 c. crushed ice in blender
until smooth. Pour into
hurricane glass. Slowly pour
rum on top. Garnish with
orange and cherry.*

🍸 BEACH BUM'S COOLER

1¼ oz. Irish cream liqueur
¾ oz. light rum
¼ oz. banana liqueur
2 oz. pinapple juice
1 tsp. cream of coconut
¼ ripe banana, sliced
2 scoops vanilla ice cream
1 splash half-and-half
Garnish: Pineapple wedges,
    paper umbrella

*Process ingredients in
blender until smooth.
Pour into hurricane glass.
Garnish with pineapple
and umbrella.*

🍸 THE BIG CHILL

1½ oz. dark rum
1 oz. pineapple juice
1 oz. fresh orange juice
1 oz. cranberry juice
2 tsp. cream of coconut
Garnish: Pineapple wedge,
    maraschino cherry

*Process ingredients in
blender with 1 c. crushed
ice until smooth. Pour into
hurricane or pilsner glass.
Garnish with pineapple and
cherry.*

♀ THE BLIZZARD

1 oz. brandy
1 oz. Irish cream liqueur
1 oz. coffee liqueur
1 oz. light rum
2 scoops vanilla ice cream
1 splash half-and-half
Garnish: Freshly ground
    nutmeg

Process ingredients in blender until smooth. Pour into large snifter. Top with nutmeg.

♀ BLUE VELVET

1 oz. black raspberry liqueur
1 oz. melon liqueur
2 scoops vanilla ice cream
Garnish: Whipped cream, blue
    curaçao, maraschino cherry

Process liqueurs and ice cream in blender until smooth. Pour into hurricane glass. Top with whipped cream and drizzle with blue curaçao. Garnish with cherry.

♀ BLUSHIN' RUSSIAN

1 oz. coffee liqueur
¾ oz. vodka
1 scoop vanilla ice cream
4 fresh or frozen strawberries
Garnish: Chocolate-covered
    strawberry

Process ingredients in blender until smooth. Pour into hurricane glass. Garnish with strawberry.

♀ THE BRASS FIDDLE

1 oz. grenadine
2 oz. peach schnapps
¾ oz. Tennessee whiskey
2 oz. pineapple juice
1 oz. fresh orange juice
Garnish: Pineapple wedge,
    maraschino cherry

Swirl grenadine inside hurricane glass to coat inside. Do not discard excess. Process remaining ingredients in blender with 1 c. ice until smooth. Pour into glass. Garnish with pineapple and cherry.

CAVANAUGH'S SPECIAL

1 oz. coffee liqueur
1 oz. white crème de cacao
1 oz. amaretto
2 scoops vanilla ice cream
Garnish: Whipped cream, chocolate sprinkles

Pour coffee liqueur into snifter. Process next three ingredients with 1 c. crushed ice in blender until smooth. Pour over coffee liqueur. Top with whipped cream and chocolate sprinkles.

CHAMPAGNE CORNUCOPIA

1 oz. cranberry juice
2 scoops rainbow sherbet
1 oz. vodka
¾ oz. peach schnapps
1 oz. chilled Champagne or sparkling wine
Garnish: Orange half-wheel

Pour cranberry juice into oversized red-wine glass. Process sherbet, vodka, and schnapps in blender until smooth. Pour over cranberry juice to produce a swirl effect and pour Champagne on top. Garnish with orange.

CHERRY REPAIR KIT

Use imported cherries for the best flavor.

6 Italian preserved cherries or domestic maraschino cherries
½ oz. half-and-half
½ oz. white crème de cacao
½ oz. amaretto
½ oz. maraschino liqueur
Garnish: Italian preserved cherry in syrup or domestic maraschino cherry

Process 6 cherries with the remaining ingredients with 1 c. crushed ice in blender until smooth. Pour into hurricane glass. Garnish with remaining cherry and serve with straw.

CHILLY IRISHMAN

3 oz. cold brewed espresso
1 oz. Irish whiskey
½ oz. coffee liqueur
½ oz. Irish cream liqueur
1 scoop vanilla ice cream
1 dash simple syrup

Process all ingredients in blender with 1 c. crushed ice until smooth. Pour into hurricane glass.

☐ CHOCO-BANANA SMASH

1¼ oz. Irish cream liqueur
½ oz. half-and-half
½ scoop vanilla ice cream
½ ripe banana, sliced
½ tsp. vanilla extract
Garnish: Maraschino cherry
   and banana chunk on
   cocktail pick, whipped
   cream, chocolate sprinkles

*Process ingredients with
1 c. crushed ice in blender
until smooth. Pour into
hurricane glass. Garnish with
skewered cherry and banana,
and top with whipped cream
and chocolate sprinkles.*

☐ CITRUS BANANA FRAPPE

2 oz. dark rum
1 oz. soda water
1 oz. fresh orange juice
1 oz. milk
½ oz. fresh lime juice
½ ripe banana, sliced
1 tsp. light brown sugar

*Process all ingredients with
1 c. crushed ice in blender
until smooth. Pour into
Collins glass.*

☐ CLOUD 9

1 oz. Irish cream liqueur
1 oz. amaretto
½ oz. black raspberry
   liqueur
2 scoops vanilla ice cream
Garnish: Whipped cream,
   chocolate–peanut butter
   cup, notched

*Process ingredients in
blender until smooth.
Pour into hurricane glass.
Top with whipped cream,
and perch a chocolate–
peanut butter cup on
the rim.*

☐ COOL OPERATOR

1 oz. melon liqueur
½ oz. vodka
½ oz. light rum
4 oz. fresh grapefruit juice
2 oz. fresh orange juice
½ oz. fresh lime juice
Garnish: Melon wedge,
   maraschino cherry

*Process ingredients with
1 c. crushed ice in blender
until smooth. Pour into
hurricane glass. Garnish
with melon and cherry.*

CRANBERRY COOLER

1½ oz. bourbon whiskey
1½ oz. cranberry juice
½ oz. fresh lime juice
½ oz. simple syrup

Process all ingredients with 1 c. crushed ice in blender until smooth. Pour into hurricane glass.

CREAMY GIN SOUR

2 oz. gin
1 oz. triple sec
½ oz. fresh lime juice
½ oz. fresh lemon juice
1 oz. heavy cream
1 oz. simple syrup

Process all ingredients with 1 c. crushed ice in blender until smooth. Pour into large red-wine glass.

DEATH BY CHOCOLATE

1 oz. Irish cream liqueur
½ oz. vodka
½ oz. dark crème de cacao
1 scoop chocolate ice cream
Garnish: Whipped cream, chocolate curls

Process ingredients in blender with 1 c. crushed ice until smooth. Pour into hurricane glass. Garnish with whipped cream and chocolate curls. Serve with straw.

DEVIL'S TAIL

1½ oz. light rum
1 oz. vodka
1½ tsp. apricot-flavored brandy
1 tbsp. fresh lime juice
1½ tsp. grenadine
Garnish: Lime twist

Process ingredients in blender with 1 c. crushed ice until smooth. Pour into champagne flute. Add lime twist.

🍸 FROSTY NOGGIN

1½ oz. light rum
¾ oz. white crème de
    menthe, plus more for
    garnish
3 oz. prepared nonalcoholic
    eggnog
2 scoops vanilla ice
    cream
Garnish: Whipped cream,
    green crème de menthe,
    chocolate-mint cookie

*Process ingredients in blender
until smooth. Pour into
hurricane glass. Top with
whipped cream, drizzle
with green crème de menthe,
and garnish with cookie.*

🍸 FROZEN BERKELEY

1½ oz. light rum
½ oz. brandy
½ oz. passion fruit syrup
½ oz. fresh lemon juice

*Process ingredients in blender
with 1 c. crushed ice until
smooth. Pour into champagne
flute.*

🍸 FROZEN CAPPUCCINO

For glass: Orange wedge,
    superfine sugar, ground
    cinnamon
½ oz. Irish cream liqueur
½ oz. coffee liqueur
½ oz. hazelnut liqueur
1 scoop vanilla ice cream
1 dash half-and-half
Garnish: Cinnamon stick

*Rim hurricane glass with
orange and blend of sugar
and cinnamon. Process
remaining ingredients in
blender with 1 c. crushed ice
until smooth. Pour
into glass. Sprinkle with
cinnamon and serve
with a straw.*

FROZEN CITRON NEON

1½ oz. citrus-flavored vodka
1 oz. melon liqueur
½ oz. blue curaçao
½ oz. fresh lime juice
½ oz. simple syrup
½ oz. fresh lemon juice
Garnish: Lemon wheel,
  maraschino cherry

*Process ingredients in blender
with 1 c. crushed ice until
smooth. Pour into hurricane
glass. Garnish with lemon
and cherry.*

FROZEN DAIQUIRIS

CLASSIC FROZEN DAIQUIRI

1½ oz. light rum
1½ oz. fresh lime juice
½ oz. simple syrup
Garnish: Maraschino cherry

*Process ingredients in blender
with 1 c. crushed ice until
smooth. Pour into champagne
flute. Garnish with cherry.*

FROZEN BLUEBERRY DACQUIRI

⅓ c. fresh or frozen
  blueberries
1½ oz. light rum
1½ oz. fresh lemon juice
¾ oz. blueberry syrup
Garnish: 1 mint sprig

*Process ingredients in blender
with 1 c. crushed ice until
smooth. Pour into white wine
glass. Garnish with mint
sprig.*

FROZEN STRAWBERRY DACQUIRI

4 large strawberries, hulled
  and sliced
1½ oz. light rum
1½ oz. fresh lime juice
¾ oz. strawberry syrup
Garnish: 1 whole
  strawberry

*Process ingredients in blender
with 1 c. crushed ice until
smooth. Pour into white wine
glass. Garnish with whole
strawberry perched on rim
of glass.*

BANANA FROZEN DAIQUIRI

1½ oz. light rum
½ oz. triple sec
1½ oz. fresh lime juice
½ oz simple syrup
1 medium banana, sliced
Garnish: Maraschino cherry

Process ingredients in blender with 1 c. crushed ice until smooth. Pour into champagne flute. Garnish with cherry.

MINT FROZEN DAIQUIRI

2 oz. light rum
¾ oz. fresh lime juice
6 fresh mint leaves
¾ oz. simple syrup

Process all ingredients in blender with 1 c. crushed ice until smooth. Pour into old-fashioned glass.

PINEAPPLE FROZEN DAIQUIRI

2 oz. light rum
4 (2-inch) pineapple chunks
¾ oz. fresh lime juice
¾ oz. simple syrup

Process all ingredients in blender with 1 c. crushed ice until smooth. Pour into champagne flute.

FROZEN FUZZY

1 oz. peach schnapps
½ oz. triple sec
½ oz. fresh lime juice
½ oz. grenadine
1 splash lemon-lime soda
Garnish: Lime wedge

Process ingredients in blender with 1 c. crushed ice until smooth. Pour into champagne flute. Garnish with lime.

FROZEN MARGARITA

Vary the flavor of your Frozen Margarita by substituting fruit schnapps for the triple sec and adding ½ c. of the desired fruit. Depending on the fruit's sweetness, you may need to add simple syrup. Try berries in season, mango, or melon.

1½ oz. tequila
¾ oz. triple sec
1 oz. fresh lime juice
Garnish: Lemon or lime wheel

Process ingredients in blender with 1 c. crushed ice until smooth. Pour into cocktail glass. Garnish with lemon or lime.

☐ FROZEN MATADOR

1½ oz. blanco tequila
2 oz. pineapple juice
½ oz. fresh lime juice
Garnish: Pineapple wedge

*Process ingredients in blender
with 1 c. crushed ice until
smooth. Pour into old-
fashioned glass. Garnish with
pineapple.*

☐ GAELIC COFFEE

1½ oz. dark crème de cacao
¾ oz. Irish whiskey
¾ oz. Irish cream liqueur
2 oz. milk
1 tsp. instant coffee or 1 oz.
cold brewed espresso
Garnish: Whipped cream,
green crème de menthe

*Process ingredients in blender
with 1 c. crushed ice until
smooth. Pour into Irish coffee glass. Top with whipped
cream and drizzle with crème
de menthe.*

☐ GOLDEN CADILLAC

2 oz. white crème de cacao
1 oz. Galliano
1 oz. half-and-half

*Combine with ½ c. crushed
ice in blender on low speed
for 10 seconds. Pour into
chilled champagne flute.*

☐ GULF STREAM

For glass: Lime wedge,
superfine sugar
1 oz. blue curaçao
1 oz. Champagne or sparkling
wine
½ oz. light rum
½ oz. brandy
4 oz. lemonade
1 oz. fresh lime juice
Garnish: Whole strawberry

*Rim hurricane glass with
lime and sugar. Process
remaining ingredients in
blender with 1 c. crushed ice
until mooth. Pour into glass.
Garnish with strawberry.*

ICED COFFEE À L'ORANGE

2 oz. cold or tepid espresso
1½ oz. triple sec
2 scoops vanilla ice cream
Garnish: Orange wheel

Process ingredients in blender until smooth. Pour into hurricane glass. Garnish with orange wheel.

ICY RUMMED CACAO

1 oz. dark rum
1 oz. dark crème de cacao
2 scoops vanilla ice cream
Garnish: Chocolate shavings

Process ingredients in blender until smooth. Pour into highball glass. Top with chocolate shavings.

IRISH DREAM

¾ oz. dark crème de cacao
½ oz. hazelnut liqueur
½ oz. Irish cream liqueur
2 scoops vanilla ice cream
Garnish: Whipped cream,
    chocolate sprinkles

Process ingredients in blender with 1 c. crushed ice until smooth. Pour into pilsner glass. Top with whipped cream and chocolate sprinkles.

JACK'S JAM

½ oz. peach schnapps
½ oz. apple schnapps
½ oz. strawberry liqueur
¼ oz. banana liqueur
2 oz. fresh lemon juice
1 oz. fresh orange juice
1 tsp. superfine sugar
Garnish: Fresh mint sprig,
    maraschino cherry

Process ingredients in blender with 1 c. crushed ice until smooth. Pour into hurricane glass. Garnish with mint and cherry.

JAMAICAN BANANA

½ oz. light rum
½ oz. white crème de cacao
½ oz. crème de banana
2 scoops vanilla ice cream
1 oz. half-and-half
1 ripe banana, sliced
Garnish: Freshly grated
    nutmeg, banana slices,
    whole strawberry

Process ingredients in blender until smooth. Pour into large snifter. Top with nutmeg and garnish with banana and strawberry.

♉ KOKOMO JOE

1 oz. light rum
1 oz. banana liqueur
5 oz. fresh orange juice
2 oz. pineapple juice
1 oz. cream of coconut
½ ripe banana, sliced
Garnish: Orange wheel

*Process ingredients in blender
with 1 c. crushed ice until
smooth. Pour into hurricane
glass. Garnish with orange.*

♉ LONELY NIGHT

1¼ oz. Irish cream liqueur
1¼ oz. hazelnut liqueur
¾ oz. coffee liqueur
1 scoop vanilla ice cream
Garnish: Whipped cream,
    chocolate shavings

*Process ingredients in blender
with 1 c. crushed ice until
smooth. Pour into hurricane
glass. Top with whipped
cream and chocolate.*

♉ MAUI BREEZE

½ oz. amaretto
½ oz. triple sec
½ oz. brandy
½ oz. simple syrup
½ oz. fresh lemon juice
2 oz. fresh orange juice
2 oz. guava juice
Garnish: Pineapple spear,
    maraschino cherry

*Process ingredients in blender
with 1 c. crushed ice until
smooth. Pour into hurricane
glass. Garnish with pineapple
and cherry.*

♈ MISSISSIPPI MUD

1½ oz. Tennessee sour mash
    whiskey
1½ oz. coffee liqueur
2 scoops chocolate ice cream
Garnish: Chocolate shavings

*Process ingredients in blender
until smooth. Pour into cocktail glass. Top with chocolate.*

♈ MONT BLANC

1 oz. black raspberry liqueur
1 oz. vodka
1 oz. half-and-half
1 scoop vanilla ice cream

*Process all ingredients in
blender until smooth. Pour
into oversized red-wine glass.*

ORANGE BLOSSOM SPECIAL

1 oz. peach schnapps
2½ oz. lemon-lime soda
1 scoop orange sherbet
1 scoop vanilla ice cream
2½ oz. half-and-half
Garnish: Orange half-wheel,
    maraschino cherry

*Process ingredients in blender
with 1 c. crushed ice until
smooth. Pour into hurricane
glass. Garnish with orange
and cherry.*

PEACH MELBA FREEZE

¾ oz. peach schnapps
¾ oz. black raspberry liqueur
¾ oz. hazelnut liqueur
2 scoops vanilla ice cream
¾ oz. half-and-half
1 oz. melba sauce or raspberry
    jam
Garnish: Fresh peach slice

*Process ingredients in blender
until smooth. Pour into hurricane glass. Garnish with
peach.*

PEACHY AMARETTO

2 oz. amaretto
4 canned peach slices with
    juice or fresh peach slices
2 scoops vanilla ice cream

*Process all ingredients in
blender until smooth. Pour
into hurricane glass.*

PEPPERMINT TWIST

1½ oz. peppermint schnapps
½ oz. white crème de cacao
3 scoops vanilla ice cream
Garnish: Fresh mint sprig,
    peppermint candy stick

*Process in blender until
smooth. Pour into large hurricane or parfait glass. Garnish
with mint and peppermint
stick. Serve with straw.*

RASPBERRY CHEESECAKE

1 tbsp. cream cheese, softened
1 oz. white crème de cacao
1 oz. black raspberry
    liqueur
2 scoops vanilla ice cream

*Process all ingredients in
blender with 1 c. crushed
ice until smooth. Pour into
hurricane glass.*

ROAD RUNNER

For the glass: Orange wedge,
 superfine sugar, freshly
 grated nutmeg
1 oz. vodka
½ oz. amaretto
2 tsp. cream of coconut
Garnish: Freshly grated nutmeg

*Rim edge of chilled cham-
pagne flute with orange and
a mixture of sugar and
nutmeg. Combine remaining
ingredients in blender with
½ c. crushed ice for 15 seconds. Pour into glass. Top
with nutmeg.*

STRAWBERRIES
AND CREAM

1 oz. strawberry schnapps
1½ oz. simple syrup
2 oz. half-and-half
2 strawberries, sliced
Garnish: Whole strawberry

*Process first three ingredients
in blender with 1 c. crushed
ice until smooth. Add sliced
strawberries and blend for
10 seconds. Pour into
hurricane glass. Garnish
with whole strawberry and
serve with straw.*

STRAWBERRY
ALEXANDRA

1 oz. white crème de cacao
1 oz. brandy
½ c. partially thawed frozen
 sliced strawberries in
 syrup
1 scoop vanilla ice cream
Garnish: Whipped cream,
 chocolate curls

*Process ingredients in blender
until smooth. Pour into
white-wine glass. Top with
whipped cream and chocolate
curls. Serve with a straw and
a spoon.*

STRAWBERRY
BANANA SPRITZ

1½ oz. crème de banana
1 c. frozen strawberries
1 scoop vanilla ice cream
¼ c. soda water
Garnish: 1 whole strawberry

*Process ingredients in blender
until smooth. Pour into
hurricane glass. Garnish
with whole strawberry.*

♀ STRAWBERRY SHORTCAKE

1 oz. amaretto
¾ oz. white crème de cacao
½ c. thawed frozen
   strawberries in syrup
2 scoops vanilla ice cream
Garnish: Whipped cream,
   whole strawberry

Process ingredients in blender until smooth. Pour into over-sized red-wine glass. Top with whipped cream and garnish with strawberry.

♀ SURF'S UP

½ oz. crème de banana
½ oz. white crème de cacao
5 oz. pineapple juice
1 oz. half-and-half
Garnish: Orange wheel,
   maraschino cherry

Process ingredients with 1 c. crushed ice until smooth. Pour into hurricane glass. Garnish with orange and cherry.

♀ SWEET-TART

2 oz. vodka
3 oz. cranberry juice
3 oz. pineapple juice
½ oz. fresh lime juice
Garnish: Lime wheel

Process ingredients in blender with 1 c. crushed ice until smooth. Pour into hurricane glass. Garnish with lime.

♀ TENNESSEE WALTZ

1¼ oz. peach schnapps
2 oz. pineapple juice
1 oz. passion fruit juice
2 scoops vanilla ice cream
Garnish: Whipped cream,
   peach slice

Process ingredients in blender until smooth. Pour into hurricane glass. Garnish with whipped cream and peach.

⌁ TEQUILA FROST

1¼ oz. tequila
1¼ oz. pineapple juice
1¼ oz. fresh grapefruit juice
½ oz. honey
½ oz. grenadine
1 scoop vanilla ice cream
Garnish: Orange wheel,
    maraschino cherry

Process ingredients in blender until smooth. Pour into hurricane glass. Garnish with orange and cherry.

⌁ TROLLEY CAR

1¾ oz. amaretto
4 fresh or frozen strawberries
2 scoops vanilla ice cream
Garnish: 1 whole strawberry

Process ingredients in blender until smooth. Pour into hurricane glass. Garnish with whole strawberry.

HOT DRINKS

HOT TODDIES, simple mixtures of hot water, sugar or honey, and a single spirit—usually bourbon, but any whiskey, rum, brandy, or even gin could be used—are remembered by many as old-fashioned cold remedies, especially by people who remember the first edition of this book. While it was thought that the spirit made you feel better, it was really the heat combined with the spirit that did the trick. Indeed, toddies are one of those classic comforts that we are loath to abandon even today. That's probably because hot drinks are both comforting and stimulating. Sipping in front of a fireplace is recommended but optional.

Remember that the best hot drinks are made with high-quality ingredients: piping hot, freshly brewed coffee or tea; old-fashioned hot chocolate made with real cocoa and milk instead of a mix; cream you've whipped yourself (really, it only takes a couple of minutes); and freshly ground spices.

At home, it's no challenge to heat the ingredients for these drinks on the stove. At a bar, use a hot plate, a microwave oven, or even the steamer of an espresso machine to do the job. Be sure that your serving utensil is heatproof. As an extra precaution against hot beverages cracking cups, you may want to place a spoon in the cup before adding hot liquids. Stemmed Irish coffee glasses are usually tempered and crack-proof. Irish coffee glasses are nice, but large coffee mugs work, too.

Perhaps the most important tip is to serve the drinks in preheated glasses. Pour very hot water into the serving cup, let it stand for a minute or two to warm the cup, and toss out the water.

ALMOND TEA TODDY

Created by JONATHAN POGASH, New York, NY

1 oz. Plymouth gin
½ oz. orange liqueur
½ oz. orgeat or almond syrup
4 oz. hot brewed chai or orange-spiced tea
Garnish: Orange half-wheel

Stir in preheated Irish coffee glass or mug. Garnish with orange.

AMARETTO TEA

6 oz. hot brewed black tea
2 oz. amaretto
Garnish: Whipped cream

Pour hot tea into preheated Irish coffee glass. Add amaretto, but do not stir. Top with whipped cream.

APRIHOT

2 oz. apricot-flavored brandy
4 oz. boiling water
Garnish: 1 dash ground cinnamon, orange or lemon wheel

Pour ingredients into preheated Irish coffee glass. Top with ground cinnamon and garnish with citrus wheel.

BLACK GOLD

¼ oz. triple sec
¼ oz. amaretto
¼ oz. Irish cream liqueur
¼ oz. hazelnut liqueur
4 oz. hot brewed coffee
1 dash cinnamon schnapps
Garnish: Whipped cream,
    chocolate shavings,
    cinnamon stick

*Pour first four ingredients
into preheated Irish cof-
fee glass. Add coffee and
schnapps and stir. Top with
whipped cream and chocolate
and add cinnamon stick.*

BOSTON CARIBBEAN COFFEE

For glass: Orange wheel,
    superfine sugar
1 oz. dark crème de cacao
1 oz. dark rum
4 oz. hot brewed coffee
Garnish: Whipped cream, ground
    cinnamon, cinnamon stick

*Rim preheated Irish coffee
glass with orange and sugar.
Pour first two ingredients
into glass. Fill with coffee.
Top with whipped cream and
sprinkle with ground cinnamon. Add cinnamon stick.*

BOURBON SPICE LATTE

Created by JONATHAN POGASH,
New York, NY

1 oz. bourbon
½ oz. coffee-flavored liqueur
¼ oz. allspice liqueur (pimento
    dram)
1 tsp. agave nectar
1 pinch pumpkin pie spice
4 oz. hot milk
Garnish: Star anise pod

*Stir in preheated Irish coffee
glass. Float star anise on top.*

BRANDY BLAZER

2 oz. brandy, warmed
1 sugar sugar
1 orange twist

*Combine first two ingredients
in preheated old-fashioned
glass. Light with a match and
stir with barspoon for a few
seconds. Pour into preheated
Irish coffee glass. Add orange
twist.*

🍵 CAFÉ & CACHAÇA

Created by JONATHAN POGASH,
New York, NY

¾ oz. Coffee-Infused Cachaça
   (recipe follows)
½ oz. cream liqueur, such as
   Coole Swan
¼ oz. triple sec
4 oz. hot brewed coffee
Garnish: Freshly grated
   nutmeg

*Stir in preheated Irish
coffee glass. Top with
nutmeg.*

COFFEE-INFUSED CACHAÇA

*Combine ⅓ c. dark
roast (Italian or French)
coffee beans with 1 c.
cachaça in a jar. Cover
tightly and let stand at room
temperature for 5–7 days.
Strain into bottle and store,
refrigerated, for up to
1 month.*

🍵 CAFÉ L'ORANGE

½ oz. cognac
1 oz. Mandarine Napoléon
½ oz. triple sec
4 oz. hot brewed coffee
Garnish: Whipped cream,
   finely chopped orange zest

*Pour first three ingredients
into preheated Irish coffee
glass. Fill with coffee. Top
with whipped cream and
sprinkle with orange zest.*

🍵 CAFFÈ DI AMARETTO

2 oz. amaretto
4 oz. hot brewed coffee
Garnish: Whipped cream

*Pour amaretto into preheated
Irish coffee glass. Fill with
coffee. Top with whipped
cream.*

🍺 CAPRICCIO

For glass: Orange wheel,
superfine sugar, ground
cinnamon
1 oz. amaretto
1 oz. simple syrup
½ oz. brandy
½ oz. crème de café or coffee
liqueur
4 oz. hot brewed coffee
Garnish: Whipped cream,
toasted sliced almonds,
maraschino cherry

*Rim preheated Irish coffee
glass with orange and blend
of sugar and cinnamon.
Pour next four ingredients
into glass. Fill with coffee
and stir. Top with whipped
cream, sliced almonds, and
cherry.*

🍺 CHOCOLATE-BERRY MOCHA

Created by JONATHAN POGASH,
New York, NY

½ oz. black raspberry liqueur
¾ oz. dark crème de cacao
1 tsp. chocolate syrup
½ oz hot milk
4 oz. brewed hot coffee
Garnish: Mini marshmallows,
pinch of cocoa powder

*Stir in preheated Irish
coffee glass. Top with marshmallows and cocoa.*

🍺 EL TIBIO

Created by CHRIS CARLSSON,
Rochester, NY

½ oz. dark rum
¼ oz. ginger liqueur
1 tsp. honey
5 oz. hot brewed Earl
Grey tea
Garnish: 1 dash Creole bitters,
cinnamon stick wrapped in
long lemon zest

*Combine rum, liqueur, and
honey in preheated Irish
coffee glass or mug. Add tea
and stir. Add bitters and
cinnamon stick.*

⎕ HOT APPLE TODDY

Created by JONATHAN POGASH,
New York, NY

4 oz. apple cider
1 tsp. mulling spices
1 oz. Calvados
½ oz. vanilla liqueur
Garnish: Orange half-wheel
    studded with 3 whole
    cloves

*Heat cider and spices
together over low heat for
10 minutes. (Mixture does
not need to boil.) Strain into
preheated Irish coffee glass
or mug. Add Calvados
and liqueur and stir.
Garnish with clove-studded
orange.*

⎕ HOT BRANDY ALEXANDER

¾ oz. brandy
¾ oz. dark crème de cacao
4 oz. steamed milk
Garnish: Whipped cream,
    chocolate shavings

*Pour ingredients into
preheated Irish coffee
glass. Top with cream and
chocolate.*

⎕ HOT BRICK TODDY

½ oz. simple syrup
1 tsp. unsalted butter
1 pinch ground cinnamon
2 oz. rye or bourbon whiskey
4 oz. boiling water

*Put first three ingredients
into preheated Irish coffee
glass. Add whiskey, fill with
boiling water, and stir.*

⎕ HOT BUTTERED RUM

Hot buttered rum is perhaps
the ultimate chill-chaser. If you
don't have Demerara syrup,
dissolve 1 tsp. Demerara sugar
(or light or dark brown sugar)
in the boiling water.

½ oz. simple syrup or
    Demerara Syrup (page 20)
4 oz. boiling water
2 oz. dark rum
1 tsp. unsalted butter
Garnish: Freshly grated
    nutmeg

*Put syrup into preheated
Irish coffee glass or mug. Fill
with boiling water. Add rum
and butter and stir. Top with
nutmeg.*

🍵 HOT BUTTERED WINE

6 oz. muscatel or other sweet wine
¼ c. very hot water (not boiling)
2 tsp. maple syrup
1 tsp. unsalted butter
Garnish: Freshly grated nutmeg

Pour wine and water into preheated Irish coffee glass. Add maple syrup and butter and stir. Top with nutmeg.

🍸 HOT GOLD

2 oz. amaretto
6 oz. fresh orange juice, heated until very warm
Garnish: Cinnamon stick

Pour amaretto into preheated red-wine glass or Irish coffee glass. Add orange juice and stir. Add cinnamon stick as stirrer.

🍵 INDIAN SUMMER

For glass: Lemon wedge, superfine sugar
2 oz. apple schnapps
4 oz. apple cider, heated
Garnish: Cinnamon stick

Rim preheated Irish coffee mug or glass with lemon and sugar. Add schnapps and cider and stir. Add cinnamon stick, if using.

🍵 IRISH COFFEE

2 sugar cubes
4 oz. hot brewed coffee
1½ oz. Irish whiskey
Garnish: Lightly whipped cream

Stir sugar cubes and coffee in preheated Irish coffee glass to dissolve sugar. Add whiskey. Float cream over back of barspoon to fill glass.

🍵 ITALIAN COFFEE

½ oz. amaretto
4 oz. hot brewed coffee
1 small scoop coffee ice cream
Garnish: Ground coriander

Pour amaretto into preheated Irish coffee glass. Fill with coffee and stir. Top with ice cream and sprinkle with coriander.

JAMAICA COFFEE

1 oz. coffee-flavored brandy
¾ oz. light rum
½ oz. simple syrup
4 oz. hot brewed coffee
Garnish: Whipped cream,
   freshly grated nutmeg

*Pour brandy, rum, and syrup
into preheated Irish coffee
glass. Fill with coffee and stir.
Top with whipped cream and
nutmeg.*

KEOKE COFFEE

See Coffee Nudge, page 213.

LUMBERJACK

Created by CHARLES MYERS,
O'Fallen, MO

2 oz. bourbon
1 tsp. light brown sugar
½ tsp. unsalted butter
8 oz. apple juice, heated
Garnish: Ground cinnamon

*Stir in preheated Irish coffee
glass. Top with cinnamon.*

MEXICAN COFFEE

1 oz. coffee liqueur
1 oz. blanco tequila
4 oz. hot brewed coffee
Garnish: Whipped cream

*Pour coffee liqueur and
tequila into preheated Irish
coffee glass. Fill with coffee
and stir. Top with whipped
cream.*

MULLED CABERNET

5 oz. cabernet sauvignon
1½ oz. fresh orange juice
½ oz. simple syrup
1 pinch ground cinnamon
1 pinch freshly ground nutmeg
1 dash Angostura bitters
Garnish: Cinnamon stick

*Heat ingredients together
until hot but not boiling.
Serve in preheated Irish
coffee glass or mug. Add
cinnamon stick.*

🍵 MULLED WINE

Created by JONATHAN POGASH,
New York, NY

The steamer spout of an
espresso machine does a great
job of heating the wine with
the spices. If you don't have
one, be careful not to let the
rum and spice come to a boil.
Make it in quantity for a large
group.

1½ oz. malbec, zinfandel, or
    other red wine with spicy
    notes
1 tsp. mulling spices
1½ oz. dark rum
1 tsp. honey
Garnish: Lemon wheel

*Heat wine and spices in
metal latte jug with steamer
spout of espresso machine.
(Or heat in a small saucepan over very low heat just
until steaming.) Pour into
preheated Irish coffee glass
or mug. Add rum and honey
and stir. Garnish with lemon.*

🍵 PEANUT BUTTER HOT CHOCOLATE

Created by JONATHAN POGASH,
New York, NY

1 oz. Castries Peanut Rum
    Crème Liqueur
¾ oz. light rum
4 oz. hot chocolate
Garnish: Mini marshmallows,
    pinch of cocoa

*Stir in preheated Irish
coffee glass or mug. Top
with marshmallows and
cocoa.*

🍵 PEANUT COFFEE

Created by JONATHAN POGASH,
New York, NY

1 oz. Castries Peanut Rum
    Crème Liqueur
¾ oz. dark rum
4 oz. hot brewed coffee

*Stir in preheated Irish
coffee glass.*

RUSSIAN COFFEE

½ oz. coffee liqueur
½ oz. hazelnut liqueur
1 oz. vodka
4 oz. hot brewed coffee
Garnish: Whipped cream

Pour liqueurs and vodka into preheated Irish coffee glass. Fill with coffee and stir. Top with whipped cream.

SNOW BUNNY

1½ oz. Grand Marnier
5 oz. hot chocolate
Garnish: Cinnamon stick

Pour liqueur into preheated Irish coffee glass. Fill with hot chocolate and stir. Add cinnamon stick.

SPANISH COFFEE

1½ oz. Spanish brandy
4½ oz. hot brewed coffee
Garnish: Whipped cream

Pour brandy into preheated Irish coffee glass. Fill with coffee and stir. Top with whipped cream.

SPICED APPLE CIDER

Created by JONATHAN POGASH, New York, NY

1 oz. rye whiskey
¾ oz. allspice liqueur
½ oz. Honey Syrup (page 21)
4 oz. hot cider
Garnish: Orange half-wheel studded with 3 whole cloves

Stir in preheated Irish coffee glass or mug. Garnish with clove-studded orange.

STEAMING PEACH

2 oz. peach schnapps
4 oz. boiling water
Garnish: Orange wheel

Pour schnapps into preheated snifter. Add boiling water and stir. Float orange on top.

☕ TOM AND JERRY

"Professor" Jerry Thomas popularized this warming drink, and it is still served as a Christmastime beverage. Here is his original recipe. It makes enough for many servings, so it would be best in a professional bar setting.

Makes about 28 servings

ORIGINAL TOM AND JERRY BATTER
3 eggs, separated
¼ tsp. cream of tartar
2¼ c. superfine sugar
2 oz. light rum
1 tsp. ground cinnamon
½ tsp. ground cloves
½ tsp. ground allspice

For 1 serving
2 oz. brandy
1 oz. Original Tom and Jerry
    Batter
4 oz. boiling water
Garnish: Freshly grated nutmeg

To make batter, beat egg whites and cream of tartar in medium bowl to stiff peaks. Beat yolks in another medium bowl until slightly thickened. Gradually beat in 1 c. of the sugar. Mix in rum, cinnamon, cloves, and allspice. Mix in remaining 1 c. sugar. Fold in whites. Cover and refrigerate until ready to serve, up to 2 days. Makes 3½ c. batter, enough for about 28 drinks.

For 1 serving, combine brandy and batter in pre-heated punch cup or coffee mug. Fill with boiling water and stir well. Top with nutmeg.

☕ TOM AND JERRY (CREAMY)

Richer and headier than the original, this Tom and Jerry is made with hot milk. This is the perfect hot punch to serve at your holiday parties.

Makes at least 10 servings

TOM AND JERRY BATTER

6 eggs, separated
2 c. superfine sugar
⅓ c. brandy
⅓ c. light rum
¼ c. bourbon

For 1 serving

1 oz. Tom and Jerry Batter
5 oz. hot milk, as needed
Garnish: Freshly grated nutmeg

To make batter, beat egg whites in large bowl to stiff peaks. Beat yolks in medium bowl until thickened. Gradually beat in sugar until very thick and pale yellow. Mix in brandy and rum. Fold in whites. (If you have a Tom and Jerry serving bowl, transfer batter to bowl.) Cover and refrigerate until ready to serve, up to 1 day.

For each serving, spoon batter into preheated punch cup or coffee mug. Add milk to fill and stir. Top with nutmeg.

EGGNOGS AND PUNCHES

EGGNOG FIRST BECAME popular during colonial times. Rum was the favorite spirit of the early Americans; they mixed it with milk, eggs, and sugar. Over the years, whiskey and brandy have been used as substitutes for rum. Today, eggnog is enjoyed mostly as a holiday drink, which is a shame.

Raw eggs can carry a bacterium that causes salmonella poisoning, but fortunately, there are solutions to the problem. One, use a prepared mix such as Mr. Boston Egg Nog. Two, use large prepasteurized eggs, available at many supermarkets. Three, if using unpasteurized eggs, make cooked eggnog on page 265. Float a block of vanilla ice cream (removed in one piece from its packaging) in the eggnog's punch bowl—the ice cream will chill and flavor the nog as it melts.

Punches are ideal for serving a large number of guests. Recipes for both cold and hot punches can be found in this section, as well as for several nonalcoholic punches. While cold punches in smaller quantities can be mixed in and served from a pitcher, larger recipes are usually served in a punch bowl from which guests help themselves. Use a block of ice, not ice cubes, to keep punch chilled.

Hot punch should be served at the proper steaming temperature. For an informal party, ladle up the drink right from the pot on the stove, or put the pot in the party area on a hot plate, keeping in mind that you might need an electric source. At a bar, the latte steamer of an espresso machine renders drinks mixed from cold ingredients hot in a few seconds.

EGGNOGS

☕ AMBASSADOR'S MORNING LIFT

Makes 10 to 12 servings
1 qt. eggnog, chilled
¾ c. cognac
3 oz. Jamaican rum, brandy, or bourbon
3 oz. dark crème de cacao
Garnish: Freshly grated nutmeg

Combine ingredients in large punch bowl. Serve in punch cups and top each serving with nutmeg.

☕ BALTIMORE EGGNOG

Makes 10 to 12 servings
1 qt. eggnog, chilled
⅔ c. brandy
⅔ c. Jamaican rum
⅔ c. madeira
Garnish: Freshly grated nutmeg

Combine ingredients in large punch bowl. Serve in punch cups and top each serving with nutmeg.

🍵 EGGNOG (COOKED)

Makes 8 to 10 servings
3 c. half-and-half
¾ c. sugar
9 large egg yolks
¾ c. golden rum
1 c. heavy cream
Garnish: Freshly grated
    nutmeg

Heat half-and-half and sugar in medium saucepan over medium heat, stirring to dissolve sugar. Whisk egg yolks in large heatproof bowl until thickened; gradually whisk in hot mixture. Return to saucepan and stir with wooden spoon over medium-low heat until custard coats spoon and reads 185°F on instant-read thermometer. Strain through wire sieve into preheated large punch bowl; let cool. Stir in rum. Cover and refrigerate until chilled, at least 4 hours. Whip cream to soft peaks and fold into custard. Serve in punch cups and top each serving with nutmeg.

🍵 CHRISTMAS YULE EGGNOG

Makes 10 to 12 servings
1 qt. eggnog, chilled
1 c. bourbon whiskey
½ c. light rum
Garnish: Freshly grated
    nutmeg

Combine ingredients in large punch bowl. Serve in punch cups and top each serving with nutmeg.

🍸 FROSTY NOG

½ c. eggnog
1 oz. amaretto
Garnish: Toasted sliced
    almonds, freshly grated
    nutmeg

Process eggnog, amaretto, and 1 c. crushed ice in blender on medium speed until smooth. Pour into hurricane glass. Top with almonds and nutmeg.

🍵 GOLDEN EGGNOG

Created by JONATHAN POGASH,
New York, NY

Your guests will feel very special when presented with gold-topped cups of nog. To transfer the edible gold (or silver) leaf to the drink, use the tip of a fine-tipped artist's brush to lift a large flake of the gold from its tissue. Touch the edge of the flake onto the surface of the eggnog and remove the paintbrush without getting the bristles wet.

1 large egg, separated
1 tsp. superfine sugar
1½ oz. vanilla liqueur
1½ oz. whole milk
Garnish: Freshly grated
   nutmeg, edible gold leaf

Beat egg white with ½ tsp. sugar until soft peaks form. Beat yolk well with remaining ½ tsp. sugar until pale and thickened. Add white and gently fold together. Add liqueur and milk and mix gently. Pour into ice-filled cocktail glass. Top with nutmeg and gold leaf.

🍵 GOLDEN EGGNOG (LARGE BATCH)

Created by JONATHAN POGASH,
New York, NY

Makes 6 servings
6 large eggs, separated
2 Tbs. superfine sugar
9 oz. vanilla liqueur
9 oz. whole milk
Garnish: Freshly grated
   nutmeg, edible gold leaf

Beat egg whites with 1 tbsp. sugar until soft peaks form. Beat yolks well with remaining 1 tbsp. sugar until pale and thickened. Add whites and gently fold together. Add liqueur and milk and mix gently. Pour into ice-filled cocktail glasses. Top each with nutmeg and gold leaf.

🍵 MAPLE EGGNOG

Makes 8 servings
1 qt. eggnog
½ c. pure maple syrup,
    preferably grade B
½ c. bourbon whiskey
Garnish: Freshly grated nutmeg

Combine ingredients in large pitcher and chill. Stir before serving. Serve in punch cups and top each serving with nutmeg.

🍵 NASHVILLE EGGNOG

Makes 10 to 12 servings
1 qt. eggnog, chilled
¾ c. bourbon whiskey
3 oz. brandy
3 oz. Jamaican rum
Garnish: Freshly grated nutmeg

Combine ingredients in large punch bowl. Serve in punch cups and top each serving with nutmeg.

🍸 NOG DE CACAO

1½ oz. white crème de cacao
1½ oz. eggnog, chilled

Pour over ice in old-fashioned glass and stir.

🍵 OLD-FASHIONED EGGNOG

Makes 8 to 10 servings
6 large eggs
1 c. sugar
½ tsp. salt
1 c. golden rum
1 pt. half-and-half
1 pt. milk
Garnish: Freshly grated nutmeg

In a large bowl, beat eggs until pale and foamy. Add sugar and salt, beating until thickened. Stir in rum, half-and-half, and milk. Chill at least 3 hours. Serve in punch cups and top each serving with nutmeg.

🍸 RUSSIAN NOG

1 oz. vodka
1 oz. coffee liqueur
1 oz. eggnog

Pour into ice-filled old-fashioned glass and stir.

🍵 SHERRY EGGNOG

Makes 10 to 12 servings
1 qt. eggnog, chilled
2¼ c. cream sherry
Garnish: Freshly grated nutmeg

Combine in large punch bowl. Serve in punch cups and top each serving with nutmeg.

🍵 SPIKED EGGNOG

Makes 10 to 12 servings
1 qt. eggnog, chilled
1½ c. brandy, golden rum, or
    bourbon
Garnish: Freshly grated nutmeg

*Combine ingredients in large
punch bowl. Serve in punch
cups and top each serving
with nutmeg.*

🍵 THE WORLD BAR EGGNOG

Created by JONATHAN POGASH,
New York, NY

1 large egg, separated
2 tsp. superfine sugar
1 oz. heavy cream
⅛ tsp. pure almond extract
⅛ tsp. pure vanilla extract
1½ oz. dark rum
Garnish: Ground cinnamon,
    freshly ground nutmeg

*Beat egg white with 1 tsp.
sugar until soft peaks form.
Beat egg yolk well until pale
and thick. Add white and
gently fold together. Beat
cream, almond, and vanilla
extracts with remaining
1 tsp. sugar until stiff. Add to
egg mixture and gently fold
together. Fold in rum. Pour
into ice-filled punch cup or
cocktail glass. Top with
cinnamon and nutmeg.*

THE WORLD BAR EGGNOG (LARGE BATCH)

Makes 18 to 20 servings
10 eggs, separated
1 c. superfine sugar
3 c. heavy cream
2 Tbs. almond extract
2 Tbs. vanilla extract
2 c. dark rum
Garnish: 1 tsp. freshly grated nutmeg, 1 tsp. ground cinnamon

Beat egg whites with ½ c. sugar until soft peaks form. Beat egg yolks well until pale and thickened. Add whites and gently fold together. Beat cream, almond and vanilla extracts, and remaining ½ c. sugar until soft peaks form. Add to egg mixture and gradually fold together. Fold in rum. Cover and refrigerate until chilled, at least 4 hours or overnight. Pour into punch bowl and top with nutmeg and cinnamon. Serve, without ice, in punch cups or cocktail glasses.

COLD PUNCHES

APRICOT ORANGE FIZZ

Makes 6 servings
1½ c. fresh orange juice
½ c. light rum
¼ c. apricot-flavored brandy
1 oz. fresh lime juice
Soda water
Garnish: Lime wheels

Combine first four ingredients in pitcher and stir. Pour into ice-filled Collins glasses, about ⅔ full. Top each with soda water and stir. Garnish with limes. Serve in punch cups.

☕ BOMBAY PUNCH

Makes 60 servings

1 (1-liter) bottle brandy
1 (1-liter) bottle dry (fino) sherry
3 c. fresh lemon juice
1½ c. simple syrup
½ c. maraschino liqueur
½ c. triple sec
4 (750-ml) bottles
    Champagne, chilled
2 qt. soda water, chilled
Garnish: Fresh seasonal fruit

*Stir first six ingredients
into large punch bowl. Add
Champagne and soda water
and stir. Add large block of
ice. Garnish with fruit. Serve
in punch cups.*

☕ BOOM BOOM PUNCH

Makes 36 servings

2 (1-liter) bottles light rum
1 qt. fresh orange juice
1 (750-ml) bottle sweet
    vermouth
1 (750-ml) Champagne, chilled
Garnish: Sliced bananas

*Stir first three ingredients
in large punch bowl. Add
Champagne and stir again.
Add large block of ice.
Garnish with bananas. Serve
in punch cups.*

☕ BRANDY PUNCH

Makes 36 servings

1.75 liters brandy
1 qt. soda water
3 c. fresh lemon juice
2 c. fresh orange juice
2 c. simple syrup
1 c. grenadine
1 c. triple sec
2 c. cold strong brewed black
    tea
Garnish: Fresh seasonal fruit

*Stir in large punch bowl. Add
large block of ice. Garnish with
fruit. Serve in punch cups.*

☕ BRUNCH PUNCH

Makes 40 servings

3 qt. tomato juice, chilled
1 (1-liter) bottle light or
    dark rum
2½ tsp. Worcestershire sauce
⅔ c. fresh lemon or lime juice
Salt and freshly ground black
    pepper to taste
Garnish: Lemon or lime wheels

*Combine in large punch bowl
and stir well. Add large block
of ice. Garnish with citrus.
Serve in punch cups.*

☕ CAPE CODDER PUNCH

Makes 40 servings
3 (32-oz.) bottles cranberry-
    apple drink
3 c. vodka
2 c. fresh orange juice
1 c. simple syrup
⅔ c. fresh lemon juice
1 (28-oz.) bottle mineral
    water, chilled

*Stir in large punch bowl. Add
large block of ice. Serve in
punch cups.*

☕ CARDINAL PUNCH

Makes 42 servings
2 qt. red wine, such as merlot
1 qt. soda water
3 c. fresh lemon juice
2 c. fresh simple syrup
2 c. brandy
2 c. light rum
2 c. cold strong brewed
    black tea
1 split Champagne
1 c. sweet vermouth

*Stir in punch bowl. Add
large block of ice. Serve in
punch cups.*

🍸 CHAMPAGNE CUP

Makes 6 servings
¾ c. soda water
2 oz. brandy
1 oz. triple sec
1 oz. simple syrup
1 pt. Champagne, chilled
Garnish: Fresh seasonal fruit,
    3 long strips of cucumber
    peel, bunch of fresh mint

*Pour first four ingredients into
pitcher and stir. Half-fill with
ice and top with Champagne.
Garnish with fruit. Insert
cucumber peels inside pitcher
and top with mint. Serve in
red-wine glasses.*

☕ CHAMPAGNE PUNCH

Makes 32 servings
3 c. fresh lemon juice
2 c. simple syrup
2 c. brandy
1 c. maraschino liqueur
1 c. triple sec
2 (750-ml) bottles
    Champagne, chilled
2 c. cold soda water
2 c. cold strong brewed black tea
Garnish: Fresh seasonal fruit

*Stir in large punch bowl. Add
large block of ice. Garnish with
fruit. Serve in punch cups.*

☕ CHAMPAGNE SHERBET PUNCH

Makes 20 servings
3 c. pineapple juice, chilled
¼ c. fresh lemon juice, chilled
1 bottle (750-ml) Champagne, chilled
1 qt. pineapple sherbet

Stir pineapple and lemon juices and Champagne in punch bowl. Add sherbet. Serve in punch cups, adding a portion of sherbet to each glass.

☕ CITRUS-BEER PUNCH

Makes 8 servings
8 lemons
2 c. sugar
1 c. fresh grapefruit juice
2 (12-oz.) cans chilled lager beer
Garnish: Lemon wheels

Remove zest from 6 lemons with vegetable peeler and reserve. Juice lemons; you should have 2 c. Bring 2 c. water and sugar to a boil in large nonreactive saucepan. Add lemon zest and remove from heat. Cover and let stand 5 minutes. Add lemon juice and grapefruit juice. Strain into large pitcher, cover, and refrigerate until chilled. Just before serving, add beer. Serve in punch cups, garnished with lemon wheels.

♀ CLARET CUP

Also known as a Loving Cup, make this with a full-bodied, fruity red wine. It you wish, substitute dry or sweet white wine, Champagne, or sparkling wine for the red wine.

Makes 6 servings
1 pt. red wine, such as cabernet-merlot blend or claret
¾ c. soda water
2 oz. brandy
2 oz. simple syrup
1 oz. triple sec
Garnish: Fresh seasonal fruit, 2 long strips of cucumber peel, bunch of fresh mint

Pour ingredients into large pitcher. Stir. Fill with ice. Garnish with fruit. Insert cucumber peels inside pitcher and top with mint. Serve in red-wine glasses.

CIDER PUNCH: Substitute apple cider for the red wine.

☕ CLARET PUNCH

Makes 40 servings
3 (750-ml) bottles red wine, such as cabernet-merlot blend
1 qt. soda water
1 qt. cold strong brewed black tea
3 c. fresh lemon juice
2 c. brandy
1 c. simple syrup
1 c. triple sec

Pour over large block of ice in punch bowl. Stir well. Serve in punch cups.

☕ EXTRA-KICK PUNCH

Makes 24 servings
2 qt. hot water
1 c. packed light or dark brown sugar
2 c. dark rum
1 c. brandy
1 c. fresh lemon juice
1 c. pineapple juice
¼ c. peach brandy

Stir hot water and brown sugar in large heatproof bowl to dissolve sugar; let cool. Stir in remaining ingredients. Cover and chill. Pour over block of ice in punch bowl. Serve in punch cups.

FISH HOUSE PUNCH

The Schuylkill Fishing Company, a gentleman's club in Philadelphia, is also known as the "Fish House," and it is the place of origin for this heady punch.

Makes 40 servings
3 c. fresh lemon juice
2 c. simple syrup
2 (750-ml) bottles brandy
1 (1-liter) bottle peach-flavored brandy
2 c. light rum
1 qt. soda water
1 pt. cold strong brewed black tea (optional)
Garnish: Fresh seasonal fruit

*Stir in punch bowl.
Add large block of ice.
Garnish with fruit. Serve
in punch cups.*

KENTUCKY PUNCH

Makes 32 servings
2 (6-oz.) cans frozen orange juice concentrate, thawed
2 (6-oz.) cans frozen lemonade concentrate, thawed
1 c. fresh lemon juice
1 (1-liter) bottle bourbon whiskey
2 (2-liter) bottles lemon-lime soda

*Stir all ingredients except
soda in large container and
chill. Pour into punch bowl
over large block of ice
and stir in soda. Serve in
punch cups.*

🍵 MINT JULEP PUNCH

Makes 44 servings

1 c. mint jelly
6 c. pineapple juice
1 (750-ml) bottle bourbon
  whiskey
½ c. fresh lime juice
7 c. lemon-lime soda
Garnish: Lime wheels, fresh
  mint leaves

*Cook mint jelly and 2 c.
water in large nonreactive
saucepan over low heat,
stirring until jelly melts. Let
cool. Stir in pineapple juice,
bourbon, 2 c. cold water, and
lime juice. Cover and chill.
Pour over block of ice in
punch bowl. Slowly pour in
soda, stirring gently. Garnish
with lime and mint. Serve
in punch cups.*

🍸 SANGRIA PUNCH

Makes 10 servings

1 (750-ml) bottle red or rosé
  wine, preferably Spanish
½ c. simple syrup
1 orange, thinly sliced
1 lime, thinly sliced
¾ c. soda water
Garnish: Fresh seasonal fruit

*Pour wine, syrup, and ½ c.
water into pitcher and stir.
Add orange and lime. Half-fill
pitcher with ice. Add soda
water and stir gently. Add
fruit. Serve in red-wine glasses,
adding fruit to each glass.*

🍵 TEQUILA PUNCH

Makes 40 servings

4 (750-ml) bottles dry white
  wine, such as pinot grigio,
  chilled
1 (1-liter) bottle tequila, chilled
1 (750-ml) bottle Champagne,
  chilled
2 c. simple syrup
1 c. fresh lime juice
2 quarts assorted fresh fruits,
  such as berries and melon
  balls

*Pour first five ingredients into
large punch bowl and stir.
Add large ice block and fruit.
Serve in punch cups.*

🍵 WEST INDIAN PUNCH

Makes 48 servings

2 (1-liter) bottles light rum
1 (750-ml) bottle crème de banana
1 qt. pineapple juice
1 qt. fresh orange juice
1 qt. fresh lemon juice
1½ c. simple syrup
1 tsp. freshly grated nutmeg
1 tsp. ground cinnamon
½ tsp. ground cloves
¾ c. soda water
Garnish: Sliced bananas

Pour ingredients into large punch bowl. Stir. Add large ice block. Garnish with bananas. Serve in punch cups.

🍵 WHISKEY SOUR PUNCH

Makes 32 servings

3 (6-oz.) frozen lemonade concentrate, thawed
1 (1-liter) bottle bourbon whiskey
3 c. fresh orange juice
1 (2-liter) bottle soda water, chilled
Garnish: Orange wheels

Combine ingredients over block of ice in punch bowl. Stir gently. Garnish with oranges. Serve in punch cups.

🍷 WHITE WINE CUP

Makes 6 servings

1 pt. dry white wine, such as pinot grigio or sauvignon blanc
2 oz. simple syrup
2 oz. brandy
1 oz. triple sec
Garnish: Fresh seasonal fruit, 3 long strips of cucumber peel, bunch of fresh mint

Pour ingredients into large pitcher. Stir. Fill with ice. Garnish with fruit. Insert cucumber peels inside pitcher and top with mint. Serve in white-wine glasses.

HOT PUNCHES

🍷 HOT APPLE BRANDY

Makes 8 servings

6 c. apple juice
1½ c. apricot-flavored brandy
3 cinnamon sticks
½ tsp. ground cloves

Simmer all ingredients over low heat for 30 minutes. Serve warm in snifters.

☕ HOT BURGUNDY PUNCH

Makes 8 to 10 servings
¼ c. Demerara or packed light brown sugar
1 c. apple juice
Zest of of ½ lemon, removed with vegetable peeler
1 cinnamon stick
6 whole allspice berries
5 whole cloves
1 (750-ml) bottle domestic pinot noir or burgundy
Garnish: Freshly grated nutmeg

Bring sugar and 1½ c. water to a boil in large nonreactive saucepan over medium heat, stirring to dissolve sugar. Add apple juice, lemon zest, cinnamon, allspice, and cloves, and bring to simmer. Cook over medium heat for 15 minutes. Strain into another saucepan and add wine. Simmer over low heat but do not boil. Serve in punch cups and top each serving with nutmeg.

☕ HOT RUMMED CIDER

Makes 8 servings
1½ qt. apple cider
⅓ c. Demerara or packed light brown sugar
3 tbsp. unsalted butter
1½ c. light rum
Garnish: Cinnamon sticks

Bring cider and sugar to a boil in large saucepan. Reduce heat and add butter. When butter is melted, add rum. Serve in punch cups, with cinnamon sticks.

☕ SMUGGLER'S BREW

Makes 8 servings
1½ c. dark rum
1 qt. cold strong brewed black tea
3 tbsp. unsalted butter
½ c. sugar
½ tsp. freshly grated nutmeg
½ c. brandy

Heat first five ingredients in large saucepan until boiling. Heat brandy in small saucepan until barely warm and add to rum mixture. Serve in punch cups.

☕ WARM WINTER CIDER

Makes 18 to 20 servings
1 gal. apple cider
6 cinnamon sticks
1½ c. spiced rum
1 c. peach-flavored brandy
¾ c. peach schnapps
Garnish: Cinnamon sticks,
   apple slices

In large saucepan, bring cider and cinnamon to a full boil over medium heat. Reduce heat and add rum, brandy, and schnapps, stirring until heated through. Serve in punch cups garnished with cinnamon sticks and apples.

NON-ALCOHOLIC PUNCHES

☕ BANANA PUNCH

Makes 40 servings
3 c. superfine sugar
2 (6-oz.) cans frozen orange
   juice concentrate, thawed
1 (46-oz.) can pineapple-
   grapefruit juice
4 ripe bananas, mashed
4 qt. soda water

Mix 1½ qt. water and sugar in large bowl to dissolve. Add juices and bananas. Pour into 4 (1-qt.) freezer containers and freeze overnight. About 1 hour before serving, unmold and transfer to large punch bowl to melt slightly. Stir in club soda. Serve in punch cups.

🍵 DOUBLE BERRY PUNCH

Makes 25 to 30 servings
2 qt. cranberry juice
3 c. raspberry-flavored soda, chilled
1 qt. raspberry sherbet
Garnish: Fresh raspberries

Chill cranberry juice with ice block in punch bowl. Just before serving, slowly pour in soda and stir gently. Add sherbet. Serve in punch cups, adding sherbet and raspberries to each serving.

⬜ FUNSHINE FIZZ

Makes 6 to 8 servings
2 c. fresh orange juice, chilled
2 c. pineapple juice, chilled
1 pint orange sherbet
1 c. soda water, chilled

Combine first three ingredients in blender in batches, blending until smooth. Pour into pitcher and stir in soda water. Serve in Collins glasses.

🍵 TROPICAL CREAM PUNCH

Makes 22 servings
1 (14-oz.) can sweetened condensed milk
1 (6-oz.) can frozen orange juice concentrate, thawed
1 (6-oz.) can frozen pineapple juice concentrate, thawed
1 bottle (2-qt) soda water, chilled
Garnish: Orange wheels

Whisk condensed milk and juice concentrates in punch bowl. Add club soda and stir gently. Add block of ice and garnish with orange. Serve in punch cups.

WINE AND BEER IN
MIXED DRINKS

SOME COCKTAILS EMPLOY classic varietal wines like chardonnay, claret (another name for Bordeaux or cabernet), or merlot. But wine is a broad term for several subcategories less familiar to classic wine drinkers until you say their names—many of which are proprietary. Do Fernet-Branca, Dubonnet, and Lillet sound familiar? How about vermouth? All of these are examples of wines that are aromatized—the basic grape flavor is augmented with the addition of flavorings such as spices, herbs, flowers, nuts, honey, quinine, or even pine resin.

Proprietary aromatics are often sipped solo in Europe either before or after a meal, whereas in the United States they more often show up in cocktails. Anyone who drinks Martinis or Manhattans is familiar with vermouth, a wine infused with herbs, alcohol, sugar, caramel, and water. There are three types of vermouth: dry, sweet, and half-sweet (sometimes called bianco).

Sparkling wine or Champagne is used in many cocktails, often splashed on top to add a touch of fizz. In the classic Champagne Cocktail, the bubbly is the main ingredient; unless specified, use a dry (brut) style of Champagne or an American wine, Spanish cava, or Italian prosecco. When chilling sparkling wine cocktails with ice, fold the ingredients together very carefully to avoid bursting the bubbles.

And don't forget beer as a mixer for cocktails. Its effervescence and slight bitterness make it the ultimate thirst quencher. Try a Shandy, where beer meets lemonade in a very happy marriage, and you'll find yourself craving another.

☐ 1815

2 oz. Ramazzotti Amaro
½ oz. fresh lemon juice
½ oz. fresh lime juice
Ginger ale
Garnish: Lemon and lime
   wedges

Shake first three ingredients with ice and strain into ice-filled Collins glass. Top with ginger ale. Garnish with lemon and lime.

☐ THE ALLSPICE FLIP

Created by NATASHA DAVID,
New York, NY

1½ oz. ruby port
½ oz. Demerara Syrup
   (page 20)
½ oz. heavy cream
¼ oz. allspice liqueur (pimento
   dram)
1 egg
1 oz. German white wheat
   beer, such as Erdinger
Garnish: Freshly grated
   nutmeg

Shake first five ingredients without ice. Add ice and shake again. Strain through wire sieve into chilled Collins glass. Top off with beer. Sprinkle with nutmeg.

◻ AMERICANO

2 oz. sweet vermouth
2 oz. Campari
Soda water
Garnish: Lemon twist

Pour vermouth and Campari into ice-filled highball glass. Fill with soda water and stir. Add lemon twist.

▽ APPLE-CINNAMON SPARKLER

Created by JONATHAN POGASH, New York, NY

1 oz. apple cider
½ oz. Cinnamon Syrup (page 20), or use store-bought
¼ oz. fresh lemon juice
4 oz. sparkling wine or Champagne, plus 1 splash to finish
Garnish: Red apple slice

Gently fold ingredients with ice in mixing glass. Strain into chilled champagne flute. Top with extra splash of sparkling wine or Champagne. Add apple.

◻ BELLA ROSA

Created by ROBERT KRUEGER, New York, NY

1¼ oz. bianco vermouth
1 oz. Campari
½ oz. fresh lemon juice
½ oz. simple syrup
½ large strawberry, sliced
3 oz. ginger beer

Shake first five ingredients with ice, shaking hard to break up strawberry. Strain into ice-filled old-fashioned glass. Top with ginger beer.

▽ BELLINI

Make your own puree from peeled and pitted fresh peaches, or buy online.

1 ounce peach puree, preferably white peach
5 ounces chilled prosecco

Pour puree into chilled Champagne flute. Carefully fill glass with prosecco (watch out for foaming).

▯ BISHOP

1 oz. fresh orange juice
¾ oz. fresh lemon juice
½ oz. simple syrup
Red wine
Garnish: Fresh seasonal fruit

*Shake first three ingredients
with ice and strain into ice-
filled highball glass. Fill with
wine, and stir well. Garnish
with fruit.*

▯ BLACKBERRY
FIZZ

Created by JONATHAN POGASH,
New York, NY

2 large fresh blackberries
¾ oz. fresh lemon juice
¾ oz. simple syrup
1 oz. Lillet Blanc
1 oz. gin
2 oz. chilled sparkling wine
Garnish: Fresh blackberry

*Muddle blackberries, lemon
juice, and syrup in mixing
glass. Add Lillet, gin, and ice
and shake. Strain into chilled
champagne flute. Top with
sparkling wine. Garnish with
blackberry.*

▯ BOSTON ORANGE

Created by VAN SCOTT JONES,
Hollywood, CA

14 oz. white Belgian ale, such
as Blue Moon
1½ oz. orange-flavored vodka
Garnish: Orange half-wheel

*Fill 1-pt. beer mug or pilsner
glass with ale, leaving room
at the top for the vodka.
Pour in vodka. Garnish with
orange.*

▯ BROOKLYN TAI

Created by JONATHAN POGASH,
New York, NY

1 oz. dark rum
½ oz. orgeat syrup
½ oz. fresh lime juice
12 oz. lager beer, preferably
Brooklyn Lager
Garnish: Fresh mint sprig, lime
wheel

*Shake first three ingredients
with ice and strain into 1-pt.
beer mug. Gently pour in
beer. Garnish with mint and
lime wheel.*

♈ BROKEN SPUR COCKTAIL

¾ oz. sweet vermouth
1½ oz. tawny port
¼ oz. triple sec

Stir with ice and strain into chilled cocktail glass.

♈ CHAMPAGNE COCKTAIL

1 sugar cube
2 dashes Angostura bitters
Chilled Champagne
Garnish: Lemon twist

Place sugar and bitters in champagne flute and fill with Champagne. Add lemon twist.

♈ CHERRY-VANILLA SPARKLER

Created by JONATHAN POGASH, New York, NY

1 oz. cherry puree
½ oz. maraschino liqueur
½ oz. vanilla liqueur
¼ oz. vanilla syrup
3 oz. sparkling wine or Champagne, plus 1 splash to finish

Gently fold ingredients with ice in mixing glass. Strain into chilled champagne flute. Top with extra splash of sparkling wine or Champagne.

♈ CHRYSANTHEMUM COCKTAIL

1½ oz. dry vermouth
¾ oz. Bénédictine
3 dashes absinthe or pastis
Garnish: Orange twist

Stir with ice and strain into chilled cocktail glass. Add orange twist.

♈ CLARET COBBLER

2 oz. soda water
½ oz. simple syrup
3 oz. red wine, such as claret or cabernet sauvignon
Garnish: Fresh seasonal fruit

Pour soda water and syrup into ice-filled red-wine glass. Add wine and stir. Garnish with fruit. Serve with straws.

CRANBERRY SPICED CHAMPAGNE

Created by JONATHAN POGASH, New York, NY

6 fresh cranberries
¼ oz. fresh lemon juice
1 tsp. agave nectar
1 pinch pumpkin pie spice
4 oz. sparkling wine or Champagne, plus 1 splash to finish
Garnish: 3 fresh cranberries

Muddle 6 cranberries with lemon juice, agave nectar, and pumpkin pie spice in mixing glass. Add sparkling wine or Champagne and ice and gently fold. Strain into chilled champagne flute. Top with extra splash of sparkling wine or Champagne. Float 3 cranberries on top.

DEATH IN THE AFTERNOON

1 oz. absinthe or pastis
5 oz. chilled Champagne

Pour absinthe into chilled flute glass. Top with Champagne.

EL MAESTRO

Created by TED KILGORE, St. Louis, MO

1 cucumber slice
1½ oz. oloroso sherry
½ oz. gin
½ oz. elderflower liqueur
½ oz. Cynar
2 dashes celery bitters
Garnish: Cucumber slice

Muddle 1 cucumber slice in mixing glass. Add remaining ingredients and stir with ice. Strain into ice-filled highball glass. Garnish with cucumber slice.

FALLING LEAVES

2 oz. Alsatian riesling or semidry white wine
1 oz. pear eau-de-vie
½ oz. Honey Syrup (page 21)
½ oz. orange curaçao
1 dash Peychaud's bitters
Garnish: Star anise pod

Shake ingredients with ice and strain into chilled cocktail glass. Garnish with star anise pod.

☿ FAR EAST SIDE

Created by KENTA GOTA,
New York, NY

2 fresh shiso leaves
2 oz. sake
¾ oz. elderflower liqueur
½ oz. blanco tequila
¼ oz. fresh lemon juice
1 pinch yuzu pepper
Garnish: Fresh shiso leaf

*Muddle 2 shiso leaves in
mixing glass. Add remaining
ingredients and stir with ice.
Strain through wire sieve
into chilled cocktail glass.
Garnish with shiso leaf.*

☿ FIELD BLEND

Created by NATASHA DAVID,
New York, NY

3 cucumber slices
3 oz. dry riesling
¾ oz. Cocchi Americano
¼ oz. pear brandy
1 oz. soda water
1 oz. sparkling wine

*Put cucumber slices in red-
wine glass and add ice. Pour
in remaining ingredients, and
stir gently.*

☿ FROSTED APRICOT

Created by MARK A. WEDDLE,
Greensboro, NC

2 oz. late-harvest riesling or
   ice wine
¾ oz. apricot-flavored brandy
¾ oz. elderflower liqueur
1 oz. white cranberry juice
½ oz. fresh lemon juice
Garnish: Orange twist

*Shake with ice and strain
into chilled cocktail glass.
Add orange twist.*

☿ THE GATHERING

Created by MARK A. WEDDLE,
Greensboro, NC

2 oz. Belgian white ale
2 oz. sauvignon blanc
1 oz. elderflower liqueur
½ oz. fresh lemon juice
Garnish: Lemon twist

*Pour into ice-filled white-
wine glass. Add lemon twist.*

🍷 THE GRAPEVINE

Created by JONATHAN
POGASH, New York, NY

3 lime wedges
8 fresh mint leaves
½ oz. simple syrup
½ oz. cabernet sauvignon
½ oz. Grand Marnier
½ oz. light rum
Soda water

*Muddle limes, mint, and
syrup in mixing glass. Add
next three ingredients and ice
and shake. Strain into ice-
filled Collins glass. Top with
soda water.*

🍸 INGRID BERGMAN

Created by MIKE SAMMONS,
Houston, TX

For an Ingmar Bergman,
substitute dry vermouth for
the sweet.

11 oz. cold lager beer
1 oz. sweet vermouth
3 dashes Angostura bitters
Garnish: Orange twist

*Pour ingredients, in order
given, into pilsner glass. Add
orange twist.*

🍸 LONDON SPECIAL

Large orange twist
1 sugar cube
2 dashes Angostura bitters
Chilled Champagne

*Put orange twist into
champagne flute. Add
sugar and bitters. Fill with
Champagne and stir.*

🍸 KIR ROYALE

Félix Kir, mayor of the French city
of Dijon, popularized this drink in
the years after World War II.

5½ oz. chilled Champagne
½ oz. crème de cassis

*Pour into large champagne
flute or white-wine glass.*

🍸 MIMOSA

1 oz. fresh orange juice
5 oz. chilled Champagne
Garnish: Orange half-wheel

*Pour orange juice into chilled
champagne flute. Gradually
add Champagne (watch out
for foaming). Garnish with
orange.*

☐ PEAR FIZZ

Created by BRENDAN DUFF,
St. Louis, MO

1 dash lemon bitters
1 oz. pear brandy
3 oz. cold sparkling wine
2 drops orange blossom water
Garnish: Pear slices

*Add lemon bitters to ice-filled
old-fashioned glass. Pour
in brandy and then slowly
top with sparkling wine.
Add orange blossom water.
Garnish with pear slices.*

☐ PEAR-VANILLA SPARKLER

Created by JONATHAN POGASH,
New York, NY

¾ oz. pear puree
½ oz. vanilla liqueur
½ oz. pear liqueur
3½ oz. sparkling wine or
    Champagne, plus 1 splash
    to finish
Garnish: Freshly grated nutmeg

*Gently fold ingredients with
ice in mixing glass. Strain
into chilled champagne flute.
Top with extra splash of sparkling wine or Champagne.
Sprinkle with nutmeg.*

☐ RED DIESEL

A relative of the Shandy,
with beer, cider, and a shot of
currant liqueur to give the color
that gives the drink its name.

8 oz. cold apple cider
8 oz. cold beer
1 oz. crème de cassis

*Pour cider and beer together
into chilled beer mug and
stir briefly. Add crème
de cassis.*

SANGRIA

☐ SANGRIA (WINTER)

3 oz. fruity red wine, such as
    merlot
¾ oz. dark rum
½ oz. allspice liqueur (pimento
    dram)
½ oz. orange liqueur
½ oz. Honey Syrup (page 21)
½ oz. fresh lemon juice
Garnish: Cinnamon stick,
    orange twist studded with
    3 whole cloves

*Shake with ice and strain
into ice-filled red-wine glass.
Garnish with cinnamon and
orange twist.*

♀ SANGRIA (RED)

Created by JONATHAN POGASH,
New York, NY

1 oz. brandy
¾ oz. black raspberry-flavored
    liqueur
½ oz. fresh lemon juice
½ oz. fresh orange juice
½ oz. simple syrup
2 oz. red wine, such as merlot
Garnish: Orange half-wheel

*Shake with ice and strain
into ice-filled red-wine glass.
Garnish with orange.*

♀ SANGRIA (WHITE)

1 oz. brandy
¾ oz. passion fruit puree
½ oz. orange liqueur
½ oz. fresh lemon juice
½ oz. simple syrup
3 oz. dry white wine, such as
    sauvignon blanc
Garnish: Lime half-wheel

*Shake with ice and strain
into ice-filled white-wine
glass. Garnish with lime.*

♀ SANGRIA (ROSÉ)

3 (1-inch) watermelon chunks
1 oz. brandy
½ oz. orange liqueur
½ oz. fresh lemon juice
½ oz. simple syrup
2 oz. rosé wine
Garnish: Fresh berries

*Muddle watermelon in mix-
ing glass. Add remaining
ingredients with ice and
shake. Strain into ice-filled
white-wine glass. Add berries.*

🍺 SHANDY

This mix of beer and lemonade
is one of the most refreshing
drinks ever invented.

8 oz. cold lemonade
8 oz. cold ale or lager beer

*Pour into chilled beer mug
and stir briefly.*

Y SHISO NO NATSU

4 fresh shiso leaves
1½ oz. sake
1 oz. gin
½ oz. dry vermouth
Garnish: 1 shiso leaf

Muddle 4 shiso leaves in mixing glass. Add remaining ingredients. Stir with ice and double-strain into chilled cocktail glass. Garnish with shiso leaf.

Y STRAWBERRY MIMOSA

½ c. partially thawed frozen sliced strawberries in syrup
2 oz. fresh orange juice
4 oz. chilled Champagne or sparkling wine
Garnish: Orange half-wheel, whole strawberry

Process strawberries and orange juice in blender until smooth. Pour into ice-filled hurricane glass. Fill with Champagne. Garnish with orange and strawberry.

Y STRAWBERRY-VANILLA SPARKLER

Created by JONATHAN POGASH, New York, NY

1 strawberry, sliced
¼ oz. simple syrup
¼ oz. fresh lemon juice
½ oz. vanilla liqueur
4 oz. sparkling wine or Champagne, plus 1 splash to finish
Garnish: Strawberry slice

Muddle sliced strawberry, syrup, and lemon juice in mixing glass. Add remaining ingredients with ice and gently fold. Strain into chilled champagne flute. Top with extra splash of sparkling wine or Champagne. Garnish with strawberry.

NONALCOHOLIC DRINKS

THERE'S A VERY GOOD chance that, among your circle of friends and acquaintances, there are those who do not consume alcohol at all. While it's certainly important that you respect their personal choice not to drink, there's no reason why nondrinkers cannot raise their glasses in a toast with a libation that's prepared with the care and creativity with which all mixed drinks and cocktails are made.

Most everyone has heard of a Virgin Mary and Shirley Temple, and recipes for these old standards are included here. But there are also nonalcoholic versions of other popular cocktails, such as the Unfuzzy Navel and Punchless Piña Colada. From the frosty Summertime Breeze to the refreshingly tangy Yellowjacket, you'll find quaffs to offer nondrinkers that are a giant step above plain old soft drinks.

You may want to make one for yourself when you're the designated driver, or order one when you're at a business meal or important meeting. Feel free to be creative and experiment with omitting the alcohol in some of the standard cocktail recipes throughout this book, especially those made with a variety of fresh fruit juices. (After all, without the alcohol, a Lime Rickey is Limeade.) And, of course, don't forget that presentation is just as important with these drinks as with any other.

APPLE-CINNAMON SODA

Created by JONATHAN POGASH, New York, NY

¾ oz. Cinnamon Syrup (page 20), or use store-bought syrup
3 oz. apple cider
3 oz. ginger beer
Garnish: Red apple slice

Pour into ice-filled pilsner glass and stir briefly. Garnish with apple.

BEACH BLANKET BINGO

3 oz. cranberry juice
3 oz. varietal white grape juice, such as chenin blanc
Soda water
Garnish: Lime wedge

Pour juices into ice-filled highball glass. Top with soda water and stir. Add lime.

BLACKBERRY SODA

Created by JONATHAN POGASH, New York, NY

4 blackberries
1 oz. Honey Syrup (page 21)
½ oz. fresh lemon juice
5 oz. ginger ale
Garnish: Blackberry and lemon wheel, skewered together

Muddle blackberries with honey syrup and lemon juice in mixing glass. Add ice and shake. Strain into ice-filled pilsner glass. Top with ginger ale and stir briefly. Garnish with skewered blackberry and lemon.

BUBBLETART

3 oz. cranberry juice
1 oz. fresh lime juice
3 oz. soda water
Garnish: Lime wheel

Shake juices with ice and pour with ice into chilled highball glass. Fill with soda water. Garnish with lime.

☐ BUBBLY ORANGEADE

¾ oz. frozen orange juice
    concentrate, thawed
6 oz. soda water
Garnish: Orange half-wheel

*Stir together in Collins glass
and add ice. Garnish with
orange.*

☐ COFFEE ALMOND FLOAT

Makes 4 to 6 servings
1 qt. milk
⅓ c. cold brewed espresso or
    French roast coffee
2 tbsp. brown sugar
¼ tsp. almond extract
Chocolate ice cream

*Combine milk, coffee, brown
sugar, and almond extract in
pitcher. Stir well. Pour into
ice-filled hurricane glasses.
Top each with a scoop of ice
cream.*

☐ COFFEE-COLA COOLER

Makes 3 or 4 servings
2 c. cold brewed coffee
1 tbsp. maple syrup
1½ c. cola, chilled
Garnish: Lemon wheels

*Combine coffee and maple
syrup in pitcher. Slowly stir
in cola. Pour into ice-filled
Collins glasses. Garnish with
lemon.*

☐ CREAMY CREAMSICLE

1 c. fresh orange juice
2 scoops vanilla ice cream
Garnish: Orange wheel

*Combine orange juice and
ice cream in blender on low
speed until smooth. Pour into
highball glass. Garnish with
orange.*

CUCUMBER PEACH SODA

Created by JONATHAN POGASH, New York, NY

2 (1-inch-thick) cucumber slices, chopped
1 oz. peach puree
½ oz. fresh lemon juice
1 tsp. agave nectar
3 oz. soda water
Garnish: Cucumber slice

Muddle chopped cucumber, peach puree, lemon, and agave nectar in mixing glass. Add ice and shake. Strain into ice-filled highball glass. Top with soda water and stir briefly. Garnish with cucumber slice.

FRUIT SMOOTHIE

1 c. fresh orange juice
1 ripe banana, sliced
½ c. berries, such as blueberries, raspberries, or sliced strawberries
Garnish: Banana slice, fresh berries, orange wheel

Process ingredients in blender on low speed until smooth. Pour into highball glass. Garnish with fruits.

FUZZY LEMON FIZZ

4 oz. peach nectar
2 oz. lemon-lime soda
Garnish: Lemon twist

Pour ingredients into ice-filled highball glass. Garnish with lemon twist.

GINGER-POMEGRANATE SODA

Created by JONATHAN POGASH, New York, NY

1½ oz. Homemade Grenadine (page 22), or use store-bought
6 oz. ginger beer
Garnish: Candied ginger, lime wedge

Pour into ice-filled pilsner glass and stir briefly. Add ginger and lime.

☐ ICED MOCHA

Makes 3 to 4 servings
2 c. milk
⅓ c. chocolate syrup
2 oz. cold brewed espresso or
    Italian roast coffee
Garnish: Whipped cream,
    chocolate shavings

*Combine ingredients in
pitcher and stir well. Pour
into ice-filled Collins glasses.
Top with whipped cream and
chocolate.*

☐ INNOCENT PASSION

4 oz. passion fruit juice
1 oz. cranberry juice
½ oz. fresh lemon juice
2 oz. soda water
Garnish: Maraschino cherry

*Combine juices in ice-filled
highball glass. Top with soda
water and stir. Garnish with
cherry.*

☐ LAVA FLOW

½ c. light cream
½ oz. cream of coconut
⅓ c. pineapple juice
½ ripe banana
½ c. sliced strawberries

*Process first four ingredients
in blender with 1 c. crushed
ice until smooth. Put
strawberries at the bottom
of a parfait glass. Quickly
pour in blended mixture for
a starburst effect.*

☐ LEMONADE

1 oz. fresh lemon juice
1 oz. simple syrup, or more
    to taste
Soda water or plain water
Garnish: Lemon slice,
    maraschino cherry
    (optional)

*Stir lemon juice and syrup in
Collins glass. Add ice, fill with
water, and stir again. Garnish
with lemon and cherry, if using.*

LEMONADE (RASPBERRY)

1 oz. fresh lemon juice
1 oz. raspberry syrup
½ oz. simple syrup
Soda water or plain water

Stir first three ingredients in Collins glass. Add ice, fill with water, and stir again.

LIMEADE

3 oz. fresh lime juice
1 oz. simple syrup
Soda water or plain water
Garnish: Lime wedge,
    maraschino cherry
    (optional)

Stir juice and syrup in Collins glass. Add ice, fill with water, and stir again. Add lime and cherry, if using.

LIME COOLER

½ oz. fresh lime juice
Tonic water
Garnish: Lime wedge

Add juice to ice-filled Collins glass. Fill with tonic water and stir. Garnish with lime.

ORANGE AND TONIC

3 oz. fresh orange juice
4 oz. tonic water
Garnish: Lime wedge

Pour juice into ice-filled highball glass. Fill with tonic water and stir. Garnish with lime.

ORANGEADE

3 oz. fresh orange juice
½ oz. simple syrup
4 oz. soda water or plain water
Garnish: Orange wheel,
    maraschino cherry
    (optional)

Stir juice and syrup in Collins glass. Add ice, fill with water, and stir again. Garnish with orange and cherry, if using.

PASSION FRUIT SPRITZER

½ c. passion fruit juice, chilled
3 oz. soda water
Garnish: Lime wedge

Pour juice into champagne flute and fill with soda water. Garnish with lime.

▯ PEACH MELBA

1 c. peach nectar, chilled
2 scoops vanilla ice cream
½ ripe peach, pitted and sliced
⅓ c. fresh raspberries
Garnish: Fresh raspberries

*Process ingredients in blender
on low speed until smooth.
Pour into highball glass and
garnish with raspberries.*

▯ PINEAPPLE-MINT SODA

Created by JONATHAN POGASH,
New York, NY

2 oz. pineapple juice
¾ oz. fresh lime juice
1 oz. Demerara Syrup (page 20)
4 oz. soda water
Garnish: Fresh mint sprigs

*Shake first three ingredients
with ice and strain into ice-
filled pilsner glass. Top with
soda water and stir briefly.
Garnish with mint.*

▯ POMEGRANATE-ALMOND SODA

Created by JONATHAN POGASH,
New York, NY

1 oz. pomegranate juice
1 oz. almond or orgeat syrup
5 oz. soda water
Garnish: Lime wedge

*Pour into ice-filled pilsner
glass and stir briefly. Add
lime.*

▯ PUNCHLESS PIÑA COLADA

1 oz. cream of coconut
1 oz. pineapple juice
¼ oz. fresh lime juice
Garnish: Pineapple slice,
    maraschino cherry

*Process ingredients in blender
with 1 c. crushed ice until
smooth. Pour into Collins
glass. Garnish with pineapple
and cherry.*

◻ RUMLESS RICKEY

1 oz. fresh lime juice
1 tsp. grenadine
1 dash Angostura bitters
4 oz. soda water
Garnish: Long lime twist

Add juice, grenadine, and bitters to ice-filled old-fashioned glass. Fill with soda water and stir. Garnish with lime.

◻ RUNNER'S MARK

4 oz. vegetable-tomato juice, such as V8
2 drops hot red pepper sauce
2 drops fresh lemon juice
1 dash Worcestershire sauce
Garnish: Celery stalk or scallion

Combine all ingredients in ice-filled old-fashioned glass. Stir. Garnish with celery or scallion.

◻ SHIRLEY TEMPLE

½ oz. grenadine
Ginger ale
Garnish: Orange slice, maraschino cherry

Add grenadine to ice-filled Collins glass; top with ginger ale. Garnish with orange and cherry.

♀ STRAWBERRY WONDERLAND

½ c. frozen strawberries
⅓ c. pineapple juice
1 oz. cream of coconut
½ oz. simple syrup
½ oz. fresh lemon juice
Garnish: Whipped cream, fresh strawberry

Process ingredients in blender with 1 c. crushed ice until smooth. Pour into snifter. Top with whipped cream and garnish with strawberry.

◻ SUMMERTIME BREEZE

Makes 2 servings
½ c. sliced fresh strawberries
½ c. chopped fresh pineapple
½ c. fresh grapefruit juice
Garnish: Pineapple wedges, whole strawberries

Process ingredients in blender with 1 c. crushed ice until smooth. Pour into Collins glasses. Garnish with pineapple and strawberries.

♀ UNFUZZY NAVEL

2 oz. peach nectar
2 oz. fresh orange juice
½ oz. fresh lemon juice
¼ oz. grenadine
Garnish: Orange wheel

*Shake with ice. Strain
into chilled red-wine glass.
Garnish with orange.*

♀ VIRGIN MARY

½ c. tomato juice
½ tsp. Worcestershire sauce
1 dash fresh lemon juice
2 drops hot red pepper sauce
1 pinch salt
1 grind freshly ground black
    pepper
Garnish: Lime wedge

*Add ingredients to ice-filled
large red-wine glass and stir.
Garnish with lime.*

☐ WAVEBENDER

1 oz. fresh orange juice
½ oz. fresh lemon juice
1 tsp. grenadine
Ginger ale

*Shake juices and grenadine
with ice and strain into ice-
filled highball glass. Fill with
ginger ale and stir.*

☐ YELLOWJACKET

3 oz. pineapple juice
3 oz. fresh orange juice
½ oz. fresh lemon juice
Garnish: Lemon wheel

*Shake with ice and strain
into ice-filled old-fashioned
glass. Garnish with lemon.*

RESOURCES

GENERAL BAR SUPPLIES

Bar Equipment World

www.barequipmentworld.com
   The name says it all.

A Best Kitchen

www.akitchen.com
   Great prices on all sorts of barware.

Barproducts.com

www.barproducts.com
   Mainly for the trade but open to consumers, it is
   a great resource for all kinds of bar supplies, from
   equipment to accessories.

Co-Rect Products

www.co-rectproducts.com
   Bar and restaurant supplies specifically for the trade.

The Boston Shaker

www.thebostonshaker.com

>   This site, with a retail shop in Somerville, MA, sells
>   only the very best cocktail equipment for the home
>   mixologist.

BAR EQUIPMENT

PUG! Muddler

www.wnjones.com/pug

>   The makers of PUG! Muddlers—sturdy wood mud-
>   dlers with a simple, beautiful design.

Riedel Vinum Martini Glasses

www.williams-sonoma.com

>   Among their many top-of-the-line barware products,
>   Williams-Sonoma carries the beautiful, classic-sized
>   Riedel Vinum Martini Glasses.

Schott Zwiesel Cocktail Glasses

www.surlatable.com

>   Sur La Table's Schott Zwiesel Cocktail Glasses have a
>   retro look and are reasonably sized.

Tovolo Perfect Cube Silicone
Ice Cube Trays

www.amazon.com

A substantial square of ice won't melt as quickly as the standard cube from your freezer's ice dispenser. Use distilled water or double-boiled and cooled water for sparkling clear cubes.

DRINKS DATABASES

Ardent Spirits

www.ardentspirits.com

A website by Gary and Mardee Regan, perhaps the most prolific authors on the subject of cocktails and spirits today; they've written several must-have books, including *New Classic Cocktails*, *The Martini Companion*, and *The Joy of Mixology*.

B.A.R.

www.beveragealcoholresource.com

Comprehensive spirits and mixology training programs designed to provide a well-rounded education in mixology and spirits can be found here.

Cocktail.com

www.cocktail.com

Paul Harrington's site's mission is simple: to bring the drink aficionados and bartenders of the world the best cocktail recipes and advice.

CocktailDB

www.cocktaildb.com

CocktailDB is the brainchild of Martin Doudoroff and Ted Haigh (aka Dr. Cocktail), offering an extensive anthology of cocktails authenticated in print, coupled with a massive ingredients database.

Cocktail Guru

www.thecocktailguru.com

The site of this book's master mixologist, Jonathan Pogash, with terrific recipes, information about his cocktail classes, and other services.

Cocktail Spirit

www.smallscreennetwork.com

Home of the wildly popular educational podcast "The Cocktail Spirit with Robert Hess."

DrinkBoy

www.drinkboy.com

Robert Hess's scholarly database incorporates history, tips, advice, and recipes—just like a proper barman.

Esquire Drinking Database

www.esquire.com/drinks

A great collection of cocktail recipes and wisdom, including much imparted by resident spirits expert David Wondrich. Every week it showcases a new recipe worth checking out.

Imbibe Magazine

www.imbibemagazine.com

Get the latest information on all beverages, from cocktails to coffee, from this lively and colorfully produced magazine.

Inside Food and Beverage

www.insidefandb.com

Insider news on the restaurant and hotel industry, with special attention paid to the importance of the spirits to the bottom line.

King Cocktail

www.kingcocktail.com

One of the most recognized bartenders in America and author of *The Craft of the Cocktail*, Dale DeGroff shares insights and recipes, plus great tips and advice.

Liquor.Com

www.liquor.com

Their motto is "An expert guide to cocktails and spirits," and they are right.

Miss Charming

www.miss-charming.com

Cheryl Charming, author of *Miss Charming's Book of Bar Amusements*, provides useful information and resources to both budding and experienced bartenders.

The Modern Mixologist

www.themodernmixologist.com

The cyberhome of one of the smoothest mixmasters on the planet, Tony Abou-Ganim, where you'll find tips and tricks of the trade. His video *Modern Mixology: Making Great Cocktails at Home* is worth seeking out.

Spirit Journal

www.spiritjournal.com

Writer Paul Pacult's newsletter rating spirits, wine, and beer.

BITTERS

Adam Elmegirab Bitters

www.atthemeadow.com

This online store, with brick-and mortar locations in New York City and Portland, OR, offers an amazing selection of bitters.

Bittermen's Bitters

www.bittermens.com

With flavors like Xocotl Mole and 'Elemakule Tiki, this firm is dedicated to expanding the possibilities for making cocktails. They also have an outlet, Bittermen's General Store, in New York City's East Village.

Fee Brothers Bitters

www.kalustyans.com

The Fee Brothers of Rochester, NY, have been making bitters and cocktail flavorings for decades, and their experience shows in their six different bitters flavors.

Peychaud's Bitters/Regan's Orange Bitters

www.buffalotrace.com

A great source for these bar essentials.

Scrappy's Bitters

www.scrappysbitters.com

High quality, small-batch bitters that are worth searching out.

FLAVORINGS AND SWEETENERS

B. A. Reynold's Syrups

www.okolemaluna.com

Handmade exotic syrups, with an emphasis on ingredients for Polynesian-style drinks.

Depaz Cane Syrup

www.igourmet.com

An excellent substitute for simple syrup, try it in
Mojitos and other tropical drinks.

Elderflower Cordial and
Wild Hibiscus Flowers
in Syrup

www.chefswarehouse.com

It's fun to browse at this well-stocked site.

Kalustyan's

www.kalustyans.com

If you've never heard of it, they have it. A good place
to get such exotics as orange blossom and rose water,
orgeat, and rose syrup (mymoune).

Pink Sanding Sugar

www.amazon.com

You will find many other food products for your bar at
amazon.com, too.

Sonoma Syrup

www.sonomasyrup.com

Great fruit and spice syrups for every cocktail.

FRUIT JUICES AND PUREES

Boiron

www.emarkys.com

French fruit purees prepared without sugar and bursting with natural flavor, the only drawback is that they come in 1kg (2.2-pound) containers, so make plans for using your entire purchase.

Ceres Juices

www.ceresjuices.com

You might find these excellent juices with minimum sweeteners at your local specialty grocer. They specialize in tropical flavors, such as passion fruit, and their pineapple is superior to the supermarket variety.

Perfect Purée of Napa Valley

www.perfectpuree.com

The Perfect Purée Company of Napa Valley produces a wonderful selection of fruit and vegetable purees, including a fabulous White Peach elixir that's perfect for Bellinis.

GARNISHES

Luxardo Cherries

www.amazon.com and www.kegworks.com

Two recommended places to buy Italian marasca cherries in syrup.

Les Parisiennes Cherries in Brandy

www.emarkys.com

Second only to real marasca cherries, these are perfect for Manhattans.

Cocktail Onions

www.sableandrosenfeld.com

A Gibson isn't a Gibson without proper onions. Sable and Rosenfeld sells other top-notch cocktail garnishes, such as a full line of flavored green olives, too.

GLOSSARY

The following list is meant to serve as a brief explanation for the ingredients and terminology used in this book.

Absinthe Banned for many years because of its supposed (and disproven) hallucinogenic qualities, absinthe is back on the market. It is a green not-too-sweet liqueur with a high alcohol content that turns cloudy when mixed with water.

Absinthe Substitutes When absinthe was illegal, licorice-flavored substitutes made without the wormwood were produced. Still sold, examples include Pernod (French) and Herbsaint (American). (See Pastis.)

Ale A type of beer, top-fermented with malt and hops (meaning that the mashed grains float on top of the liquid during fermentation) at warm temperatures.

Allspice Liqueur Also called pimento dram (pimento is another name for allspice), this Jamaican rum-based product is used in some Caribbean-style drinks.

Amaretto Italian almond-flavored liqueur distilled from bitter and/or sweet almonds.

Amaro "Bitter" in Italian, a variety of digestif liqueur with bitter herbal flavors. Some have specific proprietary names (such as Campari, Cynar, and Fernet-Branca) and others are branded by their producer (Amaro Ramazzotti and Amaro Averna).

Amer Picon A French apéritif wine with bitter orange flavor, it is currently not distributed in the United States. Torani Amer, a domestic product made in California, is an excellent substitute.

Anisette A very sweet anise-flavored liqueur.

Apéritif A liquor, often made from fortified and flavored wine, served before a meal as an appetite stimulant. (*Apéritif* comes from the Latin *aperire*, which means "to open.") Like digestifs, which are their opposite because they are served after a meal, they can also be ingredients in mixed drinks. Examples are Dubonnet, Lillet, and vermouth.

Aperol An Italian apéritif, with a discernable bitter orange flavor.

Apple Brandy A liquor distilled from fermented apples and barrel aged.

Applejack American apple brandy, originally distilled from frozen apple juice, a process called jacking. Laird's Applejack from New Jersey is the most common brand, and it is excellent.

Apricot Brandy A naturally or artificially apricot-flavored liqueur that must contain brandy.

Apricot Liqueur An apricot-flavored liqueur that does not contain brandy and is not as sweet as apricot brandy.

Aquavit A clear to light yellow distilled Scandinavian spirit flavored with herbs and caraway and other spices.

Armagnac Gascony, a region in southwest France, is the home of this brandy made from white grapes and aged in oak.

Batavia Arrack Similar to rum, a liquor distilled from sugar cane and rice, native to Indonesia. Other Asian countries make arrack from palm sugar and coconut flowers. **Arak** is an anise-flavored liquor drunk in eastern Mediterranean countries.

Beer Brewed from grain (often malted—sprouted and dried—but not always) and flavored by hops, this beverage is often drunk by itself, but makes a good mixer in the right cocktail. **White beer** is brewed from wheat.

Bénédictine Legend says that the original recipe for this sweet French liqueur with strong herbal flavors comes from a Benedictine monastery. The DOM on the label stands for *Deo Optimo Maximo*, which in Latin means "To God, most good, most great."

Black Raspberry Liqueur Chambord is a common and richly flavored brand of this sweet berry liqueur.

Bourbon Whiskey A uniquely American spirit is distilled from a mash of grains that must contain at least 51 percent corn (and can also include malted barley, rye, or corn). Bourbon is aged in new, charred barrels for at least two years before bottling. The name refers to Bourbon County, Kentucky, from which the whiskey was originally distributed.

Brandy Many countries, including France, Spain, and the United States, make this alcoholic liquor distilled from fermented grapes (although there are brandies made from other fruits, such as apples and apricots).

Cachaça Brazilian liquor made from sugar cane and similar to rum, it is the base liquor of a Caipirinha.

Calvados Apple brandy specifically from a region in Normandy, France.

Campari A high-alcohol Italian apéritif with bitter and herbal flavors.

Canadian Whisky Whisky produced in Canada is usually light-bodied, with a smooth taste, and made from a blend of whiskies distilled from multiple grains.

Cava A Spanish sparkling wine.

Chartreuse Richly flavored with herbs, this French liqueur is made by Carthusian monks from over 130 herbs. There are two colors, green (which gets its natural hue from chlorophyll) and yellow (which is lower proof, milder, and less sweet).

Cherry Brandy Red, cherry-flavored brandy, such as Cherry Heering, made from black cherries.

Cider Filtered apple juice. If allowed to ferment and develop alcohol content, it is called hard cider.

Claret A term for Bordeaux-style red wine.

Cocchi Americano An aromatized white wine from Asti, Italy, that often serves as a substitute for Kina Lillet (which has been discontinued) and can be enjoyed like dry vermouth.

Coffee Liqueur Kahlúa and Tia Maria are examples of this kind of liqueur.

Cognac Brandy made in Cognac, France, from white grapes that are good for distilling into spirits but not for fermenting into wine.

Cointreau An orange liqueur in the clear-colored, triple sec–style.

Cream of Coconut A thick, sweetened coconut puree used to make Piña Coladas and other tropical drinks.

Crème de Cacao Chocolate liqueur available dark (brown-colored) and white (clear).

Crème de Cassis Black currant liqueur.

Crème de Menthe Mint-flavored liqueur, sold in two colors: green and white (clear).

Crème de Mure Blackberry liqueur.

Crème de Noyaux Brandy-based almond liqueur.

Crème de Violette A pale purple liqueur with a floral violet flavor and aroma.

Crème Yvette An American version of crème de violette with a more pronounced vanilla flavor.

Curaçao A citrus-flavored liqueur made with the peel of the orange-like laraha fruit, a product of the island of Curaçao. It is sold in three colors: blue, white (clear), and orange.

Cynar Italian digestif made from artichokes and herbs.

Digestif A liquor containing herbs and other ingredients with traditional medicinal properties, drunk after dinner to aid digestion, but increasingly used as a cocktail ingredient. (See Amaro).

Drambuie A Scotch whisky liqueur.

Dubonnet An example of a *quinquina* (quinine-flavored) apéritif, originally developed to fight malaria. Sold in Rouge (red) and Blanc (clear pale yellow) varieties.

Falernum A spicy Caribbean syrup, it is sold in a nonalcoholic version, but many bartenders prefer John D. Taylor's Velvet Falernum liqueur.

Fernet A kind of amaro, Fernet-Branca and Luxardo Fernet are just two brands of many.

Fortified Wine Spirits (usually brandy) were added to wine to help preserve it on long ship voyages. Examples include madeira, marsala, port, sherry, and vermouth.

Galliano A very sweet bright yellow Italian liqueur made from over 30 herbs and spices, but with a distinct vanilla flavor. Named for a hero of the First Italo-Ethiopian War of the late nineteenth century.

Genever Also called *genièvre*, is a type of gin made in Holland that is the origin of today's liquor. There are two styles, young and old, which have nothing to do with age, but rather with how they are made. *Jonge* (young) is clear and almost neutral in flavor, like vodka. *Oude* (old) is made from malted grains and aged in barrels, like whiskey. In this book, genever refers to the oude style.

Gin A clear spirit made from a mash of cereal grain and flavored with botanicals (mainly juniper). London dry gin in made in a style traditionally popular in that city; Plymouth gin is similar, but must be made in Plymouth, England.

Grand Marnier Cognac-based French liqueur flavored with bitter Seville oranges.

Grappa An Italian brandy distilled from grape pomace (the remains from pressing grapes), and not from grape juice.

Hazelnut Liqueur Frangelico is a popular brand.

Irish Cream Thick-bodied cream-based liqueur flavored with Irish whiskey. Store in the refrigerator after opening.

Irish Whiskey Made in a manner similar to Scotch whisky, but distilled three times. Barley, either malted or not, is the main grain used for the mash.

Licor 43 Also known as Cuarenta y Tres, this bright yellow Spanish liqueur has citrus and vanilla flavors derived from its forty-three ingredients.

Lillet A French apéritif based on Bordeaux wine and citrus liqueur, sold in both Rouge (red) and Blanc (white) versions. Kina Lillet, a third version, was discontinued in 1986. (See Cocchi Americano.)

Limoncello An Italian lemon liqueur, traditionally made in Southern Italy from lemons.

Madeira A Portuguese fortified wine from the island of Madeira.

Mandarine Napoléon A tangerine-flavored liqueur.

Maraschino A clear Italian liqueur made from marasca cherries, bearing no resemblance to American maraschino flavoring or cherries.

Mezcal A relative of tequila, made from maguey plants, primarily near Oaxaca, Mexico.

Pastis A French licorice-flavored absinthe substitute, it turns cloudy when mixed with water. Pernod is a notable brand.

Pimm's No. 1 There were originally six different kinds of this liqueur, but the gin-based No. 1 is the only one still sold in the United States.

Pisco A colorless brandy made in Chile and Peru, with some argument as to which country can claim it as its own.

Port Originally a fortified wine from Portugal, but now made in other wine-producing countries. It is available in the following styles: white (made from white grapes), ruby (aged under four years in casks), tawny (a blend of white and ruby), late-bottle vintage (aged four to six years, then bottled, which stops the aging), and vintage (highest-quality port aged for two years in the cask, then bottled, where it continues to age). For cocktails, ruby or tawny port are good choices.

Punt e Mes An Italian apéritif similar to sweet vermouth, but more bitter.

Rum Distilled from sugar products (either molasses, sugarcane juice, or a syrup made from reduced sugarcane juice), the three main styles are light, medium, and dark. Also sold are spiced or flavored rum, aged rum, and high-proof rum.

Rye A whiskey that must include at least 51 percent rye in its mash.

Sake A brew (not quite a wine and not quite a beer) made from fermented rice. Traditionally made in Japan, there are also domestic sakes.

Sambuca Made from elderberries and anise, an Italian liqueur usually served as an after-dinner drink with three espresso beans added to the glass.

Schnapps A light-bodied, very sweet liqueur that comes in a wide variety of flavors.

Scotch The common name for Scottish whisky (spelled without an "e") from malted barley that has been dried over smoldering peat. Blended whisky is created from a combination of whiskies from different barrels. Single malt whisky is the product of a single distillery and aged for at least three years in charred oak barrels (many of which are imported from America after being used to age bourbon). The flavor of the Scotch is often dictated by the distiller's location—Islay and Skye produce the smoky whiskies called for in some cocktails.

Sherry Spanish fortified wine made in Andalucía. Varieties encompass fino (the driest flavor), manzanilla (richer than fino, but still dry), amontillado (half-dry, with nutty flavor notes), oloroso (sweet and full-bodied), cream (also sweet and heavy-bodied), and Pedro Ximénez (very sweet and rich). Use the sherry indicated in the recipe, because, as you can see, the flavors range enormously.

Sloe Gin A red liqueur made from sloe plums, but only the best versions have a gin base.

Tequila Mexican liquor distilled in the Jalisco region from blue agave, sold in four distinct styles: *blanco* (also called clear or silver), *oro* (gold, artificially colored to give the appearance of aging and generally disdained by the best bartenders), *reposado* (blanco aged in oak barrels for up to one year), and *añejo* (aged in oak for over one year).

Triple Sec A colorless orange liqueur made in the curaçao style.

Tuaca Originally Italian, and now produced in Kentucky, a liqueur with predominant citrus and vanilla notes.

Vanilla Liqueur A liqueur where the vanilla flavor is dominant without citrus or spice notes.

Vermouth A fortified wine-based apéritif aromatized with over fifty herbs and spices, in red (sweet) and white (dry) styles.

Vodka A colorless, virtually flavorless spirit distilled from grain, potatoes, or buffalo grass. Flavored vodkas, with flavors ranging from lemon to chile pepper, are also available.

Whisk(e)y A spirit distilled from cereal grains (mainly barley, corn, or rye, alone or in combination with oats and wheat), and often aged in oak barrels. (See Bourbon, Irish Whiskey, Rye, Scotch, and White Whiskey.)

White Whiskey Also called white lightning, a colorless unaged whiskey distilled from corn that was the traditional homemade liquor of the South.

Wine The fermented juice of grapes or other fruits.